Edubooks by Kathy S. Thompson

A Journey through the Triangle of Canada, Britain,
   and America
Afterlife Envision
Brown Flowers in Gloucester (Drama)
Cataract Surgery Is No Fun
Counseling Helps (27 Helps)
Creeping Greed
Crime and Rehabilitation (and The Gap Theory)
Crimes, Crime Awareness, and Crime Prevention, including the Mafia
Diary of a Drug Addict,
8 Drama Stories: Twists and Turns
Funeral Planning, Memorial Services, and
   Coping with Grief
Global Warming Causes, Solutions, and Theories
I Care For My Cats (and Other Animals)
Landscaping a Small Lot
Letters to England
Living and Travelling in the South-West
Political Write-ups
Racial Equality
13 Science Fiction Stories: Separate Worlds
Scriptwriters and Scriptwriting
Sex Trends in Society
Shingles are Awful
Stair-Temple Sites/Chilean Easter Island
Stonehenge and Other Stone-Placement Sites
Taking a Shower—Shower Savvy
The Case Study—Case by Case
The Equal Personage Concept of Children and Youth (EPCCY)
The Gap Theory for Mental Assessment and Treatment
The Outdoor Perils of Cats
The Surgery Experience
Three Careers and a Driven Life: The Life of My Father
Travellers (Sci Fi)
Writers and Writing

Poems and Short Works Books (57 in each)

Going through Life Poems and Short Works
Getting through Life Poems and Short Works
Next Poems and Short Works
Straggler Poems and Short Works
Isolates Poems and Short Works
Extra Poems and Short Works
Final Poems and Short Works
Spare Poems and Short Works
Subsequent Poems and Short Stories

Young Readers Books

Charlie and Mom Cat (early readers)
The Cygnet (young readers, and all ages)
Madame Spider (tweens, teens, and all ages)
Philpot and the Forest Animals (young readers and all ages)

THE SURGERY EXPERIENCE

A CAR ACCIDENT, DIFFERENT KINDS OF PAIN, AND SURGERY FIVE YEARS LATER— A PATIENT'S GUIDE

Kathy S. Thompson, M.A.,
Education and Counseling

authorHOUSE®

AuthorHouse™
1663 Liberty Drive
Bloomington, IN 47403
www.authorhouse.com
Phone: 833-262-8899

Published by AuthorHouse 11/23/2022

ISBN: 978-1-6655-3803-9 (sc)
ISBN: 978-1-6655-3816-9 (e)

Library of Congress Control Number: 2021918845

Print information available on the last page.

Any people depicted in stock imagery provided by Getty Images are models,
and such images are being used for illustrative purposes only.
Certain stock imagery © Getty Images.

This book is printed on acid-free paper.

Because of the dynamic nature of the Internet, any web addresses or links contained in this book may have changed
since publication and may no longer be valid. The views expressed in this work are solely those of the author and do
not necessarily reflect the views of the publisher, and the publisher hereby disclaims any responsibility for them.

The author makes no claim to the accuracy of all details in this book. The author has attempted to remove
any noted errors and has checked out what could be checked out, as well as possible. Efforts towards
accuracy have been made but the author makes no claim to there being full and complete accuracy of
all the book's contents. Names of people and places have been changed but the story is authentic.

The information, ideas, and suggestions in this book are not intended as a substitute for professional
medical advice. Before following any suggestions contained in this book, you should consult your personal
physician. Neither the author nor the publisher shall be liable or responsible for any loss or damage allegedly
arising as a consequence of your use or application of any information or suggestions in this book.

Life is real. It has its bends in the road, it's twists and turns, and you take it as it comes, one day at a time. You learn as you go, building on whatever was previous, and you make decisions as you go along life's course. Just as each person is different from other people, so is their life's course different. Even though there can be parallels, no one path is the same, and so it is that we all travel alone.

Kathy S. Thompson

CONTENTS

CONTENTS

DEDICATION

To all the people who are facing any kind of surgery or have already had any kind of surgery, and to the loved ones of those people.

APOLOGY

I know this book is not perfectly written. Though I majored in English as an undergraduate, I've forgotten some grammar, plus some grammar and even spelling rules have changed over the years and I have not kept up with those new ways, although, many of them are optional. Still, grammar can get to be a little muddled in the mind. So, apologies for any and all imperfections. Just getting the book out was the priority. Therefore, you may find some irregularity, in that the book was not professionally edited. I hope there's no typing errors (but my eyes are not so good). So, apologies go out for any and all oversights or undersights. There may be some repetition, too. Some is purposely there, to drive in a point. Some is accidentally there but is put in a different context. Because I was working on more than one book at a time, I would sometimes forget what I had already written so I occasionally put the same information in twice—almost always in a different context. Also, this book was a bit of a rush job. Because the book was somewhat rushed, all sentence construction may not be immaculate but most of the content generally makes sense in so far as I know.

Furthermore, you may think some text information does not directly relate to the included covered subjects. There is, perhaps, some borderline material in there. With what may seem extraneous, if you give it more thought, you would likely make the connection that the material does relate to the overall subject and certainly to what is generally being covered in the text. There are one or two covered areas that may be more remotely related to the principal subject but I wanted to add in those subjects and felt that they were connected. All points made tie in with the overall subject, and they generally or specifically relate. Some points that were made do, more than others. I tried to be thorough; I am a detail-oriented writer. Putting so many details in so the book would be more comprehensive was not always so easy to do and so the organization of the book is not quite all that I would have wanted it to be, but I'm not unhappy with it. Mainly, I got everything in that I wanted in and that was my priority. Again, this book was a little rushed.

WRITER'S NOTE: JUSTIFICATION AND EXPLANATION

First off, please realize that this book is written by a non-medical professional—in other words, a layperson. I have no medical background, other than health classes I took over the course of time. I also took Biology. I wanted to write a book that was about an average person experiencing medical problems and surgery. I picked up medical information along the way of my journey. As it turned out, the surgery experience was an even longer journey that I'd first expected it would be.

This book is as scholarly and researched as I could make it, but I could not write it like an actual medical doctor would have written it. I wrote it from first-hand experience, though—all the way through and all across the board. It is like the rather long cat and animals rights book I have written—I am not a veterinarian but I am so extremely interested in everything surrounding cats (including cat care) that I can be a zealot and research cats and write about them (and other animals, too, because the book is also about animals rights and includes content about other animals). During my surgery experience, I was constantly taking notes. I observed and remembered everything I could.

I purposely did not make note of any names and even changed several names (early on in the book). The book is a book of a number of experiences I had along with my recollection of those experiences and what all I'd medically picked up and experienced along the way. Again, what has been noted is, on the one hand, second-hand but on the other hand, first-hand.

I started writing this book right after I came home from the hospital, after I'd had surgery, and when I was on painkillers. Therefore, sometimes I'd forgotten what I'd previously written, or I wasn't thinking real straight. I had to go through the book and improve it, more than once. I was sleeping a lot, too, and had been tired. There could still be some occasional repetition, but it will have been woven in, in different ways.

I smoothed it all out fairly well over time, and again, any repetition is generally applied in a different context from the previous and so it is useful. Also, the book has occasional repetition that was put in on purpose because I gave progress reports about my surgery a number of times and had to note some of the same things, i.e., right after surgery, three months later, six months later, one year later, three years later and also, even subsequent to that. At that point, I hadn't known there might be a recurrence of the thoracic/abdominal and hiatus problems thirteen years following the initial surgery. Therefore, more parts had to be added to the book, which had, in the meantime, just been sitting on a shelf while I was writing other books. It's good it had been on the shelf and nothing was, yet, being done with it because I needed to add more to it. So, instead of having eight parts, it now has twelve.

Because the symptoms and healing progression are recorded at several intervals, it will seem like there is more repetition than there really is. As you read the book, try to keep in mind that a few segments or chapters cover similar material, including the progress reports and so repetition is basically because of the progress being made relative to several aspects of the surgery. Content in the chapters is different when there is what may seem to be repetition. Some repetition may seem to be there, even though it may not really be.

With the first surgery, after the five-year checkpoint, I let go of everything—i.e., I rarely thought about the surgery and its side-effects. My life continued. I still had some annoyances left over from the surgery but I was able to live with the irritations with no problem. The main lingering irritation was a muscle over the left ribs (the Serratus anterior); it never attached quite right subsequent to the first surgery and it often became dislocated and I had to re-orient my body so it would go back in place. This muscle continued to be a problem for me, from time to time over the years. If my body ever gets into a particular position, it will dislocate that muscle and there I am in temporary pain, but I can always get is re-shifted back in place by twisting my body a certain way so that part is good.

I went along for thirteen years after the split-rib thoracic surgery. Even the scar looked better by that time. Then, I began to have symptoms again, but I could have begun having problems even before that thirteen-year point. I cannot

xiv

attest to that, one way or another, but I suspect that damage in the area was slowly happening and then the stomach slipped back up, above the diaphragm. The recurrence was there to stay and so I ended out adding material to what I'd though was an already finished book. I'd thought the book had been finished, but it wasn't, since new and interesting material came to the front. There was more to the overall story and so I spent more time adding to the book and the book now has more facts and information related to pre-surgery, surgery, post-surgery, and recurrence after surgical correction. Because of the second set of symptoms, I acquired even more facts and information. I was able to build on my experiences from the first surgery. For me, in a way that was good but in a way that was bad because I was essentially back at Square One.

I'm not noting, now, if I had a second surgery. That would be a spoiler. You'll have to read all the way through to know if I did or didn't. What the future holds for me is, of course, currently not known, regardless of how the book ends because who knows what will happen in the future. I will note this—big decisions are very hard to make. You go back and forth, forth and back, and you look at everything major that affects the decision. You weigh and balance. You get a little stressed.

Again, and last, I do not want any reader to believe that everything in the book is accurate and reliable, because I am in the education and counseling fields, <u>not</u> the medical field. I made note of what I picked up along the way and presented it in as educational a way as I could. The main reference book was a set of encyclopedias, and a dictionary, that are noted in the book. I picked up knowledge from my discussions with several medical professional people along the way, by what I heard them discussing amongst themselves and by what I generally observed and experienced so again, this is not a medical book—not per se—even though there is much medical in it. The book is scholarly, but it has been written by a layperson who just happens to have an eye for detail, which has always been my strong point and why I've been able to write a number of books.

CHAPTER 1
What happened to cause me to have the surgery

Several years ago, in November of 1996, I was the brunt of a car accident. I was making a U-turn around an island and into the other part of the road, going the other way, and BAM-BOOM, I got hit, really hard. I had looked to the side for cars before I went to make the turn. I always do. I have never once failed to do that. But there were no cars traveling within the danger range for turning, and so I turned. I turned in an area where a city park was, and so I thought I was safe.

It was obvious the driver had been speeding, and speeding well in excess of what was legal for the area. For one thing, he obviously did not slow down for the city park area; that was both clear and obvious. His position was that I didn't look to see him coming. I did look, and he wasn't in range. He claimed he wasn't speeding. I believe that he was speeding and so do other people. Also, he failed to slow down, when signs and other indicators revealed that he should slow down. A commercial shopping complex was to his left, a city park was to his right, and a large city intersection was not very far away. All these were 'indicators' for him to slow down. He was likely hoping to make the light at the intersection coming up. He hit me with such force.

The officer put down that he was going 40 mph because that was the speed that the driver told him he was driving. No one could verify this speed, of course, because radar speed timing was not there, at the time of the accident. An officer has to put down the speed the driver states that he or she was driving unless the officer can prove otherwise. Since the officer had not clocked the other driver's speed, and because the officer called in was not there when the accident occurred, he could not prove that the speed the other driver told him he was driving was false.

When I was informed that I could leave the scene, I went home. After I came out of my shock a little, I went back to the scene of the accident and took photos of the area. I discovered that there was a flashing yellow light that was on a

1

sidewalk post, indicating that there was a pedestrian crossing so that people from one side of the road could safely walk over to the city park, and that this light was always flashing. This light, indicating that there was an advisory caution, was seen before the intersection of the crash site, by about two hundred feet. The blinking yellow light was approximately a block before the actual crossing, which was the area (the actual crossing spot) where I got hit. When I went back later, to see the scenario in general, I noticed this and that the flashing yellow light was actually a double flashing yellow light. There was every reason why this young man should have slowed down, but he didn't slow down, and he was going well in excess of the speed limit.

There was also a bus stop area right before the crosswalk. The stores and shopping were very close, on the other side of the street from the park. Right where I got hit, there was an entrance into the park, with a large wood sign for people to see, right there at the park entrance. The road was two-lane, to each side, but that doesn't have much to do with anything relative to the accident. All these other things relate quite specifically, except that why didn't he get over to the other lane and avoid hitting me? Was he impaired, in some way? The speed zone where the accident site was noted right before; it was 40 mph, but there were multiple advisory signs indicating that any driver should start to slow down. This driver failed to slow down when he saw the advisory signs, if he had even been looking for them, which he probably wasn't. He was in too big of a hurry. He was in his twenties—possibly his early twenties because he had a toddler with him.

Advisory signs are advisory only, reference speeds. They're essentially warning signs that indicate that drivers must now drive with caution, because there are going to be sudden changes on or near the road. They indicate that it is wise to be alert and to slow down. Again, the policeman put down that his estimate for the speed of the other driver was 40 mph. He never looked at the 'whole' area. He only looked at part of the area—the immediate area right before the collision. And again, police who weren't at the site put down the speed that a person tells them they are driving, after a car accident, because they have no choice. I personally don't believe that they should put down the stated speed. I think they should put down a question mark or the word, unknown. Or, put the speed down in quotation marks. Police also have to record the speed of the general speed zone, and not what the speed should be relative to any advisory signs that are in the vicinity. In other words, there are factors, extenuating circumstances, and lack of information relative to police reports, after accidents.

Advisory signs are black and yellow and they're found all over. The color yellow always advises caution, when driving. Judges take into consideration advisory signs in civil traffic-related matters, but when police do reports at accident sites, they don't usually consider them and so the picture is incomplete. Personally, I think there should be a place on all accident reports where advisory signs that are in the vicinity of where an accident occurs have to be noted.

Had the officer taken some time, he could have gone back a block, regarded the flashing yellow light, and realized that 40 mph was driving in excess of the advisory speed. (Then, there was the City Park and the shopping center, too.) Why this officer didn't cite the other driver for speeding is irritating but I guess it's the way they do things. The driver <u>was</u> speeding, but the officer didn't see it. He wasn't there. Accident officers don't have all that much discretion. They must follow general policy, all across the board. Again, the other driver told him "40 mph", so that's what he put down because his hands were tied. No way on Earth will I believe that the accident was not the young man's fault. My consolation is that God saw it all, and the accident is in one of God's record books.

The officer was wrong about my speed, too. I had come to a full stop at the island before making my turn so that I could look for cars before I made my turn. I'd only gone out a few feet from the island, from the full stop, and so I was not going the estimated 10-15 mph that the officer put down. I was only going around 5 mph. (The other driver hit me broadside). I wasn't fast enough in telling him what my speed was because frankly, I was in shock. His large truck wasn't hurt at all, hardly, but my car was demolished. I was driving my prized car. I was therefore being double careful about my driving, and about looking where I was going. I had seen cars, far down the road. They were quite a distance away. When I went back and did a U-turn at the same place, later on, it took me four seconds to do the U-turn. Therefore, from the time I had stopped, and then proceeded to make my turn, it couldn't have been more than two seconds. This is why I know the other driver was speeding, and, why I know I was going 5 mph, at most.

The other driver knew that he was fortunate to not be cited for speeding. I believe that he very well knew that he had been going 55-65 mph, in a 40 mph zone. I, of course, was in a state of shock immediately after the accident, just letting everything go on around me and not being capable of doing much else. When you are in shock, it is ce sera sera, what will be, will be. You are too concerned with thoughts like "am I OK? Am I going to be OK?" You're thinking "I'm afraid. I'm disoriented. Why am I here? What is happening around me?" You feel light in weight, and the whole scenario almost seems like a dream that you're in. You feel like you're being enveloped inside a giant cotton ball. You know that something real and bad has just happened, but you feel like you're on the outside, looking in.

The officer at the time cited me for not yielding to traffic at the island. This was a falsehood and an error on his part, and I will always know that I was so dazed by the accident and hardly even knew what was going on that I was unable to think clearly, and speak for myself. I heard later on that officers at accident sites have to cite whenever they even suspect there might have been a moving violation. Believe me, the violation was not mine. I looked before I proceeded. I well remember doing that. If the officer thought or believed that the other driver was only going 40 mph (and I don't know how the officer could have thought that, especially when looking at my damaged car and at how far the glass had been thrown), then it would have followed that he would have thought and believed that I was proceeding into traffic when I shouldn't have been. But, he was wrong. The premise was wrong. The officer connected the dots wrong, or rather, he didn't even connect the dots. My car was so horribly caved in, and the glass had been thrown as far as forty feet from the actual collision. If the officer had assessed the total scene and really thought about it, he would have been able to see the bigger picture, if he had wanted to.

When I went in for my hearing for my violation, the matter ended out being dropped and I had no fine to pay. At the time, I spoke my case. I was at least relieved about that. At the time, I had all my paperwork in very good order and was prepared to not only prove my case, but win my case as well. I think the judge had realized I had a good case. I had, at the time, a somewhat scientific assessment of the action, that included glass-thrown distances and related estimated speed. Again, I well recall looking, before rounding around for the turn, and there were no cars within range and it was safe to make the turn, not unsafe. I was the person who was responsible to check if it was safe to make the turn, and it had been safe to do so. The other driver was driving very fast, or I would have seen him and not gone ahead and proceeded out in the road. The last thing I wanted to happen was for my beautiful car to be hit. I truly believed it was safe.

A neighbor of mine (who at the time was the superintendent of a local school district, and was pretty astute) went to the accident site right away and measured tire skid marks and thrown glass distances. My auto glass was pale turquoise and broke up into little bits so it was easy to find. There was no other turquoise glass around. It's not too common. It was on my old car and it was the original windshield glass. I was glad to have my neighbor's help. I was a widow and I had been disoriented for a day or two, after the accident. I wasn't my usual self and couldn't think real well. The noise from the bang on the car was so loud and the impact so jolting that it had been like being bombed.

Measurements were made from point of impact. My neighbor's conclusions were that the other driver had to have been driving well in excess of the speed limit–from fifteen to twenty-five miles per hour more than the speed limit. That's assuming the speed limit was 40 mph but again, I believe it should have been even less than that because the precaution advisories called for an immediate slowing down. I personally believe there should have been a shift in speed-zone speed, down from 40 mph to around 20 mph before he even got to the accident site and this is because of all the advisory signs and because of other factors, too, but he wasn't even going 40 mph. He was going more. My neighbor calculated that the other driver had to have been going somewhere around 55 to 65 mph.

Also, my car—a 1970 Oldsmobile Cutlass Supreme—was a heavy-duty car. Some call these kinds of cars muscle cars. A heavier steel is used, when making these cars. They weigh more than today's cars weigh. Engine sizes are larger, with muscle cars. His vehicle caved in the whole right side of my vehicle, so much so,

5

that the dent was coming in close to my side—the driver's side—of the car. The side that he hit was completely smashed and dented in. Glass was broken on that side, and front windshield glass was also in little pieces.

The other driver tried to lay the blame on me, but I know who was at fault. Again, they couldn't cite him for speeding because no one saw him speed. Even if anyone had seen his car moving at the time, they couldn't have ascertained his exact speed. They could have said he was going fast, but unless speed is clocked, no one can prove the speed. No one in the area saw his car going down the road, until he hit my car. Then all heads were lifted, because of the crash sound. Otherwise, no one was watching his car. The officer cited him for driving without a license. And, it was noted that he did not provide proof of insurance, as well.

It was a stored and second car, so was okay. I had planned to sell the car I was driving that day. I had been keeping the car around for years, as an investment. I only drove the car to keep the carbon from collecting in the system and to keep the electrical system charged up. I drove the car only every so often, but not on public roads. (I live in a large community, where the streets are private). I knew a car had to routinely be driven, just from a maintenance perspective. The car had to be started up at least a couple of times a week and the car had to be driven at least short distances after having been started up. Especially if it was cold outside, I had to start the car up and let it run for a while. I had to keep the internal parts of the car in condition. I live in a private community, and I had been driving the car only on certain roads, and never too very far. I usually drove another car around town—a small runabout type.

That one day, I chose to drive the Olds. It was almost as though the accident was meant to be—the whys of which would be anyone's guess. I had to go to the credit union, only one block away from my home, so I thought "well, why not charge the Olds up. It's been sitting dormant for a while." As it turned out, that was a fateful thought indeed. Why didn't I reject that particular thought on that particular day? I had been planning a trip to northern California to see my sister and brother-in-law, and was leaving late that afternoon, and a plane departure is always a deadline. I needed the cash from the credit union for my trip. My sister was ill from cancer and so I felt I needed to take the trip. I had been trying all morning to prepare for it. Anyway, whatever the rationale or reason, I wish now that I'd driven my other car. Done was done, though, and reality had to be faced.

The car was very precious to me. It was special. I had had the car since the 1970s. For a time, the car was my only car. I had had special seat covers put on the car, that matched the original blue ones, and I had put in new carpeting, too. I still had the original hub caps. I also had had the car painted a color that matched its original blue color. Perhaps I drove my car that day because I always felt like a princess in it, whenever I drove it. I really did love to drive it. It was a beautiful car. It started up so well and drove like a dream. I had been planning to sell the car, for some extra income, but such aspirations ended on the day of the crash.

I had been wearing an over-the-belly or lap seat belt while driving the Olds. It was the original seat belt. Older cars only had over-the-belly seat belts. These did not go around the waist—they went around the belly. The over both the chest and belly ones didn't come around until later. These seat belts are supposed to prevent people from hitting a windshield with their head or the steering wheel with their chest. They're made in a Y-shaped arrangement. Thrust is distributed upon impact, in large part because of the shoulder strap. These seat belts are supposed to be safer. Possibly, fewer hiatal hernias or torn diaphragms result from the chest/belly ones. You would think so, anyway. The seat belt I had been wearing was made of very thick and strong material. The belt was at least as thick as most seatbelts were. Later on, someone told me that the over-the-belly seat belts should always be worn low. Most people wear them higher up. I probably did too, on the day of my accident. I do not recall my chest area having hit the steering wheel, but it could have. I did not have bruising there afterwards; the bruising was along my stomach area. If I had hit the steering wheel, that, too, could have caused trauma to the hiatus and diaphragm areas (but not like the seat belt did). Women have breasts as cushioning against a steering wheel, though, and, in my case, too, no ribs were broken, nor was my breastbone (the sternum) harmed.

Today, there are cars that have even more safety-connect points to their seat belts. With the around-the-belly type, there were two points because the belt attached at its two end points. A three-point belt, that went over the belly and the chest came out even before the late 1970s and was put in a few vehicle types (more so in Europe than in the United States) but they didn't come out en masse until the late 1970s. Eventually, the shoulder belt part of this type was attached to the actual seat (versus the structure of the vehicle). Seatbelts having from four to six points have been used in car seats for children. Race car drivers use the five or the six point harness or seat belt. Aerobic aircraft pilots are even more latched in but they can unlatch quickly if they must ever parachute out. Because of four to seven point belts, it can perhaps be conjectured that belts having more points will be put into general vehicles. Laws vote these kinds of things in, more often than not. Sometimes these laws come in because of previous vehicular accidents.

I think that either way—wearing seat belts high or low over the belly—can cause a person problems if they are in an accident. Whether you wear the seat belt low or higher, there can be so much pressure on the area that something internal can get hurt. The lower area is the pelvic area and something could break or get dislocated. Something could rupture or tear or split, too, in the pelvic area. Or, something could get dislodged or strangled. Up higher is more around the hip area. A hip can get dislocated because of seat-belt pressure, if a person is in an accident, and, of course, something can rupture or tear or split inside this area, too. Pressure can be put on the direct area, or pressure can go to other areas because of the pressure put on the area where the belt is. One area gets pressed or squeezed so another spot next to it does, and so it can go. The pressure and movement can be transferred over to any organ and even go as high up as the diaphragm.

During an accident and upon impact, a seat belt can automatically release from the force of the impact, especially with certain of the buckles, but this does not mean that damage was not done internally. Today, cars have air bags that release upon significant impact. They are hard to put back in once they've been expelled. New ones are hard to put in, too. Better seat belts and seat belt types will probably come about over the years.

The seat belt itself was about two and a half inches wide and the latch had been original and was made of shiny steel. Even the seat belt was blue, like the car's interior and exterior. Losing my wonderful car—that ran strong and sure and turned on a dime—caused me to be blue as well. I was always faithful about wearing a seat belt. I'd seen too many documentaries or news-clips on car accidents, which graphically showed what happened to people when they didn't wear seat belts. Odds of being hurt even worse are greatly increased if you don't wear a seat belt, compared with if you do. And this I very well knew.

It was the insurance companies that catapulted mandatory seat belt wearing by taking the matter to the courts. They'd been losing a great deal of money because people weren't wearing seat belts. Car manufacturers dragged their feet because it would have cost them so much to make new cars with improved seat belts. The fight went on but eventually, state by state, it became mandatory to wear seat belts. From 1985 to 1989, most states made it mandatory but there were a few stragglers. Mandatory seat belts wearing meant fewer vehicular deaths. The last two states—Maine and New Hampshire—voted in the requirement. Both were smaller, lower-populated states and therefore had had fewer deaths from vehicular accidents. Obviously, the child safety restraint issue came into focus immediately thereafter, en masse, which is an aside subject here. There have been quite a few oppositions on the part of pediatricians relative to back-area positioning for infants and very young children, relative to their car seats. There have been many improvements in design and comfort of child safety seats; there have been many safety improvements.

Quite possibly, wearing the seat belt saved my life. It helped me to not be thrown around and bashed inside the cavity or cab of the Olds. I ended out with a few cuts, from the flying glass, and, a few bruises. I had bruising around my waist, from the seat belt, but it didn't show up right away. (Bruises tend to show up several hours later). The area there was red, though, and it soon turned black and blue. Glass from the side windows and the windwings, and the front windshield was thrown a far distance from the point of impact. The glass that broke shattered into beautiful pale blue glass pieces, which I could have used for a huge art project if I'd wanted to. Lots of the pieces fell inside the car but many of them went all over the road, and around the turn area, too. Eventually, someone from the City came and cleaned it up, but not before my neighbor went over and did all his measurements. We both took photos, but I went back even later and got pictures of the overall setting, and of all the cautionaries, for my court date.

Kathy S. Thompson, M.A.

My neighbor's write-up about his conclusions regarding the accident follows:

TO: Whom It May Concern

FROM: Gary A. Barton
            33 West Saguaro Way
            Tucson, AZ

SUBJECT: Statement Re: Mrs. Kathleen Thompson Accident

I am Mrs. Thompson's neighbor immediately west and adjacent to her residence. After learning of her vehicle accident at a location two left turn lanes north of the intersection of Saguaro Way and El Grande, and seeing the extensive damage to her vehicle, I immediately investigated the scene of the accident myself to determine some facts. I offer the following statement based on that investigation.

I believe that Mrs. Thompson is innocent of any violations of the traffic laws of this state, based on the following information.

FACTS in EVIDENCE:

1.   Mrs. Thompson was cited by the investigating police officer for failure to yield to traffic.

2.   Mrs. Thompson made a legal U-turn in a properly marked turn lane on El Grande.

3.   Windshield glass was scattered more than 40 feet west of the scene of the accident.

4.   The ability to view on-coming traffic from the turn lane is excellent because El Grande is a wide two-lane roadway for south-bound traffic and the view is clear for at least 200 yards north of the scene of the accident.

5.   The driver of the vehicle that hit Mrs. Thompson did not have a driver's license or auto-insurance for his vehicle as required by Arizona law.

6.   The allowable speed limit for traffic on El Grande at the location of the scene of the accident is marked to be 40 mph.

SUMMARY of INVESTIGATION:

1. I went to the scene of the accident and took pictures of scattered automobile glass and discovered that glass from her vehicle was strewn west of the scene of the accident at least as much as 40 feet. Since the vehicle that hit Mrs. Thompson was traveling south on El Grande and Mrs. Thompson was making a legal U-Turn from the north-bound lane on El Grande into the south-bound lane of El Grande and the driver of the oncoming vehicle hit Mrs. Thompson's car broadside on the passenger side of her vehicle with such force that glass from Mrs. Thompson's car was scattered not only south of the accident, it was scattered more than 40 feet laterally from the accident, it is very evident that the on-coming vehicle that struck Mrs. Thompson was traveling at a very high rate of speed.

2. Mrs. Thompson's vehicle, a 1970s model Oldsmobile, hardtop, is a very sturdy and heavily built vehicle with a solid frame and body. The extent of damage to her vehicle indicates that the vehicle that struck her was traveling at a rate of speed greater than the allowable speed limit of 40 mph.

3. I drove the normal speed limit of 40 mph from the scene of the accident in the north-bound lane of El Grande for eight seconds which clearly put my vehicle a safe distance from the turn lane at which the accident occurred. I also drove the same distance at the same rate of speed in the south-bound lane and reconfirmed the distance from the scene of the accident.

4. I made the same U-turn in exactly the same location as did Mrs. Thompson. It took me exactly four seconds to make a safe U-Turn so that my vehicle was completely and safely in the south-bound lane of El Grande.

5. Mrs. Thompson has stated that she did not even see the on-coming vehicle. To my knowledge, she has no visual impairments that would have prevented her from seeing the oncoming vehicle. Considering the view from the turn lane, if the oncoming vehicle had been seen, she could have made a reasonable judgment regarding the feasibility of making a safe U-turn at that location. The fact that she did not see the vehicle nearby is another clear indication that the on-coming vehicle was traveling at a rate of speed far in excess of the allowable limit.

6. In order for the oncoming vehicle to strike Mrs. Thompson while she was making the U-turn, that vehicle would have had to be traveling at a rate of speed of 55-65 mph which is considerably more than the allowable speed

limit. If the on-coming vehicle had been traveling at the maximum speed limit of 40 mph, it would take at least eight seconds to reach the point of impact which would have given Mrs. Thompson sufficient time to make the U-turn safely and the accident would not have occurred.

In conclusion, I truly do not believe that any accident would have occurred if the on-coming vehicle had been traveling within the posted speed limit and I do not believe that Mrs. Thompson was negligent in her actions.

To Whom It May Concern:

The foregoing pages represent my own personal statement regarding the Kathleen Thompson accident. The information presented is true and accurate to the best of my knowledge based on my own research and assessment of the accident scene and the damage to Mrs. Thompson's automobile.

Signed, Gary A. Barton

I changed my neighbor's last name because he since moved away and I could not find him to get his consent to use his full name. I have copies of the signed form, though. My neighbor took time out to help me, and to write up this report. His support helped me through the ordeal. He helped me to see things I wouldn't have been able to see myself. Frankly, I was in semi-shock for several days after the accident. Full shock went away after a day, but semi-shock stayed around for a while. I wasn't able to think as clearly as my neighbor did, so I was thankful that he entered the scene and helped me, during that time. No one at the accident scene helped me like he did, I can well affirm that.

Another individual, who was visiting his parents who lived in the neighborhood and who ended out buying my wrecked car—mainly for the engine—also wrote a conclusion, based on his view of the car damage afterwards and a belief that my car had not been moving much at all, when it was hit. His conclusion was brief, but it was nevertheless a conclusion, and God Bless him for it. (I changed his name, too.) His conclusion was:

To Whom It May Concern:

I am the new owner of Mrs. Thompson's 1970 Olds Cutlass Supreme. At first look at the car it was hit at least at 55 mph; in my opinion the car is totaled.

11/30/96   Tom Anderton

<u>This is the sad dilemma regarding some and certain accidents—i.e., that no one sees the real culprit's speeding, nor can their speed be ascertained.</u> Nowadays, you can buy special camera-like apparatus that sets on the dash and films your driving so if you didn't go through a red light or turn into the wrong lane and there's an accident and/or a possible ticket, you have proof. Quite a few people have bought this. But, they didn't have it around back then.

As relates to my particular accident, and the young man who was speeding, when there is an accident and a speeder is involved, the speeder knows in his or her heart that they were speeding, but because they know it can't be proven and that there is so much at stake if they do admit the truth (that they were speeding), they cover up the truth and even lie about it and hope that no one figures out the real truth. Also, they may not want those close to them to know that they were at fault—like a parent or a spouse. After a while, they may even convince themselves that they weren't speeding, and they become delusional. Or, they know that they were speeding and do not care about the person they hit so that telling a falsehood becomes a comfort to them—a false and wrong comfort, but nonetheless, a comfort. Some people are just downright callous. They have a seared conscience. Sometimes even race differences can enter the picture, and it's too bad when that happens because, again, God sees and records all these things and there will be no escape, one day, from God. More people believe this than don't.

Drivers, policemen, and even judges of different races, can be polarized one way or another, so that truth about overall scenarios get clouded and blocked. When lives and futures are at stake, it is very painful when persons involved—directly or indirectly—are biased. It hurts everybody, in different ways. If people would look at the truth—the facts that make up the truth—and think "this person is a person is a person," and if they would consistently disregard race, color, and creed differences, and other supposedly but not necessarily legally-protected differences, our society would be better and healthier. People can be biased—witnesses, lawyers, police, judges, et al. It happens, but people don't like to talk about it.

Many things slip through the cracks concerning fair dealings and honest handlings of situations, creating a sadness and a hopelessness among those who are not treated fairly, or properly heard. Some people hear with deaf ears, or, they hear only what they want to hear. Am I trying to tell you something? Yes, I am—about society in general, and concerning many things. We just haven't arrived yet, with reference to being open to the truth about many things that affect our lives. So often, we are not as objective as we should be. We allow in too many diversions and distractions that put us on wrong paths of thought. We need to try harder to hone in on facts, and on what is genuine. 'Whosoever has an ear, well then please hear' is my admonition. Often, we judge things prematurely, and we act too rashly. We don't allow equal say. Or, we are inclined a certain way to begin with because of our race, color, creed, and even our sex. When I use the word 'we', I'm also referring to the other person and not you, necessarily (depending on the situation). And also, about the different races, God put different genes in different people, but they are all a part of God's creation and are equal in God's sight. A gene is a gene is a gene.

You cannot wash your hands of going the way of untruth, unless you genuinely become sorrowful for having done so. Being sorry <u>at the right time</u> counts for a lot. Many harden their hearts to truth, and let it bounce off, knowing that an action (or lack of action) has hurt another person. I didn't intend to go this far into these kinds of issues, but I've been able to glean a great deal from this whole, overall experience—both directly, and indirectly. If you are sorry later, and later is better than never, how will that help the aggrieved or harmed person, unless you can still make some kind of restitution, which usually, you can't. It will be too late. If you can, then do so, but often, you can't go back. Still, some kind of restitution is better than none. Often, though, the person who was aggrieved has moved on, and can't even be found. When you are truly sorry about something, you ask for forgiveness. You try to make fair restitution, too. How many really do that these days? There are sincere apologies, insincere apologies, and those that are somewhere in the middle. Apologies, and repentance, are actually relative, but they're not supposed to be; they're all supposed to be heartfelt and sincere. Deep down, people know when they are wrong and when they've done wrong.

Anyway, back to more concrete issues and to some other points. At the time of my accident, I was essentially in shock and then in semi-shock and this lasted for several days. Again, the crash I was in was traumatic because it felt like I had been in an explosion. I was shell shocked. I bumbled about, and I was insulated from thinking too much for a time. My mind went into a somewhat sedated state (possibly from endorphins), although, I was taking no sedatives. I didn't even go see the doctor because all I had were minor cuts and bruises. I had to defer my trip to California to see my sister because, for one thing, I needed to find a way to get rid of my formerly beautiful but now demolished car. I was concerned that if it sat too long, the neighbors would complain. It was a mess. To the neighbors, the car—which had been towed to my home—was likely a real eyesore. To me, the car was still beautiful, even though it had been damaged so badly. I had to let it go, though. Gone was my chance to sell a Classic Car.

Sometimes I think that had I kept the damaged car, I could have found doors and fenders for the car and fixed it up, but doing that would have been too hard on me, and too unfair for me to have to do. Plus, I'm sure the chassis needed some help—some straightening out, and some new parts perhaps—and that thought also deterred me from keeping the car. Plus, having the car around the neighborhood for a long time and as an eyesore deterred me from keeping it, too. I didn't want to have to keep looking at the car day in and day out either, over the course of time it would have taken me to fix it all up. It hurt too much to look at the car, quite frankly. For all these reasons, I was forced to part with my old Olds, and parting with it I did. I sold it for scrap, essentially, and I assume the young man I sold it to parted it out, but maybe not. He may have reconstructed the Olds and somehow been able to get it fixed and straightened out. It was a great car. Having to lose it was hard on me. I'd wanted to hold on to it as a Classic.

Later on, I tried to file suit against the other driver, but I made a mistake about the statute of limitations, relative to the lawsuit. I initially wasn't going to file suit against him, because he had no insurance. I, of course, just wanted reimbursement

15

for my car loss. (I didn't know about my medical problem yet). Because he didn't have insurance, I didn't think I would be able to collect anything on my car loss. I let it go for two years. Then suddenly I got angry about the whole thing, and thought, well surely I can at least get a minimum settlement of some amount, for the damaged car.

I had previously cut out an ad for a similar type of car, and the asking price for that Olds was $7,200 OBO. However, it was a convertible, and a 1971 two-door. Mine was a white vinyl hardtop, and a 1970 four-door. Of course mine was not of equal value to a convertible. Still, the ad served as a guide. But I strongly suspected that the other driver didn't have much money, and that I'd better ask for the minimum if I wanted to collect any money at all. I figured that I would go in for less than the minimum replacement value, i.e., what another, similar used car might cost. I considered the amount that I sold the damaged car for—$400.00—and I filed the lawsuit based on these figures. I was too late in filing it, but I didn't know that at the time.

Around that time, it would have been reasonable and just to ask for at least $6,000 for the car, especially considering that I'd put in quite a lot of money for new carpeting, seat covers, and paint, to match what had been original. I most certainly could have sold the car for $6,000 at least and possibly more, that particular year, which was 1999.

All I asked for in the lawsuit was a little over a thousand dollars. Since he had had no insurance, I figured I could at least get that humble amount. I sensed the young man was low-incomed, and poor. I did a little research, right before I filed, and I found out that the young man had not even been the owner of the truck. He had borrowed the truck from his mother-in-law, but come to find out, the owner of the car hadn't had any insurance, either. So <u>she</u> didn't have insurance <u>and</u> the driver didn't have any insurance, because his license had been revoked and he wasn't even supposed to be driving any vehicle at the time. Why would he insure even his own car if his driver's license had been revoked and he wasn't supposed to be driving. But, he wasn't in his own vehicle. Maybe he didn't own his own car. He was driving a relative's car, as it turned out, and he should have checked if she had insurance before he chose to drive her truck, but that's if he had

16

had a valid driver's license, which he didn't. Maybe he did know his relative had no insurance? But, maybe he didn't? I found out later that her license had been suspended (because of the accident), since she had allowed a person who had no license drive her truck and because her truck had been in the accident. This was getting to be a tangled mess, but I still thought that $1,000 was reasonable and likely collectible. I should have gone in for more, and done so much earlier than I did. I had good ammunition. Today, I go in for much more money than I did.

My filed case was in Small Claims Court. I had thought I had three years to file in Small Claims. As soon as the Hearing Officer researched the Statute of Limitations, he assessed that since the Statute of Limitations had ended, I was wrong to have filed the lawsuit. Why had I thought the Statute of Limitations was three years for this, and not two years, is beyond me? Somewhere along the line someone had told me that the Statute of Limitations was three years, and I genuinely believed that to be the case. At one time, it may have been three years, but at the time of the Hearing, it was only two. Everything is always changing, it seems. At least I got the people into court and was able to express my side of things. At least they got my paperwork, including my neighbor's assessment. At least the truth was lodged in an effective way so the driver could come under a conscience conviction, if he wanted to, which, probably, he didn't. I carefully observed both he and his wife. At the time, both the driver and his wife had hearts that were hardened. During the Hearing (before the Judge got wind of the dates and time deadline), they didn't want to listen to the truth—this became obvious. They wanted to bury their heads in the sand like ostriches. Hopefully, the truth eventually penetrated, but only God would know if this was the case. I'm sure the young man lied to his wife about his speeding. My neighbor's write-up would have brought the truth to her. All I can note is that there are times when you shouldn't support your husband, and times when you should. Just be silent, sometimes, if need be. I wish they'd both come under conviction and turned toward the truth, but I don't believe they did, or, at least, I didn't see it. The opportunity was there, though. It's too late for them now. They'll never see me again (in this life).

In a roundabout way, I confirmed that the other driver was continuing to live in delusion because as I was observing his behavior, it was obvious that he was oppositional. He wallowed in his own lies. Not only that, but he was now pretty arrogant, knowing that his speeding would never be exposed and that the overall matter was now, presumably, buried. Again, I do not believe that God has buried it. Approximately five years later, I was forced to have surgery because of this accident—surgery forced on me all because this young man had decided to drive a car without a driver's license and insurance and because he chose to drive too fast. Whether he had his mother-in-law's permission to drive the truck (that she had not insured) or he didn't have her permission, I never learned.

I found out later, from a different officer, that a driver (such as myself) can get cited at the scene of an accident whether they caused the accident or not. He went on to say, with reference to my particular case, that it was my responsibility to take into consideration that the other driver, who was way down the road when I went to make my turn, may have been speeding. That's really backwards when you think about it. It was I, then, who was cited, for not taking into consideration that one or more cars that were coming down the road, as I was making my turn, could have been speeding. Police reports are done up a certain way. It isn't always 'what it may seem' on police reports. Again, judges who hear civil actions take into consideration all these other things, especially if they're pointed out to them. They read between the lines in other words. At least, they're supposed to. Sometimes, they may not know something. Judges learn as they go, too.

At the time, everyone said, "You were so lucky you weren't hurt worse than you were, with that much impact." I thought that too, of course. I thought it strange that I hadn't been hurt more than I was. I didn't know that things were happening to my body, internally, because I had been in a car accident. Something had started, with a rip or a tear, which I really didn't feel at the time of the accident. I was bruised along where I wore my seat belt, and I felt the bruise at the time, so any pain around that area, I assumed, was only related to the bruise. Everything else seemed OK. So, no problem, I erroneously assumed as I went about my life.

Because of the force of the crash, my stomach had been pushed up enough to cause a diaphragm tear (the hiatus) on one side. This was because my seat belt had been tight. The hiatal is what holds the esophagus and the stomach in place and in position. Without this part, the esophagus and the stomach would be up

18

in the chest area, which is what happened to me, only it happened gradually, after the accident had occurred. Once the hiatal tears, if not immediately repaired, it will continue to tear even more over a period of time, because of pressure and body movements. My tear became big enough that the stomach moved up quite a lot, over time, and the stomach was forced to somewhat tip. Quite often, the stomach goes up a bit at a time, over time. The seat belt pressure had been great and the abdominal parts and organs had been pressed upward at the time of the accident, which tore the hiatus, up next to the diaphragm. One doctor explained to me that the diaphragm is a muscle that separates the abdomen from the chest. It must have holes in it, however, to allow blood vessels, the esophagus, etc. to pass from the top of the body to the abdomen. A hiatal hernia means that the hole that allows the esophagus to pass through the diaphragm is usually large (because of tearing), which allows a portion of the chest to bulge into the chest cavity to a lesser or greater extent, depending on the size of the tear, or rupture.

It became clear to me that when symptoms become difficult to tolerate, it was time for surgery. A hiatal hernia can become life threatening. The esophagus, and even intestines, can turn or twist and there can be strangulation. Something can cause a blockage. Infection can result if there's been food buildup that cannot move along. Infection can occur at a strangulation or blockage site and then you're in big trouble. I suspect that my body was thrust to one side—the left side—and that that is where the hiatus and diaphragm tear was. Of course, at the time of the car accident, my body went one way, and then the other, because of impact thrust and the reaction to impact thrust. At the time, I felt no pain inside of my body. I'm not so sure that an Upper GI test, Ultrasound, MRI, or CT-Scan would have, at the time, detected the tear. Possibly an MRI and a CT-Scan would have, but who knows. The tear was likely small.

You cannot feel pain in the diaphragm area, when it tears. If you could, I might have known there was damage there. But there is no nerve impulse sensation there that goes to the brain. Diaphragm trauma cannot be felt. My diaphragm—the hiatus—subsequently ripped a little at a time, after the first rip from the accident, and I didn't feel those rips either (or tears or splits, whatever you want to call them). With a torn diaphragm and hiatus, eventually, some or even much of the stomach can go into the chest. The stomach can turn or bend a little, in various ways, depending on the situation. That which is attached to the stomach, to the west or east, can get altered, and pressed, and that which is to the south can come up, because the stomach did. In other words, there can be an internal rearrangement.

All this can come about suddenly, i.e., the stomach goes up into the chest because of a diaphragm (hiatus) rupture, or, the stomach can go into the chest gradually. No one is one hundred percent sure how mine came about, whether the damage was maximally caused at the onset, from the impact of the accident, or whether it gradually worsened, over a period of time. It could have been either situation or somewhat of both. Again, had it all occurred at the same time, I may not have felt it because nerve impulses are less felt or they are not felt at all, in that part of the body. It depends on the problem, though, because there can certainly be pain around the abdomen and upward if something else is wrong. Again, I had had bruising along my belly, because of the force and the seat belt. Any pain there, I just naturally assumed was because of the bruising. The hiatus, and diaphragm, are up much higher, above the stomach and duodenum.

My doctors believed my condition took time to worsen and that it was gradual. They believed that I would have had more intensely felt symptoms, early on, had the stomach gone up into the chest upon impact. And as I thought about it, my pains and problems did seem to slowly and gradually increase. For a long time, I experienced occasional bouts and symptoms, that didn't seem excessively problematic, but right before my surgery, the pain was becoming chronic, especially after I ate.

For some time, though—years even—I went along my merry way, completely oblivious to what had happened and of what was going on inside of my body. Nothing too distinctively painful or bothersome happened for quite some time, it seemed. I lived my life normally, did whatever work was before me to do. I did a great deal of writing, which is sedentary work. I worked towards a museum, that I hope to one day establish. I ran my errands, worked, cleaned my home, repaired and maintained my home, did yard work, took care of my pets, and did whatever it was that I had to do. In short, I was a regular person, doing regular things.

Some of my writing was done during the day, but much of it was done at night and I 'burned the midnight oil'. All in all, I was up and about doing a number of projects and doing whatever I needed to do, to survive and to live a decent life. I even slept any way I wanted to—on my back, stomach, or on either of my sides. I assumed that all was well but all wasn't well so I was wrong about that.

CHAPTER 2
Becoming aware of my after-the-accident problems

After the accident but after some time, I noticed occasional pains in my side. I thought it was just normal cramps. For example, one time I was walking and I got a pain in my side. I had been fast walking. I had to stop where I was and wait for the pain to subside and go away, which it did. I said to myself "oh, I guess I just ate too much." Another time, I remember being in a lot of pain (again, to the same side) and I had to lie down, but the pain didn't go away right away, at first, but, within a fairly short period of time (like a half an hour), it did. I may have been walking then, too. When I walked around, I didn't get relief right away, so I laid down. This kind of thing happened a few times, but not enough times for me to be concerned, especially because soon after going through the pain, it would suddenly leave. The whole matter confused me. I thought that pain in the side was common and normal, if it was only felt every so often, so I would always forget about the incidents. When the pain would disappear, the greater part of me assumed it wasn't coming back. The pains I felt weren't radically high on the pain scale, but they were distinctive and incapacitating, in that I had to lie down. When I'd lie down, the pain was still there, but it would seem like less than were I walking around or sitting.

I kept getting these kinds of pains over a period of time but they were infrequent and they always went away after a short while. Only minor discomfort was felt when the symptom came around. A couple of times, however, I felt more pain than usual, to the point of having to go to a medical facility. It was always outpatient treatment, but nothing was ever learned because the pain subsided so quickly. Sometimes it would be gone before I got into the doctor's office. I tended to think that it was happening because of indigestion, or that an ulcer might even be starting. I felt pressure, and sometimes a burning feeling on my right side. But the pressure always went away, not too long after it had started. It was baffling.

The medical facility that I frequented never figured out what the problem was. I never faulted them for this because they weren't set up to be a full and complete clinic. I went there at least three times, over a span of time. Later on, I retrieved those medical records and determined that these pains started up not too long after I had been in the car accident. I felt discomfort over to the one side a few times, and the condition sometimes worsened. I eventually figured out that when it did, the discomfort and pain was present whenever I ate and drank a certain amount, with a meal. Then, afterwards, it would subside and go away. It didn't happen all the time, because I rarely ate large meals.

For some time, I never connected any dots. The condition was bothersome at first, then it became somewhat distressing, but pain was only intermittently felt until finally, a certain point was reached. That's probably when my stomach turned to a certain point, up in my chest, and went all the way up or, at least, as far as it could go. Perhaps the diaphragm (the hiatus) had completely ripped; this all makes sense. Eventually, the pressure and pain was felt even if I ate or drank less than I usually did. But even then, I still didn't figure out what was going on. I didn't know what my thoracic or abdominal anatomy was, at the time. This was one of the problems—lack of knowledge. Whatever was inside my chest and abdomen was Greek to me. Eventually, I got some diagrams of the internal areas, but even then, I couldn't make heads or tails out of what was going on. Of course, this is why we have doctors.

It never entered my mind that the off and on, recurring problems that I was having may have been related to my auto accident. The auto accident had been over and done with for some time, and again, I had been convinced at the time that I had not been physically hurt. Whatever problems I was having afterwards and over a period of time had to be completely separate from the accident, no two ways about it, and I never even remotely or at any time connected the two situations or thought them to be related. You would think that I would have, but I'm not in control of all my thoughts. None of us are. They either come or they don't. The light bulb didn't light up, until later. I didn't even think about the possibility that the two might be related. The problems I was having were puzzling, but I had no answers. My layperson's mind told me it was indigestion, constipation, or perhaps an ulcer. I was way off.

After a while, the pain not only continued but it seemed to occur more frequently, so that the problem or condition was becoming chronic. I was starting to be alarmed and to get stressed out about it. Just about every time I was eating a meal, I was getting a pain over to my right side. But before then, the pain had only came about when I had eaten a really big meal, like a Thanksgiving or Christmas dinner, or a smorgasbord meal at an eat-all-you-can restaurant. The stomach capacity was gradually getting smaller, because it was turning and bending and losing space, up in the chest area. It later became evident to me that when I ate under a certain amount, I didn't get the pain, but when I ate over a certain amount, I did get the pain. But, believe it or not, it took me a long time to even figure this out—much longer than I like to admit. I was younger then and that certainly had something to do with it.

Another problem I started to have was stress and pressure around my mid and lower spine. The whole area around there was what was later termed in my medical records as 'degenerative'. I had been believing that this spine discomfort was normal for a woman my age, especially since I'd always been a bit top-heavy, in that I wear a C-cup bra. I felt that the top weight there caused my spine to curve more because I stooped over more. I couldn't help stooping over a little. Also, my eyes have always been bad (particularly one of them) and I tend to lean forward to see. I wear glasses, but I still lean forward, perhaps out of habit. Hence, that was another contributing factor to the spine problems. I had both osteoarthritis and dextroscoliosis of the spine, according to one medical report. 'Dextro' means towards or on the right side. There was an even greater reason why my spine was curving, though.

Apparently, because my stomach wasn't where it was supposed to be and because it was over to one side, in my chest area, my spine was being forced to readjust and realign, over to the right. This happened over a fairly long period of time, too. My spine was being forced to curve over and out a little, around the area where the stomach now was, so that pressure on the connective tissue and the bones caused some degeneration. Right before the diagnosis of my stomach-in-chest condition, I was having more back discomfort. I was having to lay flat on my back because this seemed to give the area some temporary relief. Close in to my surgery date, my overall diagnosis report included a notation that there had been 'degenerative changes at multiple levels along the mid and lower thoracic spine'. At my age, too, I was starting to get osteoporosis, and I had, for some time, thought that this was the sole cause of my back discomfort. For some time, I had no idea my stomach wasn't where it should be, so any back discomfort I had, had to be due to other reasons. Obviously, though, this was misleading.

Osteoporosis is very common in the spine and hip but spine fractures are twice as apt to occur, compared with hip fractures. Weak bones, or porous bones, which is what osteoporosis is, increase the risk of experiencing bone fractures. A fracture can suddenly happen because bones have been depleted of a significant amount of calcium, sometimes up to fifty percent of needed calcium. I had some osteoporosis, on top of the spine realignment problem, because my bone density had been decreasing because I'm an older woman. Because of my osteoporosis, and the fact that my stomach ended out in a new location, there was more pressure and stress on the spine than there would have been, had I only had the osteoporosis, but how was I to know this because, for a long time, I didn't even know about the osteoporosis, let alone the curved-to-one-side spine.

When symptoms had been affecting my life for a while, I made an appointment with a physician (Dr. Allen S. Finn), now that the main symptom had become clearer and I was having trouble living a normal life. When you cannot live a normal life, then that is the time when you must consider surgery. Fortunately, this particular doctor knew enough to order a chest X-ray. Why this wasn't suggested sooner by other doctors, I do not know. No one before him had even thought to do this. When the results of the chest X-ray came in, the physician contacted me for follow-up. I, of course, was apprehensive, and on pins and needles. I was thinking the worst, and fighting those thoughts. Perhaps I had an ulcer, a liver going bad, or a strange disease or even cancer. Perhaps I had a large growth somewhere that was getting bigger.

These thoughts were background. Then the chest X-ray results came in. When I'd had the chest X-ray, the young man who took the X-ray photos, looked at one of them on the lighted screen and he acted a little strange. He was a little too nice to me, so I became suspicious about my results. I sheepishly asked him if everything looked OK. He said that he wasn't allowed to discuss the results with me. Only the doctor could. Great, I thought. Just great.

Sitting in his office, my mouth dropped when the doctor told me that I had a ruptured diaphragm (the hiatus). The chest X-ray revealed a large, dark space in the area where my stomach was supposed to be. It was actually a black area on the screen. I could see my ribs, and everything looked OK, except for that black space. He asked me a number of questions, one being "were you in an accident before the beginning of your symptoms?" Click. On went the light bulb. I answered that "yes, I had been, come to think of it." And I told him about my car accident that had a little over four and a half years earlier.

My symptoms had actually started soon after my accident, only I was too oblivious to connect any dots. The symptoms were so mild or minor at first. This doctor, thankfully, finally connected the dots for me, using the chest X-ray as guide. Suddenly, everything made sense, and many thoughts began to enter my mind. I couldn't believe that that much time had gone by before an accurate diagnosis was made. I had seen several doctors relative to symptoms and my eating problem, and none of them had figured it out. I had been in a fog, for sure. At least, now, the fog had been lifted.

My initial visit with Dr. Finn was during May of 2001. At the time, his rank was 1st Lieutenant. I was then transferred to another doctor—an actual surgeon—and it was this man who ended out performing my surgery. His name was Dr. Jason P. Reynolds and he was Chief of Surgery at a Medical Group at the local Air Force Base. At the time, his rank was Major. The first, diagnosing doctor also informed me that the particular type of ruptured diaphragm (hiatus) that I had tended to occur because of trauma, as, for example, from a car accident. As I had experienced no other kind of trauma, other than the car accident, it was concluded by the doctor (and then by me because I knew he was right), that the ruptured or torn area had originated because of trauma caused by the car accident. My previous car accident had been the sole cause of my medical issues, and the puzzle pieces all seemed to fit in together quite well.

I didn't know that such things happened when a person was in a car accident. I had heard about ruptured or torn body parts, but not much about rearranged body parts. I didn't even know where the diaphragm or hiatus was located or what a diaphragm or hiatus was used for. I thought the diaphragm had something to do with breathing, but I wasn't sure exactly how it related to breathing. In Webster's New World Dictionary, the definition of a diaphragm is 'the partition of muscles and tendons between the chest cavity and the abdominal cavity'. Muscles go around the abdominal organs and system; the diaphragm is one of those muscles. It is between the liver, duodenum, and stomach, and the lungs and heart. The hiatus is between the diaphragm and the esophagus goes in through where the hiatus is so when the hiatus tears, the esophagus is affected, along with the stomach. I didn't realize that these kinds of body damages could occur. If ever I did know this, I didn't 'know' know it, if you know what I mean. There are levels concerning knowing about something. There are levels of awareness. There is conceptualization.

Another problem I had been having, and that I never related to the possibility that my stomach could be up in my chest, was that of breathing. Many times I noticed problems with breathing, mainly when I exerted myself and had been doing something on the strenuous side, like vacuuming. "Oh, it's just the dust," I'd reason. But ultimately, I figured out that before my accident I had never had a problem with breathing, so why should I be having a problem with breathing now. Well, as it turned out, my stomach was now pressing up against one lung, affording me much less lung capacity, on the one side. When I'd be out of breath more easily, I had previously thought, "well, the old girl just ain't what she used to be," when really, it was my one lung that wasn't what it used to be.

The side of my body that had the problem was not the side where I felt the symptoms. Don't ask me how this 'transfer pain' works, but because of nerves, nerve endings, and nerve stimuli, a person can feel aggravation or pain in one area of the body when the actual problem is elsewhere in the body. Right up until the Friday before my surgery, I had thought the surgery would be more to my right side, because that is where the pain was. But the doctor explained to me that no, the surgery would be on the left side, even though the pain had been felt on the right side. This was difficult for me to soak in, because it didn't seem logical to me, and it was only because I trusted my doctor that I accepted that bit of knowledge. I don't know that it related to everything I had been feeling, but to some things, it did.

Right before I had the surgery, my stomach was over to one side, and most of it—about eighty percent—was in my chest area, over to the left side. The diaphragm and the hiatus had torn. I felt the pain and discomfort on my right side, and felt absolutely no pain or discomfort on my left side. I thought this paradox to be very strange. One wonders, what would doctors of earlier times have done, surgically, with such a person as myself? They did not have the benefit of X-rays, years ago. They probably would have opened me up on the right side, where the pain was, when the area that really needed surgery was on the left side. They may have even operated on the wrong part, and woe would have been me. Such a thought made me glad that I was living in the Twenty-First Century.

Before my diagnosis, I genuinely believed I only had indigestion or something minor, or perhaps that I was starting an ulcer. The whole time that I was having symptoms, I believed these things, even after they had worsened. I thought the symptoms might have had something to do with foods and diet. As a result, I thought I'd stay away from acidy foods and foods with rough edges, like potato and tortilla chips. I reduced my salt intake. I began to eat better, but the symptoms still kept occurring. The principal symptom was that of feeling pressure against or on my one side. Sometimes, my stomach did feel as if the acidity was high. And sometimes the symptom was a sharp pain, which may have been from food with sharp edges. Sometimes my right side just felt tight. Sometimes I experienced all the symptoms at the same time, but again, the pain always went away soon after it came on. (This is because the food was digested.) It might be felt for a half hour to an hour after I ate, for example, but then the pain would be gone. It just disappeared, as if some demon had been driven out.

It took me a long time to realize that the pain went away because a certain amount of my food had been digested (so that there was no more pressure on the area). Some demon! When I ate a certain amount of food, there would be the pressure and pain, because my stomach's capacity to hold food had been reduced in size. I was only able to use a portion of my stomach, and that portion kept decreasing, as my stomach was going up in my chest, and was perhaps even turning.

The shape of my stomach had bent and changed, up in my chest. I could only use a portion of my stomach and this portion got smaller and smaller, over a period of time, as my stomach moved more and more up in the chest area. Also, there was one part of my esophagus that became constricted, either because the part of the stomach was pressing against it or because it was turned or bent a little. Something was causing my food to get clogged or stuck, at least occasionally. If the food was 'thick' food, or if I ate too much too fast, I sometimes vomited. This didn't happen too often, but it happened enough for me to notice it and to begin to be bothered about it. Mainly, this had started to happen fairly close in to my surgery date. I was not living a normal life.

The symptoms weren't so acute until right before the diagnosis, and they worsened between the time of the diagnosis and the surgery. I had previously let the matter go, thinking it was just indigestion or something minor, or maybe the start of an ulcer. I even began taking liquid antacid, whenever any or all of the symptoms hit, which was always after eating, if I ate over a certain amount. Until the diagnosis, nobody figured out what was wrong with me—not me, not my friends, and not my loved ones. I didn't tell too many people about my problems anyway, so of course, they wouldn't figure much out. For a long time, my situation didn't seem like a problem to me. People in my life only knew fragments of what was happening, so it wasn't enough for them to piece anything together. Nobody really knew what a problem it had become. I only knew fragments myself, and I'm the one who is supposed to be in charge of my life. I still can't believe that I went along for essentially five years before I finally had surgery, which of course, was a new and different ordeal for me. It came on me unexpectedly, but there it was, like a bright neon sign.

I think it was because I was so sedentary and busy with working and writing during those five years (when I experienced the miscellaneous, growing symptoms), that I didn't focus in too much on doing something about the problems I was experiencing. I was all by myself, and I didn't have a significant other around, encouraging me, or pushing me to get the symptoms and problems thoroughly diagnosed. I maybe would have resisted doing that anyway, at least in the beginning, because the symptoms, for some time, were infrequently experienced and were so minor. And again, they went away fast, at least in the beginning.

I kept thinking that I was OK, because nothing seemed chronic or severe. This is another reason why I most likely would have resisted pressing in on the problem. Truly, I didn't think the problem was major, and I thought that it was something I could manage without medical attention. I started to eat better so I thought that this would take care of the problem. The biggest reason I probably did not whirlwind into the problem is because, most of the time, I felt fine. I lived the 'same ole, same ole' life, doing everything I was used to doing and that I needed to do, and I did everything with gusto and zeal. I wasn't all that inconvenienced, in other words.

The day finally came when I began to take notice, though, as my condition became quite noticeable. I had been selling general items and collectibles on the side and on weekends, to help with my finances and bills. I had been doing all of my writing when I wasn't working on or selling items. I finally got to the point where I couldn't handle boxes and maneuver them in and out of my car. They weren't all that heavy but it got to be too much anyway. This had more to do with my back than anything else. It was becoming more and more sore.

None of the boxes were very large—most were apple, orange, and tomato boxes that I'd found at supermarkets—but my spine was getting so out of alignment (because of the reorganizing of inside body parts) that whenever I tried to handle the boxes of items I wanted to sell, my back felt very stressed. It hurt too much so I had to stop handling the boxes. Then, after a while, my back was hurting all the time, no matter what I was doing throughout the day. Even if I was just sitting, my back would hurt. It was the distorted alignment, the osteoporosis, and the dextroscoliosis that was putting stress on my spine (as it curved, some, to the right).

When the surgeon noticed the back problems on the X-ray, he didn't give too much attention to the degeneration. It had been caused by the torn diaphragm (and hiatus) and the stomach's relocation and other shifts, but there was nothing that could be done about my back, per se. The attention was predominantly on my torn diaphragm and hiatus. No back surgery could be done. Only surgery to sew up the torn diaphragm and hiatus could be done, after the stomach (and all else) was put back into their original places. Once this surgery was done, the back would make efforts to realign accordingly, which would mean more discomfort but so be it. For a time, because realigning would be a process, I would have some back discomfort after the surgery, assuming I elected to have the surgery. I would probably have back discomfort for the rest of my life, actually. My back may never realign all that well, especially because of the osteoarthritis and scoliosis. This idea didn't bother me too much, though, because I'd already learned to live with the discomfort. It wasn't too major, but the discomfort was a nuisance.

I suspect that my stomach slipped up in my chest significantly more, right before my diagnosis. It may have been a sudden change and it may have even been a minor change or shift, but the point is that whatever happened was enough for me to sit up and take notice. I was starting to notice the eating problems particularly around that time, and the pain. I made an appointment to go see the doctor and he was experienced enough to know to order the chest X-ray. That is what started the ball rolling.

I don't really know when all of my stomach finally pushed through the diaphragm and hiatal area. Like the doctors, I too believe that the tearing had been gradual. Eventually the stomach completely pushed through those areas and it went up into the chest and that is all I know and really need to know. I know I had had symptoms for years, but that they were random, irregular, and hard to figure out. Again, for quite a while the symptoms had only been minor. Another factor that deterred me from figuring out what the problem was, was that I didn't usually eat big meals. I ate throughout the day, but I didn't eat all that much during any one sitting. It was only when my stomach got filled to a certain point that I would experience the symptoms and pain.

When I ate over a certain amount, it seemed like my stomach was being pressed by something, but I assumed my stomach was in normal placement. Actually, I didn't even think about this, for some time. I didn't try to figure it out. Again, what was happening was that my stomach was going up into my chest and was turning and bending so that only so much food was able to fit inside the stomach, in the non-bended portion, and this part of my stomach was getting smaller over time, as the stomach gradually went more up into my chest area. The bend got to be lower down on the stomach itself until finally the stomach stayed in one place and couldn't go anywhere else. At that point, there wasn't very much stomach around for any food to set in, because of the bend, and because most of my stomach was up higher in a position where the food couldn't go. I could be off the mark here, but at least I've got the gist.

Once I found out what the general situation was, I was relieved. At long last, here was my answer. What had been affecting me for so long was no longer a mystery. The doctor who diagnosed the condition said that it was not life-threatening at the present time (but it could become life-threatening). For this reason, I paced myself and didn't feel the need to panic.

I, at first, thought I could live with the problem, now that I knew what the problem was. I was relieved it wasn't any of the other things that I had thought it could be. I reasoned that I could adapt to the medical condition, and figure out ways to cope with it. In other words, I could somewhat avoid and dodge the problem. But, the symptoms got even worse, and I was forced to contact the same doctor, again. At that point, the doctor must have figured out that I had figured out that I couldn't live with the problem anymore. So, as it turned out, the diagnosing doctor set it up for me to go see the surgeon. At that point, he probably knew that I needed to have surgery, but he never mentioned it to me, although, referring me over to a surgeon is a message all to itself, isn't it.

In the beginning, the diagnosing doctor had stated that some people can live their whole lives with this condition. When he said this, I thought "well, if some people can, then I can." I held on to that thought for as long as I could, even up to just a few days before my surgery. That thought actually comforted me, and for a while, it eased my stress. It was an escape release for me to think that I maybe didn't have to have surgery. I would just learn to manage the problem, like other people had, and everything would be OK. This would be my approach, and how I would deal with the problem. Surgery was for other people to have, not me. I was invincible, after all.

Still, I went in to see the surgeon. Don't ask me why. Curiosity was perhaps the reason, but it wasn't because I thought I needed surgery, or because I was seeking surgery. About the last thing I thought would result from my appointment with the surgeon was that I would actually have surgery. In other words, I was going to see the surgeon because I could at least learn some new things that might be useful to me on down the road, but I kept the appointment with him for no other reason. "Maybe he could prescribe something for my stomach problems" was one of my overriding thoughts, I do remember that. I would just eat less per meal, let that food digest, and then eat more. And so it would go for the rest of my life.

I was also thinking that if surgery was to be had at all, I could probably defer it indefinitely because, after all, I was going to manage this medical condition by only eating small portions at a sitting. I was also thinking that I might never have to have surgery. "I've lived with this problem this long, so why can't I live with the problem until I die a natural death?" was what I would reason. This was another one of my idealistic and unrealistic thoughts. If I went to see the surgeon, maybe he, too, would tell me that he thought I could live with the problem and just manage it. This is what I was hoping would happen. A novice to it all, and living in a dream world, I decided to face the surgeon.

CHAPTER 3
Mentally preparing for surgery

Once the surgeon got me into his office and went over the chest X-ray results with me, he strongly suspected that this was a surgery situation. He was wise to not initially spell that out to me, however—i.e., S-U-R-G-E-R-Y—because I was surgery skittish, both consciously and unconsciously. Surgery was for other people to have. It was not for me. Surgery was never going to grab hold of me. No siree, Bob. No way, José.

The surgeon ordered a series of more conclusive and revealing X-rays. I had to drink liquid barium so the lines and contours of exactly where my stomach was and how it set in the chest area could be seen more clearly. The whole digestive system needed to be looked at. The technicians had me flat on a bed, to different sides, and even upright, when they took the X-rays. Drinking the barium wasn't too bad; it tasted a little like marshmallow.

After this group of X-rays was seen by the doctor I was seeing—i.e., the surgeon—he gently began introducing the word 'surgery'. I, of course, wasn't ready to hear it. It went in one ear and only slightly registered. Then it went out the other ear. Suddenly, I grew feathers and acquired a bad case of chickenitis. I said to myself "oh no, not me, I'm not going to have surgery." I was going to avoid having surgery, to find a way to live with this problem without having surgery, and to just cope with everything like I'd been doing up to this present time. Even though my condition had worsened, I was going to try to live with it.

To add to my case of chickenitis, I heard the doctor say (though I tried to convince myself that I didn't) "I'm going to consult with other physicians about your case, and try to determine whether the surgery should be done from the side, or from the front." I wasn't ready to hear the word 'surgery', let alone to hear about how they were going to cut me open. All of these words just barely registered with me. "Wait," I thought, "you're talking too fast." "Stop", I thought, "I don't like what you're saying." Because I heard him mention the possibility of going in through the front, I, at first, thought the surgery he wanted to do was going to be frontal, should I decide to have it done.

The surgeon had repaired similar tears or ruptures by entering through the front, but my tear and condition was older than the ones he had previously done, so there were certain negatives to doing the surgery by way of front entry. The doctor was concerned about adhesions for one thing. After a time, the stomach bonds with other organs and to other areas in the chest cavity and so the surgery becomes more involved because the stomach has to gently be cut and separated from other organs or areas. Other organs or parts that had moved around may have needed separating, too.

Going in through the side and through the ribs is more often done when the injury and internal problems are known to be older, because bonding and adhering develop the longer the stomach is not in its normal, usual position. The stomach is in the area of other internal organs; there can be pressing and bonding. Disconnecting what needs to be disconnected so that everything is put back into place takes longer and requires more working room, so the doctor goes through the ribs, but also, by going through the ribs, he can better get to what he needs to get to. This all gets to be very technical, though. It's much more technical than laypeople (who are not surgeons) realize.

The doctor needed to be able to see everything and to get into where everything was and this was the main reason why the surgeon wanted to go in from the side. The surgery goes faster and is less dangerous when the surgeon can well see what he or she is doing. The surgeon knew he could see everything better, if he went in from the side, so that was the way things were going to be. The surgeon called the shots. The doctors he met with about the subject all felt that my surgery should be a side-entry one.

I somewhat went back and forth with the surgeon about the issue of side versus front entry. It was ping and pong. I wanted front entry because the healing is easier and comes about faster and also because the scar isn't as large, or as bad looking, after the surgery. You can hide the scar from a front-entry operation with a one-piece bathing suit, but you can't hide a scar in back with a one-piece bathing suit. My pong ended out getting pinged and it was decided that side entry would be the procedure. One problem with front entry, according to the surgeon, was that it would be too hard to get in under the front ribs, and into the chest area. This I learned later on, so for a while I was a bit put out that the doctor was insisting on going in through the side. I wanted to avoid my ribs being split. There were probably several reasons why the doctor wanted to go in from the side—reasons that were too technical for me to understand at the time and probably still are because Medicine is not my field.

To get down in the diaphragm and hiatus area, and to be better able to see what needed to be seen, the incision was best made at the side, and, in fact, as it turned out, this was the only way that the doctor could proceed because so much was up in my chest and under the ribs that set in front of the problem areas. This decision meant that a rib splitter had to be used, so that the surgeon could get down into the area to do all the operating. A rib splitter is a medical apparatus that is used to split ribs apart and to hold them apart, during an operation. The operation was going to be rather involved, but I didn't know how involved until after the surgery had been done. Before I had the surgery, I looked at everything medical rather simplistically. After the surgery, I began to be aware of the complexity of it all. And I did some studies.

<u>I knew the surgery would be difficult, but I didn't know how difficult until I took the journey.</u> Ribs have been known to break during this type of operation, whenever ribs are split apart. Usually only one rib breaks, and I was thinking the worse—i.e. that one or more rib would break. I was frightened enough about the surgery as it was. Being cut into and opened up is not exactly my cup of tea. A broken rib, I did not want, on top of everything else. Broken ribs are supposed to smart—big time.

When I heard about the possibility of getting a broken rib, or even of more than one rib breaking, and that the surgeon was most likely going to have to go in through the side, which would be more painful and take more time to heal, I balked, and I silently bawked. It was ye ole chicken bawk. Remember, I had a bad case of chickenitis. My defense mechanisms immediately kicked in. I tried to escape, whatever way I could. I tried to find a rational way out. Even an irrational way out would work. I wasn't going to be particular.

I quickly thought "hey, living like this isn't so bad." All I have to keep doing, and I had started doing this several months earlier, was to just eat portions of meals. I quickly reverted to this line of thought. I had figured out that if I ate about a cup of a combination of food and liquid and waited until that food completely digested, that I could eat another cup after a while. And so it would go. For the rest of my life. I wouldn't starve. I would be nourished. I could keep on eating a certain amount of food several times a day, instead of eating three meals a day. "Why would such a life be so bad," I thought. "Some people eat like that anyway, and there isn't even anything wrong with them."

I was getting used to eating small amounts anyway and had come to realize what my 'quota amount' was, as well. I got to where I had a sense for when I was at my quota capacity, and so I'd stop eating. If I went over that quota amount I would feel that side pain. The minute I began to feel any pain at all, I'd just stop eating. Yes, this would be my solution to the problem. I wouldn't have the surgery. I kept going back and forth about this. "Why, I don't need the surgery. I'm perfectly fine, and eating like this is not that much of a problem", is what dominated my thinking. I'd just keep eating like this and the condition would be tolerable and managed. I'd be OK, wouldn't I?

I had various talks with the surgeon. By this time, he was nudging me along and encouraging me to have the surgery. Every time the ball seemed to be in my court, I'd say "well, I can keep living like this, no problem." I wasn't being insolent or pushy, I just didn't want to have the surgery. A part of me really did believe I could coax along through life, eating small portions only, and not be significantly affected by it. This rationale or 'ball back in your court, doctor' went on for a while. This temporary conclusion on my part was my ace in the hole, and I played it every chance I got, mostly in my own mind because it was comforting to do so. Meanwhile, during the times when I was talking to the surgeon, and with various other people, I was accumulating needed knowledge. All the time, however, I kept thinking "I don't really need to have this operation. I can take it or leave it. And I'd rather leave it." Such an escapist mentality kept me going, comforted me, and buffeted the idea that surgery would be happening. It kept me encouraged, for a while.

If I thought that I'd deserved to have surgery, I may have felt different about having it. But here I was, a woman who'd been run into by someone who had been speeding and driving without a license. True, I should have taken into account that he may have been speeding when I made that turn, and I'm remorseful about that, but I at least hadn't been speeding and I at least had had a valid driver's license. And, while 'I'm' living within the realm of truth about the accident, the driver chose to not embrace the truth, because of ego, convenience, and fear. I've always wondered if his actions after the accident were laced with hate. He seemed to carry a lot of that kind of stuff inside of him. That's the kind of person he seemed to be, quite frankly. I have a Master's Degree in Counseling, so I'm sensitive to these things. I tune into people's behaviors.

The surgeon informed me that if I didn't have the surgery, something inside me could eventually twist or get pressed in so badly that blood flow in those areas would be cut off and I would then end up in the emergency room, if I even made it to the emergency room. I could die if something like that were to happen, was his admonishment. Such an emergency surgery, he went on to say, would be a much more difficult surgery than this one would be. You never know who is going to do an emergency surgery, either, he warned. It could end out being done by someone who doesn't have very much experience with doing the type of operation that would be needed. With emergency situations, you don't always have your choice of doctors.

The doctor also said that it seemed my stomach was up as much as it was going to go, but that it could possibly go up more and if it did, the intestines would have to follow even if it was but a short distance. The intestines could then twist or turn, causing major problems. Of course, still being an escapist, I'm thinking to myself "several years have already gone by and everything is probably in the place where it is going to stay now because, after all, it's been like this for some time so why should it suddenly change?" Therefore, I concluded (to myself), "everything will stay intact and just like it is now, and all I have to do is always remember to eat small portions and drink small amounts throughout the day." I didn't let the ball stay in my court very long, in other words. Back it went, over to the surgeon's court. The surgeon was very patient, towards his patient. (He was a good man, and I was lucky to have him. He was a strong Mormon.)

I had an answer to the problem, I thought, but certain key points got through to me, from various encounters and talks that I was having with a number of people, and not just the surgeon. Notice that at this point I don't refer to the surgeon as my doctor or my surgeon, only the doctor or the surgeon. I consciously and unconsciously tried to distance myself from the idea of surgery in general, any way I could. I'd just keep the surgeon at arm's length, so his ideas and conclusions would have to stay at arm's length. I'd stay detached from him, and from his ideas and conclusions; that way, I could keep the surgery away. This was nothing against the surgeon. It's just the way things were going to be, wasn't it?

The surgeon never pushed me. He never scolded, derided, cajoled, nor did anything negative. He wasn't patronizing, either. At one point (once he knew the fish was hooked), he became firm, but he wasn't anything beyond or beside that. All the way through he was a nudger, and he tried to inform me in the best way he knew to do. I was coming in as a novice, and he wasn't at all overbearing or condescending. Again, I was fortunate to have had a surgeon who was like that, and I hope he never changes because surgeons like this are needed, not only to help people who are under doctor care, but to be examples to other professionals— surgeons, regular doctors, nurses, general staff, et al.—so that they won't become or stay overbearing, impatient, or intolerant. Some professionals are this way and some put themselves on too high a pedestal. Some are very bad at communicating, too. Some do not give patients enough information. Thank God the Internet came in and kicked these too-guarded doctors in the rear. Some of these non-communicative doctors are patronizing, while others aren't. Some just need to improve communication skills. Some doctors have a poor bedside manner with patients. A doctor can bring in dark or they can bring in light. They can intimidate and make fearful or they can smooth everything over. They can add to mental stress or reduce mental stress. Et. al.

The surgeon knew, of course, that I was an educated person, and that I had taught school and had also been a counselor. He also knew I'd been doing some writing. The writing phase of my life had started soon after my car accident but

I really didn't start up writing because of my accident, per se, except that, for a while, I really didn't feel like driving too many places and so being sedentary at home, and writing, is what I naturally turned to. I quickly discovered that I enjoyed it. I took several years out to write. I ended out writing several books, of varying length. I even wrote poems and short works books.

About my writing, I hadn't really planned to write. It just happened. I didn't know I could write. Once a pen got in my hand, and ideas filled my mind, I realized that I needed to write. I couldn't dance, sing, act, or be an artist. But, I could write. And so write I did, for many years, non-stop. (I kept writing several years after my surgery.) In a way, once you've had hiatal hernia/diaphragm surgery, you become handicapped. (In my case, I became very sedentary, and was compelled to turn to writing.) You are handicapped in one sense—you don't want the repair to deteriorate and to, then, need to have another prototype surgery, which does happen. The more active you are, then, the more apt you are to disturb the sewn-in mesh (if mesh was used) that holds the hiatus and diaphragm intact. I know that my turning to writing, as much as I did, had to do with my conscious (but more subconscious) awareness of that threat. However, I had already started to write some books even before the surgery; I'd planned to finish them and they would not be too very long; the surgery and the time it took for me to heal caused me to make the books I'd started to write longer, and to start some other books so then on and on I went down the writing path. At this juncture, I may even write in my old age, if I live long enough. But enough about my writing, because I've diverted from the subject at-hand. Again, at the time of my surgery, I'd started a few books and assumed they were almost done, but they weren't done—not by a long shot. And again, more were to come. This book probably would not have been written had other books not already been started. It may also not have been written had I had the surgery from the front and not through the ribs because it's hard to bend and sit at a desk if you've been cut open in the front. The incision would be up more than where the bend would be when you are sitting, but still, sitting for long periods of time might be harder with a front-area incision. It wouldn't cause harm, though, unless you had to stoop over too much while sitting and sat too long.

I'm the kind of person who investigates everything—turns stones over as it were. I research things and ask a lot of questions. Perhaps I was a surgeon's nightmare, I don't know. I'm sure they see all kinds of reactions to impending surgeries. One thing I know they are aware of is balking. They are aware of defense mechanisms, in general. Defense mechanism is a psychological term, but it can be a medical term, too. It can be, for example, 'a body's reaction against disease organisms'. In the psychological realm, it refers to 'the usually unconscious mental process that a person goes through to avoid conscious conflict or anxiety'. These definitions come from the *DK Illustrated Oxford Dictionary*.

Believe me, the thought of having surgery is a 'conscious conflict and anxiety'. One does want to avoid it, if at all possible. I've never encountered anyone who wanted to go under the knife. Even when a person has to, the person still doesn't want to. This is the conflict. You look for an escape route so you can escape. I mean, a man (or woman) you barely know is going to cut into your body, work on it, and close you up. Strangers are going to be giving you anesthesia and doing other things to your body. Strangers, I say, not people you've known for a long time, or even for a short time. The people in the OR (operating room) are all going to be strangers, except for your surgeon, who is really, essentially a stranger. Most people don't know their surgeons at all or all that well when they go in to have their surgery. There are no ties that bind there—at all. He owes you nothing, per se. The professionals in the OR don't owe you anything, either. You are going to be putty in their hands once you sign the consent form and once the operation begins. You gamble with your own body.

This thought leads me to some other reasons why I didn't want to have the surgery. These reasons added to my 'conscious conflict and anxiety'. My mother had had a couple of surgeries—neither of which took all that well. The first one was on her back. A vertebrate slipped, and had to be fused, or maybe she was missing a vertebrate (from birth), I don't exactly recall that particular detail. This surgery occurred around 1959, when surgeries were not what they are today. She had it when we were living up in Canada. Back surgeries are known to be relatively successful now, but back then they were chancy. The surgery, after everything had healed, was not real successful, and my mother had back discomfort for the rest of her life. Because she didn't want to go through with a second back surgery, she continued to be inconvenienced by the discomfort that she had after she had had her first back surgery.

Then in the late 1980s, my mother went in for a knee replacement operation. She chose the partial-knee replacement, instead of the whole-knee replacement. Both were an option at the time. It was believed, by some, that whole-knee replacement was better than partial-knee replacement, even if only the partial was needed. Yet, the partial-knee replacement seemed to be the more logical way to go, since, why have the whole knee replaced when only part of the knee was defective. My mother was torn. She ended out choosing the partial, and, after the healing and the physical therapy, she had knee pain. She ended out having a problem with walking and at first she sometimes used a walker, and later, she had to use a cane. She sat down more frequently, too, because of her knee pain, and she stayed seated for longer periods of time. (This inactivity did not help her weight problem, either). So, these remembrances, that I had regarding my mother's past surgeries, caused me to have a mental block against having surgery.

But, then there was my sister's surgery. It was actually macabre, but presumably, because of an accumulation of medical tests she had, it was necessary for her to have the surgery. She had cancer, and the cancer was spreading. It was not caught in Stage One, for sure. She'd had radiation, and also chemotherapy before she had the surgery, at which time cancer had to be cut out. It was strongly and fervently believed that she needed to have radical surgery, to cut out the many cancerous areas. She knew it was going to be bad. She just didn't know how badly. No one did, except maybe her doctors there at David Grant Hospital in Fairfield, California. (David Grant Hospital is where by husband had died, from cancer.)

When she awoke from the rather lengthy surgery, my sister had not been sewn up in certain areas. They couldn't sew her up. She had an open wound in her chest. They had cut out bones—part of her sternum and one clavicle, and they had cut out some ribs. Apparently the bone areas had been eaten up or were being eaten up by the cancer. They'd also removed lots of tissue under and around the bones. Over the years, she had other operations, and they removed more bone and tissue during those times, as well. This surgery was horrendous, though, and it is a type of surgery few ever even hear about. No one wants to hear about it or talk about it because people are squeamish and the surgery and her whole cancer case were very unsettling and disturbing. When you hear about it or talk about it, it first turns your stomach. Then, sympathy floods in.

A permanent dressing had to always be over my sister's open chest. It was redressed, and redressed, and redressed, because the dressing had to always cover the open area and it got soiled. They kept hoping that when they removed more of the cancer that they got all of the cancer. And for several years, my sister continued to live, although her life was far from pain-free or normal. That she still lived so long was amazing, when you think about it. The initial cancer was removed during the surgery, and this did prolong her life. Unfortunately, some did come back, after a time. More was cut out, extending her life, but the day came when they could remove no more or it would kill her. Everyone knew she was on borrowed time.

My sister's life had to be hell. The open wound had to be hell. I saw it only once when the dressing was off, and it turned my stomach and made me feel extremely queasy. I wanted my sister to be like she was before the operations, but that could not be. My sister lived about twelve years with this open area in her chest. Her faith in God, her family and friends, helped to pull her through these really difficult times. Her affliction showed her very little mercy. Cancer is a mean disease.

The pain and stress my sister went through, very few of us on planet Earth will ever realize. How can anyone relate to or identify with such a lengthy ordeal. Certainly not me. I can't relate to it. I can relate a little more to it now, because I've had surgery, but it's only 'in part' that I can relate to it. Before my surgery, I couldn't relate to it at all. Because I'd seen what surgery had done to my sister, I consciously and subconsciously feared having surgery. I 'feared' surgery because of what had happened to my sister and because of what she had been forced to suffer. Eventually my sister died because a tumor that they couldn't operate on was growing against her esophagus, so her breathing slowly got cut off. Can anyone relate to that?! No one can tell me that these remembrances weren't in the back of my mind, as I was considering whether or not to have surgery.

At one point, one of the resident doctors at the hospital threw a curve at me, and I spun out and decided, absolutely, that I wasn't going to have the surgery. I hadn't formally met him, but I spoke with him on the phone. Sometime, young resident doctors have a way of acting like they're experienced doctors, when they're really just starting out, and they say things they shouldn't be saying. Later, the established surgeon (mine) said that the resident was essentially responsible for administrative duties, but at the time, I saw all doctors as being blended together. They were all the same to me.

Around this time, I got hold of a book, titled, *Take This Book to the Hospital with You–A Consumer Guide to Surviving Your Hospital Stay,* by Charles B. Inlander and Ed Weiner. This book is written with patient's rights in mind—all across the board. By reading this book, I got well informed about hospital on-goings. I learned much. One thing I learned was that resident doctors are not real high on the scale and so what they say will likely not be the end all be all. They aren't doctors in the fullest sense of the word—not yet. I knew this before, but I didn't 'know' know it, if you know what I mean.

When residents complete their residency requirements, then and only then are they full-fledged doctors. (But they still don't have a great deal of experience). Before then, for example, they can write prescriptions but they're under the supervision of established doctors when and if they do. Actually, they are under the supervision of established doctors with reference to everything, until they are done with their residency program. They have some free rein and latitude but it's limited. Their experience is not at all great and when it comes to surgery, they've never had to take full charge of anything, on their own. They observe and assist, and study a great deal. Some of them don't make it, quite frankly, for whatever the reason or reasons. Still, certain of them will throw their weight around, before they are licensed doctors.

At the time of my encounter with this one resident, I was still trying to find my way through the maze—should I have the surgery, should I not have the surgery? During my conversation with the resident, I was telling him about my sister's cancer, and the rather large chest opening that she had had and continually had to dress. Whereupon the young resident interjected "and, Mrs. Thompson, you too could end out with a permanent open wound." My mouth fell open as I went into a mental-shock state. He was so matter-of-fact when he said this, like he was thinking "well, so what if you do". I couldn't believe it. If he's going to be a doctor, he sure has a lot to learn.

I thought about my sister's pain and stress, because of the open wound she had to live with for such a long time. I thought about something else, too, that somewhat related to everything. I had met a young man, just the week before my surgery was scheduled. He was the neighbor of someone I knew from church. While we were all talking in her living room, the subject of my impending surgery came up and he showed me a spot in his front area under his shirt that had a rubber bag placed over a hole in his skin. It was to his side, near a rib. The bag was necessary because it is where his urine went into. He'd had an operation because of a birth defect and he couldn't urinate the usual way. His urine had to come through a hole in his front area, and the rubber bag filled up with his urine. The subject only came up because I had been talking about possibly having surgery or I'm sure he would never have shown me the hole and the bag. This fellow seemed to have a good attitude about his handicap, which is exactly what it was.

When I left the friend's home, I thought about the fact that some doctor had cut out a hole in the fellow's body and rerouted things so that he could urinate in a bag, which always had to be attached to his body. The fellow was just a toddler when this was done, and he, at that very young age, knew he had to live like that for the rest of his life. This fellow's condition had been affecting my thoughts about surgery, too, because I had just met him. This, my sister's condition and some other things, had been on my mind when the young resident said that I, too, might end out with a permanent hole in my body.

Quickly I said to the resident "what do you mean, how can that be." And he suddenly said he had to go because he got a pager call. "Great. Just great," I thought to myself. "I can't go to sleep tonight with this thing hanging over my head." It was looking like I was needing the surgery and so now I was panicked. So, I called the young man back and asked that he be paged because he was in the hospital somewhere. I finally got him on the line, and again, he got off the phone quickly because he was 'busy'. He got off the phone quickly, as if he was the only person who had rights in the universe. I thought, "What a jerk! What an insensitive!" How could he say something like what he said and then drive me away with aloofness and insensitivity without any further comment. Is he a sadist or something—someone who enjoys tormenting another person?

I immediately called the surgeon, who had by this time already set up a date and time for my surgery. I left a message for him that relayed that I had canceled the surgery because that is what I had just done, because of my new compounded fears. I didn't want to have a surgery that was going to leave me with a hole in my body—not if I could help it!

The surgeon had previously set up a surgery scheduling for me because another doctor, who headed the Cardio-Thoracic section there, had agreed to be there with him (Cardio-Thoracic surgeons are sometimes just typed as Thoracic surgeons.) The Cardio-Thoracic surgeon who was to supervise him had done plenty of surgeries himself, but, he wasn't my proposed, prospective, primary surgeon. The surgeon I'd been discussing everything with was a 'general' surgeon (as opposed to a Cardio-Thoracic surgeon) and he was to be the main surgeon for my surgery. He would likely never be a Cardio-Thoracic surgeon by specialty, like the doctor who was to supervise him was, but he had done plenty of thoracic-related surgeries. My surgery date had been set and up until my conversation with the insensitive young resident, I had planned to go through with it, though just barely. I was very fragile, and could turn on a dime, and I did turn on a dime.

So, to follow up with the story, the general surgeon called me the next morning and he wiggled out of me everything that had happened or that had been said and he reassured me that the odds of my ending out with a permanent open wound was essentially nil. He affirmed that it was 'a million to one' chance that something like that would happen. Other things were said too, and the result was that he smoothed out all the wrinkles and made my apprehension, almost, go away. Then he said, "I'll keep the surgery date open". So, the ball was back in my court. Oh that darn ball.

I was also really nervous about the fact that so many people were going to be in the OR during my surgery. OR means Operating Room. I made a separate call to the surgeon to specifically tell him I was worried about germs. Germs are 'any microscopic organism, especially, one of the bacteria types that can cause disease'. (Webster's New World Dictionary) Any one of these professionals in the OR could bring in unwanted germs, one way or another. (Germs are the main reason why they wear sterilized foot coverings over their feet, sterilized clothing, masks over their faces, and a covering over their heads).

I have to add here that I'm sure glad there were coverings over their feet because I'm not so sure that hospital floors are scrubbed enough times throughout the day. They may not always be scrubbed well enough, either. Hospitals are prone to having Staphylococcus aureus infection. These bacteria can cause a number of infections or a number of toxins in humans and animals. Food poisoning sometimes causes Staph. Burns and rashes can be open and bring about Staph. Blood sitting around for a while can bring it about, too. It is bad when staph bacteria get in deeper into the body and enter the bloodstream and its circuitry. Staph can get into the heart and lungs; it can even get into joints and bones. Antibiotics have to be given. Some common antibiotics are resistant to some staph types. A hospital may have to send out for particular or special antibiotics. Germs multiply in certain liquid environments. Staph bacteria can be brought in by staff, but hospital workers are trained to keep staph at bay.

Regardless of precautions that professionals take, I was still nervous about germs. I thought about Howard Hughes, and about the rumor that he had been totally paranoid about germs. He therefore isolated himself in a germ-free environment. (Is there such a place as a germ-free environment?) The surgeon assured me that everything is under strict germ control, relative to clothing worn, sanitation, sterilizing, and to the overall environment. Instruments were always sterilized. Gloves were worn. I, of course, knew all this, on one level, but I had to hear it, at that particular point in time. Infection happens, during operations. It can increase after the operation. It can start up for the first time after the operation, too, so you can't always know how the infection got started. Infection can occur inside or outside of a body during or after a surgery. I didn't want that to happen, and when the doctor assured me that every precaution would be made to prevent infection during the surgery process, the red light that was in my mind turned to green.

I had to jump over all the hurdles before the surgery because that's the kind of person I am. Right before my final decision to have the surgery, I spoke with my cousin, who is a Pathologist with an M.D. after her name. She said that the odds of my ending out with an open wound were 'a million to one', just like the surgeon had said. She used the exact same phrase that the surgeon had used, which I thought was rather coincidental and even odd. She didn't even know my surgeon, and, I'd never mentioned the 'a million to one' adage to her. My cousin and I talked for a while, and she knew quite a lot about medical facts that were outside of the range of her specialty. Doctors learn general Medicine along the way, because it ties in with their specialty field, one way or another. The human body and all related is the basis for the overall field of Medicine, in other words. Plus, she'd learned a lot in medical school (plus her residency).

I had already been talking about the overall subject of my medical problem and possible surgery with various people, but especially with the prospective surgeon who had ended out with my case (poor fellow), and, I'd read quite a lot, too. I'm quite the perpetual student. I already knew a lot by the time that I spoke with my cousin. In fact, I actually carried most of the conversation with my cousin, because I already knew so much about the overall situation. It was my situation, and not hers. It was current with me and not her. She listened. I talked. That was good. My cousin and I batted the subject around for thirty or forty minutes on the phone. She perhaps learned more from me than I did from her. Or, she was simply reminded of some things she already knew. This was not her specialty and she'd never done any surgery. She had probably forgot many things from med school. I know I would have, and I have a pretty good memory. My cousin is younger than I am too, which really didn't matter, in this case. There wasn't that much age difference between us. My cousin's first husband had had his ribs split apart during an operation, early in their marriage, so my cousin was up on the rib-splitting part. My cousin certainly knows a lot about Pathology, and probably about Oncology. She knows more than I'll ever know about the field. I was never even interested in Microbiology and using a microscope. I took Biology and we did some of that in that course, but I jumped over it as fast as I could. Germs and diseases—no thanks, not my interest for life-long work.

Kathy S. Thompson, M.A.

I was actually fortunate to have completed Biology. At the first college I went to, the course was eight credits for my first year—four for the first semester and four for the second. The course was all theory and no lab. But, when I transferred to a larger university, their Biology course was set up three credits for theory and one credit for laboratory (lab) each semester. I was able to avoid Biology lab because I'd already taken the required eight units and satisfied that requirement. In lab, dissection took place, including the dissecting of frogs. I could never have dissected a frog because I was too squeamish and I loved all animals. Psychologically, I could not have cut up even a dead frog. Some surgeon I would have made! Surgeons are all about 'cutting' but all their cutting is in line with what is practical and needed, and is in line with their Hippocratic Oath. My cousin had not done any surgeries. Her work involved using the microscope and contributing to getting the findings into medical reports that other doctors relied on for their work.

Relative to the Hippocratic Oath, most U.S. med students swear some kind of oath. (In France, med students actually sign to their oath.) The Hippocratic Oath has been modified at some places; there have been completely new oaths sworn to at other places. Still, it is good that some kind of 'do no harm' oath (or nil nocere oath) is sworn by most med students, which means that when they become M.D.s, they will, in all probability, continue to honor that oath. The oaths are not necessarily said before God but they're said in good conscience.

The conversation with my cousin was a beneficial one. During the conversation, certain things that my cousin said shined pretty bright, like neon lights in Las Vegas, which is where my cousin was living at the time. You know how some conversations can go. And, you talk with someone and certain ideas end out staying with you either by what they had said or by what you yourself had said. You also have afterthoughts, after conversations. It was those certain ideas and afterthoughts that caused me to finally let go, and to decide to have the much-dreaded operation. My talk with my cousin tipped the scales, in other words. I was glad she was there. I would have been there for her too, if she needed me, because you want to be there for family, if and when they seem to want or need your help.

50

Another piece of information that tipped the scales was that the lastability of this type of operation was in the ninety-percent range. This fact came directly from the surgeon. He claimed that once the operation was done and the diaphragm area healed up, that the diaphragm would stay well stitched and intact. He further claimed that I'd have to have some pretty bad trauma done to the diaphragm, like being punched really hard or being in another accident, before it would tear again and become a problem. These comments were encouraging and reassuring. I was at last convinced, and could escape the surgery no more. (I learned later on that the surgery was not such an invincible one, but at the time, I believed it would have permanency.)

It is important to discuss your prospective surgery with people in the know, if and when you can. The answers, or the knowledge, come in gradually and it accumulates, if you seek out such knowledge. If surgery is at all elective, and often it is not, you can easily go from the 'no' realm to the 'yes' realm, because of the knowledge you accumulate about the surgery. This is how it was for me. Sometimes a surgery may seem elective on the surface, but it really isn't elective, at all. I gradually came to realize that my surgery wasn't really elective, but again, for some time, I believed that it was.

I discussed various elements about my surgery with neighbors, people at church, friends, my father and other relatives, and even strangers, if you can believe that. For example, I encountered people while I was grocery shopping and the subject would come up. So, I discussed the subject with perfect strangers. Well, why not! Each time I spoke, ideas and concepts got ingrained. Pity the very shy type of person who has to have surgery, because, whereas they may have some peace of mind about going into it, they won't have as much peace of mind as the person whose mind has been more mentally prepared to have the surgery would have. If and whenever possible, a mind should be prepared to have surgery. Knowledge can bring about comfort and peace. The more preparation, the better. One must always ask questions, and be a careful listener. When it comes to having surgery, reality has to permeate, and, acquired knowledge brings about reality.

It is not good if a person ends out changing a surgery date. Time is being held aside for the surgery, and when there is a cancellation, they have to fill that space,

51

if there is time. If the cancellation is a sudden one, it puts the hospital, doctors, and staff in a difficult place or position. So, you learn all you can <u>before</u> your surgery date. You take it upon yourself to do this. You make the date. And you keep the date. You convince yourself that God is never too early and never too late, and you hold on to your faith and hold to your acquired peace.

There are hospital professionals who are sometimes available to speak with people about their fears and concerns, relative to their impending surgery. But the person who is going to be doing the surgery should be available to a patient they will be doing the surgery on, right before the surgery. If I needed some ready answers, I should be able to call the doctor's office. Usually my doctor wasn't instantly available but I always left a message for him to return my call, so he called me back as soon as he had time for a discussion. Whoever a person's doctor is, he or she should be available, in person or by phone, to answer the many questions that will flood into the person's mind before a surgery. I kept writing my questions down on paper so that when I was able to talk things over with my main doctor (on the telephone, usually), I would go down my list of questions and not forget to ask him something. Being a list-type of person can be of benefit, in more ways than one.

Of course, there are many times when a person must suddenly have a non-elective surgery. Surgery cannot be prepared for. The patient is lucky to even have a brief discussion about the surgery so forget asking any questions. That's just not going to happen. Some sudden-surgery situations can be emergency ones, and there may be no time at all to talk about anything. My medical situation had been paced.

The day before my surgery, I spoke with a Registered Nurse, or an RN, and her job was to answer questions and ease the mind of people who were about to have surgery. Some good soul at the hospital steered me over to her. She was quite informed and helpful, but about one subject in particular—pain management. She was able to tell me, in advance, what all was going to happen to me but she educated me at the same time, about the pain management that was to be used throughout the surgery process. She got pretty specific, too. It was because of my meeting with her that I acquired a final peace, before going in to have the surgery.

All of a sudden I became trusting of everyone and everything. I held back maybe just a little, but I was really liberated, because of this woman. She was a qualified, convincing person, and I know she does a lot of good for other individuals, who need knowledge about their up-and-coming surgery. Coincidentally, she had the same first name as my sister, who is presently living in the afterlife somewhere. I thought about my sister. I wanted to join her in the afterlife, but I wasn't ready to go just yet.

Concerning knowledge, in advance, about one's surgery, studies have been done and around ninety-five percent of people who go into surgery would like to have as much knowledge about their surgery as they can acquire, before they have their surgery. Books and the Internet are very helpful, in the acquiring of medical knowledge. You don't want to be a bump on a log and learn little to nothing. You want to access as many resourceful people as you can, too, because talking things over with people who are working right in the thick of it all will also provide a patient with knowledge and important information.

I had had minor surgeries, but none were as involved as this surgery was going to be. I'd had Radial Keratotomy on my eyes, whereby all around my corneas small cuts were made so my corneas would change in shape and my vision would improve. This surgery was not real painful. It was more of an inconvenience than anything else, because of all the appointments that had to be made before the actual surgery, and afterwards, too. The Ophthalmologist had to cut slits in each cornea in both my eyes at two different sittings, too, which I ended out being unhappy about because he made the cuts too long and this ended out affecting my vision, over the years. I could see better for a while, but soon afterwards, my eyes once again required eyeglasses, which was why I had had the wreck to begin with (i.e., to avoid having to wear eyeglasses). So, this surgery wasn't exactly a success story and I'm not sure I should have even had it. Not all surgeries are successful or completely successful. Such experiences, and results, float around in your mind. Today, they are using laser, and have a higher success rate with corneas and people's vision. Back then, they made tiny cuts and the machine that was used to ascertain anything relative to the cuttings was good, but all machines require some amount of human handling and this is where error can occur, including with computers.

I'd also had minor plastic surgery. There wasn't much pain associated with that, either. I was up and about a few days after the plastic surgery. It was just some liposuction (and not all that much of it). This surgery didn't really involve cutting though, and it is cuts that take a while to heal. The cuts I ended out with after my through-the-ribs surgery were like no cuts I had ever had or ever thought I would ever have to have. Of course, I've had children, too, but that isn't really surgery, unless a woman has to have a caesarian section, which I never had to have. Childbirth is painful, but it's managed pain, and healing doesn't take that long after giving birth and there isn't too much pain after a baby is born. The body bounces back quite fast. The body has been stretched and inconvenienced, but it hasn't been cut into. I had no idea what I was getting into when I decided to have this enter-by-the-side surgery, but I was about to find out. The clock was ticking, and everything was closing in on me.

With the surgery I was to have, nothing was going to be removed. Sometimes something is even replaced, or transplanted, but this did not apply to me. My surgery was to be 'repair only.' After all my talks with the surgeon, he began to make more and more sense. He didn't force me into having the surgery. No one should be forced into doing something they don't want to do, at least in most cases. Again, he had been a nudger and I assume he was this way with all his patients. This is the manner that doctors should have (up to a point and whenever possible). Doctors should let the person having the surgery make the final decision and they should help them along the way. They should go over pros and cons, and fees of course, and they can even give their opinion, but they should be sober and reserved when they do. The trick for the doctor, I guess, is to cause the patient to think that they are making the decision, when it may really be of the doctor and other professionals who are over-riding the patient's conscious choice.

When it comes right down to it though, people have free will and they decide their own destinies. Still, my prospective surgery wasn't really elective. I had thought it was, at one time, but I couldn't keep living with the problems and still have a good quality of life. Plus, in time, I could have died from a cause that was related to the condition. Essentially, both the diagnosing doctor, and the surgeon, most likely saved my life, and in the event this was the case, I will forever be grateful. I'm grateful to them no matter what, though, because I had the surgery, and the surgery was successful.

CHAPTER 4
The surgery itself, and immediately after the surgery

My father came through for me, as I knew he would. He picked me up at my home and drove me to the hospital that morning. His lady friend, Edna, was along for the ride. Several years earlier my mother had died and he had met Edna and struck up a relationship with her. I liked Edna and grew to like her more over the years. Later, Edna became an Alzheimer's patient and was institutionalized (which greatly distressed me). It would have been hard to get up early in the morning and drive myself to the surgery, quite frankly. I was glad the two were there for me. I was feeling moderate emotions of fear and dread, despite everything I had previously learned. Fear and dread were subdued enough, however. I was even at peace, for the most part. I had resigned myself to have the surgery and everything was being put in motion. It's so much better when you go in to a hospital to be calmly driven in. It beats having to be taken in by an ambulance. Many times, people who go in by ambulance because of an emergency end out having surgery while they're at the hospital. Fortunately, my condition wasn't an emergency, per se.

I knew I was entrusting my body to a group of professionals, some of whom I had never seen or met before. It was a masks-on-faces type of thing. I also knew that I was entrusting my body to my surgeon. (Note that I am now referring to him as my surgeon and not the surgeon). I knew that he had done a large number of front-entry surgeries, but that he'd only done thirty-some side-entry surgeries. Still, thirty some side-entry surgeries does indicate experience. I figured that after doing even a few side-entry surgeries, he'd have it pretty well down because he seemed like the quick-learner type. Actually, he had to be a quick-learner type or he couldn't have made it all the way through to being a surgeon.

The man who was his assistant, an established and experienced Thoracic surgeon, had done loads of similar types of operations as mine was to be, and he was there as a supervisor. Dr. Viktor Lund was Chief of Cardio-Thoracic

Surgery, there at the hospital. The thoracic area goes from the bottom of the neck down to the abdomen. The diaphragm is the muscular partition between the chest cavity and the abdominal cavity. Inside of the chest or the thoracic cavity are the heart, the esophagus, and the lungs. The diaphragm is attached to the lumbar vertebrate, the sternum (breastplate) and the lower ribs, and there are three openings in the diaphragm. These three openings are essential because the lymphatic and thoracic ducts, veins, nerves, the esophagus, and the aorta are allowed to function (from passage) because of them. The diaphragm is lower in the rear and higher in the front. It slants upward in other words. Surgeons have to know these details and then some. Likely such details are elementary to surgeons. But, what surgeons have to have is a good memory. They have to think as they go. They have to constantly remember where everything is and how everything works. That is where their smarts come in.

Later on, my surgeon mentioned that Dr. Lund had left the room, soon after my surgery had started and I had initially been told that he would be in the room the whole time. At the very least, I had wanted him to supervise the surgery. I guess some physicians can leave during a surgery, depending on what is going on. He was Chief physician and the head of Thoracic at the hospital, after all, and my surgeon was a good surgeon. My surgeon had just started using that hospital for his surgeries, I have to add, but he had been in Surgery for many years, elsewhere. I would have wanted 'the Chief' to supervise the last part of the surgery, especially, and to have looked very carefully at both of my lungs, since they were in the way and had to be deflated so the surgery could be done. The lungs have to be put back to normal before the close-up. I have to add that my surgeon was clearly concerned about my breathing ability, right after my surgery (possibly a little overly concerned). He insisted I do special breathing exercises, using a small, special hand-held breathing apparatus, which I did but it did not seem to help improve my breathing. However one or both lungs ended out after the surgery is what I as stuck with so que sera, sera.

The diaphragm contracts when a person breathes. It expands, and when a person exhales, the diaphragm relaxes. When the diaphragm contracts, there is pressure on the abdomen. This pressure is believed to help digestion but when my diaphragm was ruptured and my stomach was up in my chest, the food I ate was still digested. When a person hiccups, it is because the diaphragm is involuntarily contracting. I never had a problem with hiccups, though. Had I had either symptom—poor digestion or hiccups, I would know that something was wrong. Since my surgery, I haven't had a problem with digestion or hiccups, but I suppose this is immaterial, except for the digestion part. Everyone has to be able to digest their food. Why I was able to digest food as well as I did, after my diaphragm and hiatus had been torn and damaged and my stomach had gone up into my chest is odd, but food follows a certain path in the digestive system regardless of a misplaced or tipped stomach. The ileum or small intestine area stays intact for the most part, and so do the large intestine areas, of which there are three—the Ascending Intestine, on the right side, the Traverse Intestine, on the top of the jejunum and ileum, and the Descending Intestine area, that goes down to the colon. If the stomach moves up, the intestines can, too, but digestion still goes on. The stomach can end out being completely above the diaphragm, if the hiatal hernia is a large one. Mine was above it about 75 to 80% the first time, and the same the second time. It could go up 100%. The hiatus can get very, very stretched because of the stomach's going up. The diaphragm is a muscle and isn't really used in digestion; it's essentially a separator. It is mainly used for breathing. Right now my stomach is pressing up on one lung and it is very close to my heart.

I was glad that my surgeon was going to have a Cardio-Thoracic specialist in the room with him when he performed my surgery. This other doctor, whom I met briefly in the hospital hallway on the day I signed my consent form, was calm and impressive. He was from Sweden, with a Swedish accent and all. He said about my operation, "piece of cake", and he said it in such a way that I knew he was on top of things. Soon after, I had the insight that, yes; the operation may have been a piece of cake for him, but not exactly a piece of cake for me.

I had trust in my doctors, by this time. I also had trust in the hospital in general. It seemed to be a well-run, efficient institution, and it was an up-to-date hospital. It had state-of-the-art equipment, and did not seem to be understaffed. I was up on my medical insurance, and at the time had no pending financial obligations. Financially, it was an open time for me to proceed with the surgery, and to also take time out to heal from the surgery, in that healing was going to take time. I did some counseling on the side, but could put that on hold. Previously, I had been finishing up some writing, and now I was pretty much caught up with it, in as much as I was able to do. (I started writing this book as soon as I got home from the hospital, though). All lights seemed to be green going into the surgery—time-wise, education/information-wise, financial-wise, and, support-wise. My father and Edna were my strongest support base.

My father had had experience with the medical world, in general, and with being there for other people when they had had surgery. He had had surgery four or five times. His surgeries were not real major, but any surgery is serious to the person having it. Actually, any surgery is serious, and dangerous, especially if a person has to go under anesthesia. General anesthesia is easier on a person. A person can have a surgery done and only have local anesthesia, like with dentistry. A couple of my father's surgeries had been semi-major and a couple of them had been minor. There are light surgeries and there are heavy surgeries and then there are those in-between. There are also multiple surgeries (at the same time). You don't want any of your loved ones to ever have to have major surgery. My father has had a lot of experience in life, on a number of levels and with regards to a number of issues and situations. His have been different from my own, and we have complete education-exposure differences so we don't always think alike, but a lot of times, we do. When the chips are down I can count on him, though. Any outside issues would take a back seat to any present crisis. All families should be this way, and it starts with the parents or the patriarch and matriarch. I have written a book about my father titled *A Driven Life*. I wrote it after I'd had this surgery.

Operations are not all the same, at all. Before having my own surgery, I tended to see all surgeries as the same but this really is not the case. All operations are different from other operations because they each vary as to area, length of time, difficulty, and actually cutting. The word, surgery, according to *Webster's New World Dictionary*, means 'working with the hands'. More expansively, the word means 'the treatment of disease, injury, or deformity by manual or instrumental operations, as the removal of diseased parts or tissue, by cutting'.

My father was there for my mother through her surgeries, and the related physical therapies. And, he was there when my sister had her first cancer surgery, and then the next ones as well. He visited my sister many times, when she had her cancer. He was there many times right before she died and during her time of death, as well. He caught midnight Air Force hops from Air Force base to Air Force base, so he could spend time with my sister and also be with her husband (who was going through hell but not as much as my sister was). My brother-in-law learned the meaning of 'deny thyself' because his life became one of sacrifice. My father is pretty tough, but my sister's cancer broke him up. I should have known he would be there for me, too, when I was to have surgery. He rallies around family, especially when the chips are down. That's one of his strong points. You can count on him being there, when hardship or calamity hits. He's there when the chips are down, too.

There were some pre-surgery instructions I had to follow or carry out. I was not supposed to eat or drink anything after midnight, the night before. I was to shower well, before the surgery. And of course, the day before the surgery I had to register with admissions. Last, I was instructed to leave my valuables at home. In other words, any watches or jewelry were not to be with me, at the hospital. None of this was too hard to do or carry out, but I was a little zombie-like as I went about carrying out these pre-surgery instructions. I suppose some dread was there, and resignation.

That morning, on the way to the hospital, it was comforting to have my father with me, and Edna too. Just to be able to talk, whether about simple things or about things pertaining to the surgery, helped to occupy my thoughts and to cushion my mind. I had to go in the pre-op receiving room, and to say goodbye to my father and Edna. Such a parting was not an easy parting for me. When undergoing surgery, people have been known to die during the surgery, for some reason or other. In the back of my mind, there was this little seed of fear that 'yes, I could die within the next several hours'.

At some point in time I took it upon myself to look into the subject of the history of medicine and surgery, and although a person can hop around like a kangaroo or rabbit, looking through numerous books in order to find, synthesize, and consolidate collected information about a topic or subject, I simply walked over to my bookcase instead, and pulled out different volumes from a set of encyclopedias that had been put out by Funk & Wagnall's Company in 1983. What can I say? That was the last time these were made, and I absolutely loved (and still love) the set because they are thorough 'enough' but not as wordy as Encyclopedia Britannia sets tend to be (which can sometimes be a bit much). There are 28 volumes in my Funk & Wagnall's set and the number 29 is the Index; there is also a two-volume dictionary to the set. I've bought several encyclopedia sets over the course of time (all were used), and the F and W set is the set I mainly use. The set is now in the rare books group; they are very hard to find and mine stay just a few feet from my desk. Some people used to make fun of Funk and Wagnall's but I surely don't see why. The ones I have are superb. The write-ups are excellent and are loaded with well-researched facts. They aren't too long, or too short. I was fortunate to have come across them at a garage sale, years ago. The Encyclopedia America set is actually very good for looking up medical information. Write-ups in the set tend to be longer and often more technical. Encyclopedia Britannica is education oriented to the max, for books of that type. Today, there is so much medical information on the Internet that is helpful. I found a lot of what I needed, relative to medical history, in these books. Historical facts and data do not often change. They're generally constant. I love the F and W set and rely on it all the time. It's so basic. The write-ups can be read fairly quickly yet you still get the complete gist. The next few pages, about the history of medicine and surgery, are credited to these trusty encyclopedias (and some miscellaneous other material I've learned along the way. I, of course, added in a few points, here and there, and have laid it all out in an organized manner. Anyone who has had or will have surgery should learn about the history of medicine. Medicine has come such a long way. Medical knowledge has snowballed, like snow rolling down a hill gets rounder and rounder until it is finally huge.

In the beginning days of surgery, early records go back to the third century B.C. The ancient Egyptians are believed to have performed the following surgical procedures: eye operations, amputations, bladder stone removals, and castrations. Early Greek surgeries, that took place mainly after battlefield injuries, seemed to be modeled after Egyptian surgeries. In India, among those who were of the Hindu faith, removal of bladder stones took place, and fractures were surgically treated. This group is believed to have started certain types of plastic surgery. There are no statistics on success rates of anything from the early days. There was some record keeping but no authentic statistics. There was little to no mass assemblage of knowledge. Even the foregoing information is pretty sketchy. Still, it is something.

In Rome, surgeries were also being done around this general time. The Romans had been affected by the Greek physician, Hippocrates. Hippocrates kept some records, and somewhat set a trend for doing so. His studies, practice, experiences, and results were written and preserved as records for future physicians. It was only around 230 B.C. that the study of human anatomy became essential to surgery. But for some reason, and for some time, anatomy was slow to be explored. Eventually, though, anatomy contributed to more accurate and consistent diagnoses and treatment. Once anatomy was learned, physicians were able to become bolder about performing surgeries. Still, much surgery was trial-and-error, since there was much to learn. At times, surgeries were incorrectly done, but the surgeons did not always realize this.

For years, the Greeks were the medical leaders. It was the physician, Herophilus, who explored and established investigative study. Medicine and Surgery began to become a formal discipline, because of both Hippocrates and Herophilus. Their foundations carried through to the present, but there have been thousands of medical contributions along the way.

Ancient medical practices were relative to Medicine (or Pharmacy), General Practice, and Surgery. Knowledge spread all around Europe through medieval days. Certain surgeons made their mark, in various countries of Europe. Because Europe is not that large of a continent, a great deal of medical information was able to be pooled. Still, the Romans and the Greeks continued to lead. Italy, in particular, produced many surgeons.

During the 1200s, Medicine (Pharmacy) and Surgery clearly became separate. In France, a group of surgeons who were strictly surgeons rose up. This became the trend around the rest of Europe and by the 1400s, surgeons were all over

Europe. Therefore, it was during all subsequent centuries that much knowledge about surgery was gathered, recorded, and pooled. The knowledge essentially snowballed.

In the 1500s, Ambroise Paré of France (1510-90) began to ligate arteries to control hemorrhaging. Before, arteries were cauterized with a fired-up iron instrument. Paré is considered to be the father of modern surgery because of his new approaches. He also did away with cauterizing wounds by using oil, just boiled. He improved on how fractures were treated and he was a proponent of artificial limbs and helped to promote their use. He implemented many new practical skills or methods in the field of surgery. He was extremely humane, in his approaches. Being humane became more accentuated in the field of surgery. More humane methods in the field were sought after, relative to the acquiring of knowledge and the application of that knowledge.

Paré wrote up everything in French rather than Latin. Previously, medical work and records had been written in Latin so that only a select few were able to read and understand the material. Now, the public could read and understand what was written. Paré had a long life for those days. He was born in 1510 and he died in 1590. He had been a military surgeon first, but then became a royal surgeon with obvious royal patronage, and this patronage and sponsorship enabled him to explore and accomplish as much as he did.

Around the early 1600s, William Harvey of England (1578-1657) presented his view that the heart propelled the blood in a circular course. He observed the course of the heart and blood in animals (just how, I do not know and do not like to think about it). He did numerous dissections to arrive at his conclusions. He included capillaries in his conclusions, as being a part of the blood circulation course.

Sadly, many physicians used dogs in their experiments. This has been the case since medicine began. In some countries, it was heavy-duty. When the study of medicine became more serious and began to advance, dogs and other animals were used more frequently. Even in the 1800s and 1900s, animals have been used. They're still being used, often 'secretly'. As a patient, and an animal lover, this subject angers me. Sometimes the research was done when it was obvious what the outcome was going to be, which was sick. So often, the research was so overdone, duplicated, and not really needed, but I don't like it that any of it was ever done. We're here to help animals and protect them, not hurt them. So much can be learned without the use of animals. So much knowledge has already been accumulated—accurate knowledge, too.

When the Dutch lens maker, Anton van Leeuwenhoek (1632-1723), perfected the microscope, the English scientist, Robert Hooke (1635-1703), was able to discover cellular composition of plants. Cellular composition of blood was then discovered by Marcello Malpighi (1628-94), an Italian anatomist (or physiologist). He also explored blood circulation (like so many others did and still do). Microscopes are now able to obtain enlarged visual or photographic images of minute objects or details of objects. It is the compound microscope that developed gradually. It is a two-lens system. Each lens is arranged in specific ways and they're each very technical, involving mathematics, physics, and optics. For something that looks so simple, it is extremely complex. An improved microscope paved the way for new discoveries in the fields of Pathology and Bacteriology. In other words, it did much towards battling disease.

During the 1600s and the 1700s, it was France and Britain that became the leaders in the field of surgery, for the most part. They superseded Greece and Italy. The United States of America jumped into the scene, and America began to make a mark in the 1800s. Around that time, ovaries were removed by Ephraim McDowell (Kentucky) (1771-1830) and by Nathan Smith (Massachusetts) (1762-1829). Valentine Mott (1785-1865) ligated blood vessels that had expanded (aneurysms). Valentine Mott was the most prominent of American surgeons during the first half of the 1800s. He was born in New York and was trained in New York, but he went over to England and Scotland and met with surgeons over in Europe. He performed hundreds of different kinds of artery or blood vessel surgeries and he is known as the father of American vascular surgery. Valentine Mott also lived to be eighty years old, like Ambroise Paré had, back in the 1500s. I bring this up because, since these two men were doctors, they were able to afford to live longer than other people, during those times. Plus, they had to know how to take better care of themselves than others did. Paré had also ligated arteries but much less was known about the subject (and many other medical subjects) when he was living. In 1847, Valentine Mott translated Alfred Velpeau's book, *New Elements of Operative Surgery*. Mott taught medicine in New York. (Many prominent physicians were educators, as well.) James Marion Sims (Alabama and New York) (1813-1883) became the founder of modern Gynecology. Samuel D. Gross (1805-1884) became prominently known in Philadelphia, as being an exceptional surgeon. (He also taught in the field.) Most all these noted physicians did various types of medical research and work. Many of them had a distributive practice and medical life. Several were trauma surgeons.

Many of these men were alive when anesthesia was discovered, in the 1840s. Anesthesia gave a great boost to the field of Medicine. Much more could be done, and done longer, during surgery. At the time, anesthesia was a modern-day marvel. Up until then, hemp, opium, or just alcohol was used, to manage pain. Quite a few people who needed to manage their pain (and if they had the money for it), became opium addicts, and ended out dying because of their opium use.

When Louis Pasteur (1822-1895) did his work in France, he developed a theory about germs, and he learned that fermentation was really the increasing of 'multiple upon multiple' microorganisms. He developed vaccines for Rabies, and for several other diseases. He taught pasteurization, which is a process named after him. By heating certain liquids that have bacteria in them, to a high enough temperature, the bacteria are killed. At a certain point, if the liquid is at a certain pressure and temperature, the liquid can be bottled and sealed, and then be safe for public consumption, at least for a time. Pasteur contributed much to Microbiology, which had application to surgery and surgery safety.

Joseph Lister (1827-1912), a doctor in England, developed antiseptic techniques in the mid-1800s. Lister introduced a sterilized catgut, in silk, and also sterilized gauze, so that surgeries would be more sanitary. He also began to apply purified carbonic acid to wounds, to kill germs on and around wound sites or sites cut for surgery. Lister applied Pasteur's contributions to surgery. He formulated a theory that was essentially about unsanitary versus sanitary. That which is putrid, rancid, and 'sepsis' can be avoided, changed, and eliminated by 'antisepsis'. A 'sepsis' is any agent, as a microorganism, that is capable of causing disease. 'Antisepsis' is the technique of preventing infection or the growth of microorganisms. (These definitions come from *Webster's New World Dictionary*).

James Simpson (1811-1870) contributed a great deal to the field of Anesthesiology. He specialized in Obstetrics (in Edinburgh, Scotland) and he believed that using anesthetics was better than bloodletting, when a woman delivered a baby. First, he used ether. Then, he decided that chloroform was the better of the two. Again, anesthetics started to be used in the 1840s, when his medical practice was thriving. When he used the chloroform, many criticized him. But chloroform gained in popularity anyway.

The microscope caused doctors to realize that it was germs that caused disease, and, once the microscope was perfected, blood types were learned and blood transfusions became more successful. Blood transfusions somewhat started in 1667 when Jean-Baptiste Denys (1643-1704) injected lamb's blood into humans. Out of three people, only one died. This was an injection method, but it was rather different from what we have today. In 1829, in England, James Blundell (1791-1878) saved the lives of women during and after childbirth, by giving them blood transfusions. However, blood typing had not yet been learned, so transfusions were hit and miss. It was this way for a while.

Finally, in 1901, a Viennese doctor, Karl Landsteiner (1868-1943), found out that some red corpuscles clumped together when they were mixed with other ones, from a different person. He categorized blood types into A, B, and C, but he learned that C type was not a mix of A and B, it was absent in both A and B types, so he typed it O, for zero. In 1940, he worked with two colleagues, Philip Levine and Alexander S. Wiener, to discover the Rh factor in blood. He learned that Rh⁺ and Rh⁻ blood are the two factors. Approximately 85% of the population is Rh⁺ and 15% are Rh⁻. When people marry and have babies, this factor must be realized. Blood for blood transfusions must always be typed so there are no mistakes.

Happily, Karl Landsteiner became an American citizen in 1929. He had moved to America in 1922 because medical research had slowed down in Vienna, and then in The Hague, Netherlands, which is where he had most recently lived. World War I had devastated Europe's finances. He was awarded the Nobel Prize

Kathy S. Thompson, M.A.

for Physiology (Medicine) in 1930. His work had been in Serology, but the overall scope of his work was in Physiology. He is considered to be the father of transfusion medicine. He received a Laskar Award in 1946, which is the year they began to be given out.

It is interesting to learn about these historical people who contributed to Medicine. Although certain men made a significant mark, many contributions have been overlooked and some aren't even on record. Women entered medical practice and research later on. For years, women were helpers and contributors, though. They were very much needed and significant, in the overall field of Medicine. Quite a few women worked in research. Nurses have been around since after Christ (A.D.). Christian women attended the sick. Many Catholic nuns have been and are nurses. Early nursing often just meant doing routine tasks that weren't of a medical nature, per se. Often, they were housekeeping tasks, and meal preparation and serving. Florence Nightingale made a contribution to Nursing during the Crimean War, and thereafter. Nursing became more important as the field of Medicine advanced. Nurses today perform some medical-related tasks, some of which require skill and special training.

For centuries, many people died because of infection. The surgical instruments that were used weren't all that clean. Germs abounded in the surgical room, and even on the surgeon. Germs got into opened-up bodies, in various ways. Once this problem was tackled, surgery had a much higher success rate. Medical personnel are constantly concerned about microorganisms now, because they know all about them. When you can see them under a microscope, and see what they do under a microscope, you know that they exist, and multiply. New strains of germs—bacterial and viral—come about on occasion. Some of them are dangerous. They have to be fought, medically. Vaccines and anti-viral drugs have to be prepared for these strains because they are killers. Radical warmongers have used germ warfare and many people have died because of it. In some areas, contagion of a disease can be rapid. All countries make efforts to be prepared to fight diseases. Countries try to work to together to combat disease. Germs can be and are in hospitals. They can spread around. It's something to be extra careful about in every country of the world.

68

Since the mid-1800s, there have been constant advancements in all areas of the medical world, including surgery. Today, people are safer, if they have surgery. Bone and skeletal (including the spine), spinal cord, brain, head and neck, trunk, muscles, blood vessels, the respiratory system, the digestive system, the gastro-intestinal tract, the vascular system (including the heart), vessels, the genitourinary tract (including the reproductive system), the endocrine system, glands, the lymphatic system, the thorax area, the abdomen area, the pelvic area, shoulder, arm and hand areas, thigh area, leg and foot areas, and nerves are all areas in which surgery has greatly improved, and all areas of the body, really, see more surgery successes than they did during those darker, less enlightened, earlier times.

Medicine is essentially divided up into systems and areas. The ABCs of Medicine is to first learn those basics and then to learn what comprises those systems and areas. Learning what system and area is found in each and how everything in each system and area works together becomes extensions from the basics. Figuring out how it all works together is what takes doctors years and years of study. The body is very intricate and complicated. If you'll excuse the pun, there is much beneath the surface. There are machines within machines.

My surgery involved the respiratory system, the gastro-intestinal tract, and the vascular system. The respiratory system was involved because my stomach had adhered to one lung and my stomach was pressing against that lung. It involved the gastro-intestinal tract because my stomach, intestines, and esophagus were involved. And it involved the vascular system because my stomach had settled in next to my heart and the two had to be separated during surgery because they had adhered, or grown together, at some point in time. The heart really is shaped a little like a valentine, and the point is at the bottom. The heart area is a vulnerable area to be cutting around. My surgery related to both my abdomen and my thorax.

Since several systems within my body were involved in the surgical process, my surgery was not that simple. I assumed it would be much simpler than it was. How wrong I was. Like with a car, the body has many systems inside it. All the systems are separate and important, but they work together, in unison. They're all needed, for performance. They're all packed in, jumbled as it were, and everybody looks a little different because of size, build, weight, and, of course, sex. Because all bodies are different, I imagine that surgeons aren't always that 'cool' before and during the surgeries they complete. No surgery is the same as others, in other words.

Presently, there are interesting medical and even surgery museums that can be visited. A number of them have folded up, though. You can sometimes see old surgical tools and devices, and various medical artifacts in general, at these museums. Even old iron lungs and microscopes are in certain medical museums. Some maladies of the past have been preserved in formaldehyde and the like. Samples of tissues, cancer lumps and tumors, diseased organs and areas, and even conjoined twins have been preserved. Old techniques are revealed. Some of these are now considered to have been harmful to medical advancement. Sometimes these museums are actually at universities.

Learning about electricity greatly helped the field of Medicine to progress. Now, with electronics and the computer, the sky seems to be the limit. Surgery has come a long way, since ancient times and the Egyptians. The Chinese were interested in medicine, early on, too. A plethora of knowledge has entered the scene, and whatever was of merit stayed around. Knowledge has been extended from and expanded on over the years, up to this present day. Medical research is ongoing and there are new revelations every day. Many prestigious awards have been given out, because of medical achievements. With all this in mind, the fear of having surgery has been greatly and significantly reduced. Hospitals are better now, too; they're more efficiently run but of course, they aren't cheap. Oh my, they certainly aren't cheap.

My surgery was to last approximately three hours. On a 'difficult, dangerous surgery scale', I was told it would register about a 6 out of 10. Certain (not all) brain and heart surgeries register 7 and 8 and on occasion, will register higher. 9 and 10 is for surgeries that involve several procedures at a time that are high risk. These ones are usually very long surgeries. I felt fortunate to not be having a surgery that registered higher on the scale. There is also a scale for amount of time it takes for healing from the different surgeries. One of my doctors told me it would take me a good three months to be well healed, and another three months to be really well healed, so in other words, I should be mobile and agile, without hesitation or slowness, six months after the date of my surgery. Someone mentioned that it would take me a whole year to be completely healed though, to where I didn't feel any irritation, aggravation, or tenderness. (I'm not sure I believed that though). "So," I thought, "I have a three-month checkpoint, a six-month checkpoint, and a one-year checkpoint. And probably there'll be checkpoints after those ones. Never having had this type of surgery before, and not knowing anyone who had, I couldn't even come close to guessing how my healing might go, but I was finally resigned to have this surgery and thought to myself "ok, then, on with the show...let 'er rip..."

My surgery was performed December 5, 2001, so Christmas was in the air. Weather outside was crisp and a little chilly. I was glad to be in a Sunbelt area during the winter, and not somewhere else. The day before my surgery, I noticed things more—trees, buildings, people, sidewalks, signs, etc. All was so crisp. Everything looked so sharp and clear—much more so than usual. I thought "I'm alive today. Will I be alive tomorrow?"

For some odd reason, I became very in tune with the weather, right before my surgery. I noticed it more when I was walking to different buildings for my group of medical tests, that I had to have administered the day before my surgery. These were EKG, blood, and X-ray. They wanted to know if my heart could stand the surgery, if my blood was of a certain thinness, or thickness (however you want to look at it), whether or not I was anemic or had a disease, and if anything had shifted in my stomach and chest area. I'm sure that other important things were derived from the tests, too, just hours before the actual surgery. It is incumbent on surgeons to look through the results of these tests because they help the surgeon to double-check everything and to confirm that the surgery will go on according to schedule.

Well, I guess I passed all the tests because they performed surgery on me that next morning. I was fortunate to be a very healthy woman. I was physically tougher and stronger than someone who wasn't healthy, so this made the surgery prognosis a better one. On the morning of my surgery, I put on my surgical gown—dress, robe, whatever—at the pre-op admitting room. (I like the word robe best). My father and Edna went on home, to Edna's house, which was closer to the hospital than my father's house was. They planned to meet with the doctor in the waiting room three hours later, which of course happened but I was still out like a light, in ICU or the Intensive Care Unit. I was placed there, in a separate room, to be consistently monitored after my surgery. Before my surgery started, my father had left a phone number with the pre-op nurse, just in case it might be needed.

On the morning of my surgery, I was escorted from the pre-op admitting room into another room, where there were several people and a bed (with wheels) that was awaiting me. I was escorted onto this bed (that was eventually wheeled into the actual surgery room). I'm not positive if I stayed on this bed with wheels throughout my surgery or if I was put on another bed, without wheels. Not that it really matters. I became unconscious early on so whatever happened reference any beds is not noted. I at least do know this—I was on 'a' bed, during the surgery, and after the surgery. It probably had wheels that were able to lock, but that is a guess.

When I first got in the room, a number of medical professionals were moving all about, doing their work. As soon as I was given anesthesia, things faded out real fast. Oxygen was given to me through a tube that was put in my nose, and a breathing apparatus was put down my throat. The level of oxygen in my body had to constantly be monitored. A certain amount of oxygen had to always be going to my brain.

My heart pumped all through the surgery. I was glad I wasn't having heart surgery, actually. I hope I never have to. Heart surgery is very expensive. Heart surgeons that are specialists have two and a half years more education than general surgeons have. Of course, if anything does happen to your heart during any surgery, there are people around the room who know what to do. This applies to any emergency, in addition to a heart emergency but that's if you are in a surgery room, with doctors present.

Because of the administered anesthesia, I was actually dead during the surgery. I was supposed to be. Everyone is. It is because of all these various tubes going in you that you are alive, but, you are actually dead, just being kept alive, during a surgery. That is a main reason why close observation and monitoring is so crucial. Observation and monitoring is crucial from the start of surgery and to the day that you are given approval to leave the critical care unit. During surgery, tubes keep you breathing. If it weren't for the oxygen, it would be 'bye-bye world'.

What is scary about anesthetics is that if it isn't closely monitored, for each person, and carefully administered, a patient's heart can give out, their breathing can stop, and other things can happen. One's life is in the hands of the Anesthesiologist and the Anesthetist, during the surgery process. One person who died during surgery (many years back) was the singer, Bobby Darin. He had had Rheumatic Fever, though, and his heart was weak to begin with, so whether it was the anesthetics or the weak heart that caused him to die on the operating table is something that was hard to prove. Still, such stories were in my memory bank and I was concerned about becoming a statistic before I got old.

Actually, I was most concerned about this part of the surgery process. I was genuinely concerned that I might die sometime during the surgery. I'd heard about this happening to other people aside from Bobby Darin, so I couldn't shake the thought. A young man I grew up with in high school had surgery and he never came out of the anesthesia and he remained in a coma for several years until he finally died. Jimmie (my friend) had also been from my neighborhood, besides being a classmate of mine. I couldn't get the notion out of my mind—i.e. that I could soon die. Also, a young man I dated in college had been in a car accident and he was in a coma for some time. He, too, never came out of his coma, and finally died. I never found out if the coma was from the accident itself, or from surgeries (and anesthesia) that he had to have immediately after the car accident. It could have been the one, the other, or a combination of the two. My memories about these deaths were vivid. I wasn't naïve about going into surgery. I knew I could die and was aware that death could be around the corner. I had prepared my Will (as best I could for my age), before going in to surgery. "Better safe than sorry," I thought.

When a person has the kind of surgery I had, or a similar kind of surgery, they're given general anesthesia, which puts them into a sleep-like state. Generalized muscles relax. Pain is relieved. Multiple drugs are also given, in varying amounts. Some reduce the anxiety before the surgery and calm the person down. They also support the functioning of the lungs, and the heart. Other drugs make pain minimal during and after the surgery. Pain relief medication is prescribed after surgery, since pain has to be managed. No one is pain free after a surgery.

The general anesthesia is rather powerful, and you lose most or all consciousness. Still, drugs that relieve pain are necessary, even though you are unconscious. In my case, because of the length of time my surgery was to take and because of the severity of the surgery, I lost all consciousness, all the way through. I don't remember a thing. I was out like a light. Anything they gave me was well scrutinized and assessed, and amounts related to my weight, degree of health, and even age. Amounts related to length of time for the surgery, too.

I had both general and local anesthetics. They sure took effect fast. Anesthetics will both put you to sleep and stop you from feeling pain, during a surgery. They surely do work. They worked very well with me. First I was given an injection to relax me and to prepare me to receive the anesthetics. The epidural I had was an injection placed into the area of the spinal cord. It was an inserted needle taped on securely so it couldn't come out. This anesthetic prevented pain stimuli from coming into that area, so pain could not be transmitted to the brain and become known and therefore felt. I was feeling no pain, from around the waist down and to the tip of my toes. I felt nothing. Then the general anesthesia always knocks you out and makes you completely unconscious. It certainly did me. Once they administered the general, I was dead to the world.

The operation wasn't a very bloody one (compared with other types of operations), but they had my type of blood on file, just in case they needed any blood. My cousin had advised me that I could go in early and donate some of my own blood, to be used for the operation, but there really wasn't time for me to do that, because of my surgery date. (She had mentioned this right before the surgery). They didn't need any extra blood, though, as it turned out. Nothing unexpected ended out happening. The hospital was a well-equipped one, all across the board, and they kept reserves of blood in the event blood might be needed.

I had tubes all over my body. I was the Tube Woman. At the time of my wake-up, tubes were on my wrist, on my arm, in my urethra, on my back, on my side, in my mouth, and in my nose. If I hadn't been under sedation, I might have gone berserk because of all the tubes I was experiencing after the surgery. Some of these were put in me after I blacked out from the anesthesia. That's exactly what I did. I blacked out. I don't remember a thing. Not one thing. Every one of the tubes that were put in me were necessary, or the operation could not have been done with me being out like a light, not feeling pain, maintaining my fluids, eliminating my fluids, being able to breathe, and being able to perform other functions. I'm sure antibiotics were in there, too. Tubes come down from IVs. Tubes are necessary, no doubt about it.

Everything used for the operation is sterilized. Even sutures are. To prevent infection, involved medical professional people will scrub themselves for ten minutes or so, to rid themselves of bacteria and germs. At least, they're supposed to scrub that long. We are all more familiar with hand scrubbing since the onset of COVID-19; we all know about hand sanitizers now, too. Medical professional people wear masks to minimize germs being exhaled by breathing. (We are all quite familiar with mask wearing, as well.) They wear surgical caps so hair doesn't fall out during surgery. Hair can fall inside an open surgical area when a body is unconscious and on the surgical bed. Dandruff can, too. The surgical team's clothes are specially cleaned and sanitized in advance. I was actually dressed in the same manner, almost, as the medical professionals were, except that there was an open area of the garment I had on, because the incision had to be made and the area had to be opened up for working. Maybe I ended out having nothing on, I wouldn't know. And I don't really want to think about that.

I was on my right side during the whole surgery, which went along according to the doctor's schedule. He expected to complete it in three hours, and he did. Some of this time may have been prep and clean-up, though. As I think about it, cutting into a person and doing this and that inside of their body is really some job. Three hours is an awfully long time to be working inside of and on a body. When it's your body, you think about these kinds of things. Later on, I thought about the fact that all these people were able to see my blood and guts, and even some of my uncovered body—maybe all of it. Somehow this didn't bother me that much because everything was so clinical and was done within a medical perspective. Some residents were in there, observing and assisting, and even that didn't bother me when I thought about it later on. (I won't let it bother me. I know they must continue their learning in the operating theater.) These people see it all, and they're professionals.

The last thing I remember, before becoming completely unconscious, was a woman putting long white leggings on my legs, which were very tight. I didn't remember everything she did, just the first part, but I found out later that bands went around those stockings and air was pumped into the bands so they would get tight and then loosen, over and over, so there would be circulation in my legs and blood couldn't clot anywhere. In other words, the bands were air cushions pumped by a machine. If blood vessels tighten or blood collects somewhere in a vessel, then blood, which carries oxygen, can't get to the brain area. During my surgery, my oxygen level was constantly being monitored, very closely. It was someone's job to do this but I don't know whose. Needless to say, blood clots are not good to have during a surgery or after a surgery. You can die from a blood clot. Walking helps circulation, after a surgery, but during the surgery, I was going nowhere.

Right before I entered the unconscious realm, I also remember a nice young man, a Nurse Anesthetist, coming around trying to at least generally explain to me what was going to happen to me, relative to his part of the process. I wasn't exactly able to concentrate on what he was saying. I got some of it. I do recall him saying that he would be there, monitoring the anesthesia. Then, I noticed the doctor who was going to be supervising and assisting my surgeon—the Swedish doctor—=who was the head of the Cardio-Thoracic section at the hospital. He had a surgical mask on. His outfit was medium green, I think, but I'm not positive about that because I was a little out of it. It could have been blue, but I know it wasn't white. My general surgeon wore the same color and type of garment. I assumed the Cardio-Thoracic surgeon would be working on me, too.

Right before the surgery, in the pre-op admitting room, the nurse in the room had my general surgeon and a resident doctor listed as being the ones doing my surgery. I was distressed because I expected the Cardio-Thoracic doctor, who was quite experienced, to be listed with my general surgeon. I thought they'd done a switcharoo. She called in to double-check, and sure enough, the Cardio-Thoracic doctor was still assisting my general surgeon. I found out later on that the Cardio-Thoracic surgeon was there at the beginning of the surgery, then left for a while, but came back, and inspected the work that my surgeon had done before my surgeon closed me up. He stayed while I was being closed up, I hope, but I don't know that for sure. At one point, I wondered if my surgeon did all of the surgery himself, or had one of the residents done some of the surgery, too, but then I reasoned that, no, the residents could only assist, not take much initiative, so only my surgeon was working inside of and on my body. My surgeon confirmed this for me later on, too. I hated to think of myself somewhat and very unclothed, around so many nice looking young men, and well, anyone, really, but what could I do? I was out like a light.

Again, a number of professionals were watching my surgeon and the surgery, during those three hours. They'd seen it all before. Of course, my surgeon checked everything really well, before he finally closed me up, but I have to say that I would have felt better if the other doctor (the Cardio-Thoracic surgeon) had stayed in the Operating Room the whole time that I was having surgery. I expected he would when I went under, but he ended out leaving the room, and of course, I had no control over that. How could I. I was completely out. My surgeon told me later on that he felt very good about how everything went, which roundaboutly meant that he was generally pleased with his work.

I wish I could see an actual film of my surgery. If you'll excuse the pun, I think I could stomach it. I would find it fascinating to watch, very frankly. But, only to see my own surgery and not others' surgery would be my desire. My surgery wasn't filmed, however, so I missed the show. At least, I don't think it was filmed.

I don't know how surgeons do what they do, day in and day out. I guess they get used to it. Practice, practice, practice will make it so that doing surgery becomes routine for them. Still, the pressure surgeons have to work under, when there are lives at stake and when precision means whether or not, and to what degree, a surgery will be successful, is enormous. All professionals related to surgeries are under pressure. They work as a team—a surgical team—so all the pressure gets shared, except that the lead surgeon is definitely the one in the hot seat, and everyone else is secondary but major.

Way more woman are going into the field of surgery these days, than ever before. Some medical classes now have more prospective female surgeons in them than prospective male surgeons. Assuming all the women get through the medical programs, there may be more female surgeons than male surgeons in the United States by the time the year 2020 rolls around. Having babies sets some women back. Women tend to have babies when they're young and that is when most women go to Med school. It can be a conflict. It is better to get schooling over when you are young.

During the surgery, I was barely aware of the nurses. But they were constantly busy. One of them was directly assigned to me, to tend to me during the operation. I do not recall meeting him, or her. This nurse made sure all supplies were in the operating room, and generally prepared the operating room. Keeping me warm and comfortable was this professional's job, and flanking me until I went into recovery was, too. Another nurse assisted my surgeon by handing him surgery-related items. There was also a main supervising nurse who was responsible for the operating room—that everything was there and working, that everything got or was sterilized properly, and that the necessary people were present during the surgery. These are details I learned after the surgery. I'm sure there are variations at other places where surgeries are performed but I think you get the gist of it all.

While I was under, the surgeon cut me open, and then used the rib splitter to open up the area where he needed to work. (That must have been some job). Just the thought of it makes me cringe. He did some cutting, separating, and then he proceeded to do the sewing and mending, after the stomach had been dislodged, separated from the heart, the esophagus, and the one lung, and put into its normal place and position. My diaphragm was sewn up, in whatever way it needed to be. The hiatus was repaired. Special mesh had been considered to use for the repairs, but it had to be sewn in. Different surgeons prefer different meshes. There are several on the market. As it turned out, my surgeon didn't have to use the mesh, which still leaves me scratching my head but he said he didn't need it so go figure.

To add, and what was also done during the surgery, is that my lung had to first be deflated, so there would be room for my surgeon to work. The lung is rather large, and it gets in the way during certain surgeries. Fortunately, my surgeon didn't have to cut through any vessels or arteries, and then have to ligate them. He only had to cut through some capillaries. The ligations of vessels and arteries are usually successful, but the very thought of having mine cut, and ligated, sends shivers up my spine. I'm glad it didn't happen. Once everything was finished in the thoracic area, the lung was filled with air again, before I was stitched up. Then, I believe that two of my muscles were sewn up because they had been cut so the surgeon could get down into the area to work. Last, my outer skin was sewn up. As I think about it, that is a lot to have to do. And a lot of sewing and stitching. I sure hope he was good at sewing and stitching. I'm sure it is taught in medical and surgery school.

Surgeons have to work within a time limit. Surgeries have to be finished by a certain time. Anesthesia is administered in accordance with expected amount of time for a surgery. They factor in the weight of the person and so mathematics plays a part. Anesthesia amount that is administered is one of the criteria for length of time for surgery and so a surgeon can't be wasting any time during surgery. No time out to do a crossword puzzle, watch the News, or run to the bank or a store. The surgeon has to work steadily and carefully. If something happens during surgery that was unexpected, or if a mistake was made, it can lead to real problems. Surgeons always 'try' to give the loved ones of their patients a general time range for length of surgery, and they're almost always right, unless there are complications. If there are complications and more time is needed, they have to decide if more anesthesia can be administered so the surgery can continue. Sometimes it can't, so they have to do another surgery, later on.

While my surgeon was doing the surgery, he kept a lookout for anything that appeared irregular and he told me later that everything looked fine and that no biopsies needed to be taken. After I was closed up, a drain tube was put in to my chest, and it stayed in for a while so that my lung, that had been deflated but was now inflated, could stay inflated. The drain tube helped to decrease swelling in that area, so there would be room for the lung to stay expanded to the max. Swelling is present because a surgical area is more liquidy or watery, so the drain tube was needed to drain this liquid so that the lung could continue to be expanded, at its usual size. Excessive swelling would have constricted the lung and it would have been a problem so I had to have the drain tube.

The muscles that were cut were the Serratus anterior, that is a small one, along the side and in the area under the arm, and the Latissimus dorsi, that is a large one, in back. Most people know where the Latissimus dorsi is. Actually, the two ribs that had been split apart were sewn together, too, so that they would stay close in together, like they were before. Otherwise, they would have had a tendency to be separated, and that would have been a problem. The stitches along my side and back that closed up the surgical opening, of course had to go all the way through the skin of the cut opening. They weren't topical, like stitches that a small cut might get. They went all the way through the whole layer of skin, on both sides of the cut opening. Ouch! The surgeon did a good job of stitching up the opening, so I believe he likely followed suit and had done a good job with all the other stitching, that was internal and couldn't be seen. It seems logical to assume that and so do I.

My scar on the outside starts under the outer edge of my left breast, under my arm, and it extends, with a bit of a curving, out about ten inches towards the center of my back. It is somewhat thick. I had hoped it would become thinner, as it healed. (It didn't; in fact, the stress from natural movement and pulling over a period of time caused it to end out being even thicker.) My scar had tape sewn through the stitches, over the surgical wound. The tape was used to better hold the stitches in place. Gradually, the tape deteriorated and fell off. The stitches dissolved, but not until the skin had bonded really well. Material was used that lasted as long as the wound needed the stitches.

I was told that my scar would stay reddish for up to three months, and that then it would begin to fade. By six months, the scar would be completely faded, or so I believed. At six months, it wasn't red but it was pink and noticeable and there is no way I am going to ever get away from this scar. Anyway, it doesn't matter to me that I have it. I'm now older, and I accept the fact that my looks are starting to leave me anyway. My scar will always be covered, and over the years I won't be looking at my scar at all, because I don't want to look at it. Most of it is in back, so it's not in my usual view. The part of my scar that is under my arm, I'll never have to look at, either.

The stitches that were used, in the various areas, were of polysynthetic suture material. The stronger suture material was used around the diaphragm. They are non-dissolving sutures so I guess they'll always be there. The diaphragm and hiatus areas gradually and permanently bond together, but the stitches stay intact. The stitches around my muscles were dissolving ones. Several knots (and not just one) were tied at the ends of where all the stitches started and ended. My diaphragm did not need to have a mesh material used, to bond it together, because the tear was a straight, clean tear, and it stitched together nicely. Sometime mesh material is used to hold everything in place there if the tear is not all that easy to sew, so I was glad to hear that my tear was more of a straight and simple tear. (If one can be glad about such a thing.)

The ribs are a solid unit, front to back. The back area is where they were split open. The stress and pulling from the rigors of this kind of operation also ends out affecting the front rib area. The rib stress and the pulling in back ended out putting stress on and pulling at the front area too, most particularly the front area where cartilage attaches to the ribs. At least, this is what happened to me. That area ended out being severely pulled. The cartilage there is not ligament. It is rubbery, smooth, cushiony, and bendable—at least to a point. As a person gets older, cartilage hardens and becomes more brittle. It can actually break if it is bent too much.

Fortunately, my cartilage there didn't break when it was pulled. I was still fairly young so my cartilage was still pliable. Again, the area to the back side area was split open and an opening was made for working. The working in the area is what forced my front area to get stressed, pulled, and stretched during the surgery. This situation had little to do with the surgery, directly, but it was related to it indirectly. It was an unfortunate result that went along with the total package of the surgery and the healing. I wasn't expecting this one, pulled frontal area, but I had to deal with it, along with the other sore areas and pains.

After the surgery, I woke up in the Intensive Care Unit (ICU) and was under strict pain management by competent and well-trained people. One person was assigned to me alone, and professionals were nearby, in case anything unexpected happened, like excessive breathing difficulty, for example. Each patient in ICU had a flanker. I don't know how many times the shifts changed at the ICU, but I was there almost three days. It was probably two and a half days. I slept most of the time. There were about fifteen rooms in the ICU that I was in. I had young men (RN's) monitoring me—one per shift. They sat in a small booth, with a window that looked into my room but the RN could also look out to the corridor. That flanker was always right by my room, sitting in that windowed booth. There was a buzzer right at my bedside, and if I needed help with anything, I'd ring the buzzer.

One thing I didn't like about coming out of the unconsciousness was finding out that I had a catheter stuck in me. Catheters are encumbrances and they are embarrassing, if you're at all modest. The catheter was a urological one (though there are other uses for them). Urine had to be drained from my bladder. It went through my urethra and into my bladder so my urine could drain during and after my surgery. It was kept in after the surgery, for a time, which seemed like an eternity to me. There is always a drainage bag associated with a catheter. Urine volume is usually measured for more than one reason. One reason is to co-relate that volume with fluid-intake volume.

People who have surgery and are attached to an IV do not eat for a while. IV fluids seem to reduce or eliminate hunger pains. Anesthesia often does. IV bags have substances in them that are mixed with water, so urination becomes necessary. The urinary bladder is an organ and it is where urine collects. The kidneys excrete urine into the bladder. A person is so incapacitated right after a surgery that they cannot walk over to a bathroom. They sleep almost constantly, so urine must be eliminated some way—hence, a catheter.

After surgery, people have trouble breathing. They can get pneumonia, and often they do. In my case, my lung had purposely been collapsed because they needed to deflate it so there would be room in the area to work. The lung went through some maneuvering, more than once. The gist of that is, my lung had been somewhat traumatized, so it affected my breathing afterwards. Also, there is mucous down in the throat that has to be sucked out after a surgery. The mucous affects breathing, too.

Breathing treatments start immediately after the kind of surgery I had. You blow into a breathalyzer-type of apparatus, and your strength of breathing can be medically measured. You actually do breathing exercises, every day, and these exercises reveal your breathing strength. There is another apparatus used for a breathing treatment. It helps to clear out the mucous in the throat. You suck in a vapor from a container and the vapor goes in and clears out your passageway. You do this several times in a row. Each time you take a new breath, the vapor is inhaled, through the mouth. You exhale the vapor. A couple of different people (one at a time) came around with this unit, fairly regularly. They kept a chart on each person who needed this treatment. I found it hard to get used to the smell of the vapor. It was strong, and not real pleasant.

In ICU, one young lady brought in a small hand-sized vibrator to put on my back. It was supposed to be used to loosen my mucous and to clear the area out. I really got upset about this when the vibrator was vibrating, and I started to cry from the pain because she did it close to the stitches and the wound and to where a needle and tube was still stuck. I told her to stop. She knew to stop, because I was crying from the pain. She never came around again, thankfully. Doing something like that close to and even on the surgical site was more than unwise. How could she not have known that? She was very, very young. Perhaps that is why. I wonder—do they let student nurses work in ICU? There were other ways to deal with the mucous problem, and the other treatments were the only way to go.

I ended out getting my breathing fairly well restored right before I was released from the hospital. I had breathing treatments at generally regular times. When I left, I wasn't breathing 'maximally' well, however, and my breathing was still a little weak. Therefore, I had to do exercises at home with a plastic exercise unit, for a short while. My surgeon insisted on it. My lung was not yet healed, probably. I don't think it healed up properly for some time after the surgery. One X-ray done on the area afterwards revealed some non-specific scarring in my left lung base, but I do not yet know why there was scarring. Perhaps it was from separating during the surgery; some of it had to be done by cutting. Organs that shouldn't have joined and grown together, did. Some things that the surgeon did weren't in his write-up afterwards so I don't know everything that was done. They don't put absolutely every little thing in their reports. Some of their reports are quite brief. The after-surgery write-up is what I call 'briefly thorough'. It is often one page, and single spaced. It is written in sequential order for the most part.

For some reason, I had no breathing treatment in the next area I went to, the Step-Down Unit, but I was only there for a half a day. The Step-Down Unit is where you go after ICU. They keep you there until they are sure you are eating well, keeping down food, and generally functioning OK. Then, you are wheeled to General Ward Care (GWC), where other patients are staying for surgery recovery but they're there for other reasons, too, besides surgery recovery. They were understaffed in Step-Down, so they tried to get me into General Ward Care as quickly as possible.

It seemed odd, waking up out of surgery. You are so sedated. You know why you are there and what all has happened to you, but you sure can't recite a poem or do anything like that, if you know what I mean. You sleep a lot, because of the sedation and painkillers. You are given morphine. At least, I was. I pressed a button every so often, if I wanted morphine. The button only gave me an IV (intravenous) dose of morphine every twenty minutes, though, so I couldn't accidentally overdose myself. When you're highly sedated, it is easy to get confused and forget when you push the button to get more morphine, especially when you can't have a watch in the hospital, because it is jewelry. Maybe my relatives could have brought me my watch from home but I didn't think to ask them to do this. I wasn't sure if it was just during surgery that you weren't supposed to have jewelry or if this rule applied to the whole hospital stay. I think it applied to the whole hospital stay. Any valuables are returned to you upon release.

In the Step-Down Unit, you got morphine by pill and it was monitored as to dosage amount. Morphine can depress breathing, if you get too much of it, and I wasn't breathing real well after the surgery anyway, so obviously any morphine that went into my system had to be well monitored for that reason too. A person can build up a tolerance to morphine if they take too much of it. Learning that fact made me reflect back to my sister, who had died of cancer. I thought "I hope she was able to be benefited by the morphine she was given, in the days preceding her death". She had taken quite a lot of it even before her last days.

Again, there was lots of swelling after my surgery. It was inside and out. All those cells had been grievously disturbed, and they were reacting. When there is swelling, the swollen area is large because of liquid and trauma. It didn't take too long for the excessive swelling to go down in the outer area around my side and my back—a week, maybe two—but the area still remained swollen, and was very tender, for a long time after that, and I do mean for a long time. The front cartilage area remained swollen, tender, and sore for a long time, too. (At the six-month and the twelve-month checkpoint, both the area around the scar, and the front cartilage area was still very tender, but not super sore, unless I pulled or bumped the area. If I pulled or bumped either area, it would become horribly sore, real fast. (I had to be careful to not do that).

Because you are still under the original sedation when you go into ICU, and because they monitor you so closely, one on one, I consider ICU to be a part of the actual, overall surgery experience and maybe even process. When new sedation and medication comes in—ring in the new, ring out the old—then I believe the surgery phase is over and the healing phase has begun. For me, I started my healing phase when I was in ICU, and this was when the original anesthetics wore off and I woke up. New sedation and medication came in and took over. Whereas before, the anesthesia caused me to black out, so the surgery could be done, now I was given medication that served to kill or dull pain. It didn't knock me out. It actually takes a while for a person to come out of the anesthesia after a surgery, because so much is administered. A person will go in and out of a deep-sleep state for many hours. They may not realize that this is happening or remember that it happened. When they finally awake to awareness, to say that they are groggy or dopey is an understatement.

My healing phase started when I woke up and was able to stay awake for a while. That's when the surgery phase had ended. I was 'out of the woods', as they say. Since the doctor had told my father and Edna that he had felt that everything had gone well, they relayed this to me when I woke up from all the drugs and anesthetics. This note of optimism was music to my ears. I wasn't at all mobile, and that was a burden, but at least everything was generally all right and I was actually alive. I hadn't died, during the surgery.

I was allowed visitors in both ICU and Step Down. When you are wheeled into General Ward Care, it is only because you are considered well enough to not be flanked and constantly monitored. And, of course, I was allowed visitors in GWC. After three and a half days, I was in a general ward and was under care there. They still watch you pretty well there, though—in GWC. All these days were days that I'd rather not have had to spend, but spend them I did. Specifically, I was in ICU for two and a half days, the Step-Down Unit for a half a day, and then I was in General Ward Care for three days (but perhaps only two). I think that's how it went.

I slept almost the whole time when I was in ICU. It didn't seem like I was there for as long as two and a half days, because I was sleeping so much. My body had been through trauma, and it was worn out and tired and stressed. Anesthesia and painkiller's affects do not just suddenly go away. They subside and steadily decrease in effect. (In fact, drugs in general stay in the body for a long time). Hence, I was very relaxed the whole time, and sleeping was never a problem. Plus, I had the morphine, which was given through a tube but was carefully rationed. While in ICU, I was unable to think very well. I could think linearly, and respond in a simple way to things, but I wasn't able to abstract or reason too well.

Before and even after the surgery, I didn't realize just how important and involved the Anesthesiologist and Nurse Anesthetist were. They were there before the actual surgery, during the surgery, and after the surgery. They determined what anesthetics were to be used, for which patients, who were all of differing ages, weights, fitness levels, and general health quality. These professionals determine initial amounts, and sustaining amounts, of all anesthetics used. Again, more than one drug or anesthetic is used. These professionals administer everything; they monitor everything. There's more to it than meets the eye and no wonder these medical professionals are paid so much. They have medical degrees.

Of course, the surgeon (or surgeons) is actively involved in the anesthesia process too, but to a lesser extent. They are apprised of what is being administered, relative to each operation. If something seems off-the-wall, believe me, the surgeon has a say about changing or altering the anesthesia. Surgeons supervise the decisions made, relative to anesthesia. But, the Anesthesiologist has a great deal of latitude, because after all, anesthesia is their specialty. The anesthesia part is separate from the surgery part. Once the anesthesia is administered, time is of the essence, and all must perform their work methodically and deliberately. The OR is not a place for dawdlers and slowpokes, or people who are arguing about type or amount of anesthesia to use.

There are many kinds of anesthesia. And, there are many ways to administer the different kinds of anesthesia. Then, too, necessary drugs are administered in many cases, along with the anesthesia. Surgery patients have to have antibiotics because they've been cut into, and antibiotics prevent infection by killing germs. Drugs given contribute to making the anesthesia more effective. In some cases, they help to reduce certain side effects, from the anesthesia. My general anesthesia was a variety or a mix, for example. Today, they no longer use chloroform, ether, nitrous oxide, sodium pentothal, as well as certain other chemical mixes, for anesthesia. And, of course, opium is out of the question, as is hemp or marijuana. Hospital people do not like marijuana to be on the premises. In some places (but not actual medical facilities), marijuana is allowed for the management of pain, but it's never allowed as an anesthetic. Hospital-used anesthetics are quite strong. They have to be if someone had a difficult surgery. Marijuana is always against federal law, too, even though state and/or local law might affirm medical marijuana. Federal authorities can arrest, and prosecute.

Anesthetics have improved over the years and what is now used has better effects. During my surgery, one of the IV bags administered antibiotics to prevent infection. The surgical team doesn't miss a thing. The human body is managed and protected from several angles, during major surgery. If a patient is in pain, anyone around them figures this out really fast and if any adjustments must be made, they are made. There is always a button a patient can push if there's too much pain. It goes right to the nurses' station and they respond very fast.

There is something to note regarding 'length of time' for anesthesia, and drug (or narcotic). When a specific anesthetic or drug is administered, it has to be noted on a record or chart, along with the amount. How much to use during surgery is a technical matter, requiring accurate record keeping. Anesthesiologists and Nurse Anesthetists keep these records, throughout the surgery process. It is their responsibility. Ongoing decisions are made based on these records. After surgery, too, records of this type are kept. Occasionally, hospitals end out missing drugs from their shelves. They get stolen. Or lost, but more likely they're stolen. They keep account of everything. If something doesn't get recorded, a staff member could be suspected of theft. Computers are used extensively in the medical field now. Doctors are well schooled on computer use. They rely on computers every day.

A person going into surgery, who has a general knowledge about anesthetics, can sometimes choose what anesthetics are to be used during their surgery. But they can only 'ask' for a particular anesthetic or particular anesthetics; they cannot be dictatorial about this. They do not have final say in the matter because the Anesthesiologist does. When it comes right down to it, the Nurse Anesthetist has to defer to the Anesthesiologist, when it comes to these issues and decisions. Anesthesiologists are MD's with a specialty. They have final say, but they are also the ones who are responsible for things going right, or wrong. They are the overseers, who are supposed to have the eagle eyes.

I had neither thought nor say about my anesthetics. I put the whole matter in the hands of the professionals. I had no knowledge of anesthetics and they did, simple as that. They had the knowledge, the training, the experience, and the right to administer the anesthetics. When I signed my consent form, to have the surgery, I was also giving consent to the anesthetics and the anesthetic-related decisions of the professionals. I gave consent for them to do whatever they considered best for me. I signed to consent too many other things, too, when I signed the consent form. Essentially, my body was on loan to the professionals, for a time. They could do with it whatever they needed to do.

After the surgery, the Anesthesiologist and Nurse Anesthetist will supervise the patient too, and they will take care of, in as much as possible, whatever complications are remaining from the use of the anesthetics, that were administered during the surgical process. If there are after-affects or side-affects, they are there to help. These professionals are very busy, all the way through, and, their overall responsibility is awesome when you think about it. No wonder they are paid so well. You don't get to know these people—not usually—which seems odd considering they have so much control over your body. But you only see them right before your surgery, for a very short time, and maybe briefly, after your surgery. You're lucky to even be introduced to them, or to have them introduce themselves. As soon as you go in and place yourself on the surgical bed, or are guided on to it is more likely, everything happens so fast and there's not a lot of time for formal introductions. It isn't a social time. It's a surgical time.

Surgery-room professionals are the last people you see before you check into Hotel Unconscious. They generally try to put your mind to rest. They try to help you feel mentally relaxed and at ease and they talk quietly and reassuringly. They can't be real social because brevity is all they can afford as far as time goes. They have to keep their focus and concentration on what they are doing. I noticed this professionalism right before I became unconscious and this, in itself, put my mind at rest. So, my mind was at rest, and then, being unconscious, my mind was really at rest. Having general peace of mind sure beats being fearful or panicked. I eased into unconsciousness, and then, I eased out of it, after the surgery. The professionals made it ease-y for me, or maybe it was God's presence that did this. Likely, it was a combination of the two.

CHAPTER 5
Ward care, and hospital release

In the hospital I healed and bounced back fairly quickly, all across the board, except that total healing was way down the road for me. But, I did well in ICU, at the Step-Down Unit, and in General Ward Care. I was released on Day Six of my stay and my only being in General Ward Care for three days surprised everybody. (The day I left was only a half day so I was really only in GWC for two full days, and then that half day (the day I was released.) I found out later that early releases can be a way of saving money, relative to staff and employee costs. You would think it would be the opposite though, that the longer the stay, the more the money would come in for the hospital, and the staff at-hand. Some things don't make any sense at all. This is one of those things. But, I wasn't in a private hospital, I was in a government hospital, so I guess it all makes sense.

Anyway, General Ward Care was the most interesting place of all. (Of course, it was the only place where I was pretty lucid while being there). During my time at GWC, I felt a little like Alice of *Alice in Wonderland*. I met all types. More people came in and out of my room than you could imagine. The only difference is, they weren't wearing costumes or strange clothes. Each shift it seemed like there were different people. Some were a little strange, or was that just me? Shifts changed, and new people would come in to my room. Most were female. A few were male.

Each employee had something to do, such as check on progress, check my heartbeat, take my temperature, take blood pressure, check the IV, change IV packs, give a shot, bring in medication, bring food and remove trays, help with a shower, give breathing treatments, clean the room, change soiled linen, and do various other tasks. It was a constant Merry-Go-Round of people. It kept things interesting for me, even though I was leery of germs. The employees came around both day and night. Nobody touched my surgical wound though, so the only germs that could form there were from the surgical areas themselves. So far, I was free of infection, both inside my body and outside my body. I didn't even have a dressing over my surgical wound, which I thought odd. I guess stitched areas are different from other kinds of wounds, like scrapes or fire burns.

My temperature was regularly taken. Had it increased from a normal range, it could have been an indicator that infection was building up somewhere in my body. I surely didn't want to pick up a virus or germs from someone's flu or cold, while I was in my hospital room, and with so many people entering and exiting, odds were greater that I could. Your immune system is already down, because of the surgery, so getting sick can happen rather easily.

Some hospital employees, around the nation, have contributed to causing infections. It's been proven that many hospital workers, who go about their business in various wards and rooms, do not wash their hands enough. They can pick up viruses, bacteria, and germs in general in one room and carry them in to another. There have been many deaths relating to hospital infections. Unsanitary conditions, germ-laden instruments, unwashed hands, dirty floors, too much coughing and sneezing, and employees who are carriers of flu viruses and germs from colds and flu are some of the reasons for these deaths. Some hospitals have been cited for uncleanliness. Hospitals are regularly inspected, by outside people. Some are cleaner than others are. All have to be clean to a certain point, though, or there's big trouble.

A person can come down with a cold at any time, including when they are at home, after their hospital stay. A cold can possibly bring on or contribute to an infection. A person may not take proper care of their surgical wound, either. In my case, I was to leave my wound alone, except for showering. When I showered, I could gently apply a liquid bacterial soap to the area and let the shower water rinse it off. If I perceived the area might be dirty, into the shower I'd go. I don't know how laden with bacteria perspiration is, but I was careful about that because of my scar's location.

Infection occurs at hospitals. It is spread in several ways. Germs can be left in the body after surgery. Germs can be transferred by visitors or staff members. This happens more than people realize. Mainly, with regards to internal infections, they are usually easy to spot because the person will suddenly have a very high temperature, and feel just awful. Hospitals will always have antibiotics on hand, in the event infection sets in. In a few cases, antibiotics don't work because there are some bacteria they just don't work on. For this reason, patients die. It can happen really fast. This is one reason the buzzer is always by the bed. This is also why your temperature is regularly taken, while you are staying at the hospital. You will not be released from the hospital if your temperature isn't normal. Other readings have to be normal, too. Most hospital personnel, inside of the surgery room and out, do what they can to prevent infection from happening. Of course, if it happens, who will be responsible for that part of the bill? (i.e., paying for the care and treatment of the infection, and the extra time at the hospital.)

The hospital I was at clearly took precautions to prevent falls. Those convalescing from surgery are very prone to falling or slipping. The hospital issued nonskid slippers. Lots of people who are convalescing are dizzy, and weak and feeble. Some need special help with walking. Some people need wheelchairs, and can't walk at all. They may be able to walk eventually, but, not for a while. Wheelchairs are always available at hospitals. Some people who are convalescing can only walk very short distances. Some are lucky just to make it over to the bathroom. For some, walking a certain distance can be slow, awkward, and painful. Some people have to hold on to something or someone, or lean against something or someone as they go from one area to another. (This was me, at first.)

If a patient is hooked up to an intravenous or IV unit, they have to drag it along with them wherever they go. I call these units 'dance partners'. They're metal, tall, and on wheels. They need to be plugged into an outlet but they can be unplugged because they can run on batteries; it is advised to not run them on batteries for more than so many hours, though, so they'll need to be plugged back into the wall after they've been taken away from their usual spot for a time. Patients are connected to the IV unit with one or more needles, usually in the arm. A needle is stuck in a vein and taped down tight against the arm and a tube goes from the needles up to bags that are hoisted up on the IV unit. I was so relieved when they finally removed my catheter and its related bag. All bags are hung on the IV unit. IVs are a way of getting fluids into a person so they aren't dehydrated. IVs are used for chemotherapy, in cancer cases. Bags can be filled with medication, antibiotics sugar or glucose, potassium, and whatever else is needed. The contents needed for each bag gets mixed in with actual water. Bags can even be filled with blood (for transfusions). The IV unit has buttons and readings on it so there can be pumping, starting and stopping, accelerating, decelerating, and monitoring. Nurses come in and remove the used-up bags and put up new ones.

I was concerned about walking at first, because I got dizzy. I was dizzy more than once, which happens to people who have been lying down for a long time and then try to get up. Circulation stagnates. For a while I was weak, and an unsteady walker, so I walked very slowly. I only got dizzy when I tried to get up out of bed and then when I'd try to stand up. Several times I was on the edge of blacking out, and I had to lie back down. This was a horrible feeling and it was scary, too. When I lay back down, the fainting spell went away. Then I'd sit up, more slowly. The bed had a rail on the side you got out of bed from. It covered 50 or 60% of that one side so you could still get out of bed, at the end. You'd ease down a bit and sit up, using the bed rail if you had to. The other side of the bed was against the wall. The rail was there to keep you from falling out of bed, or to give you something to hold on to, if you needed to.

Dizziness or fainting happens because of the effects of surgery and the lingering effect of anesthetics. Lying down for a long period of time significantly decreases circulation, so if a person suddenly gets up, since their blood flow and oxygen level has been low for a while, they black out. Blood carries oxygen to the brain but if there isn't enough blood circulating and going to where it is supposed to be going, then there isn't enough oxygen, and this causes the blackouts. Movement actually helps to push the blood through the vessels. People who have had surgery must get up and walk around, as soon as possible, and they must do this as often as possible. The patient doesn't have to walk all that long or all that far, but some intermittent walking is important to do. It can also help to prevent blood clots. Circulation of blood is important because blood clots can form, if blood collects somewhere and hardens or clots. Adequate circulation protects blood from clotting, so regular walking and moving around is important for this reason, too. Some kind of walking program needs to be implemented, even if it's just walking up and down the halls.

Most of my tubes were removed fairly early on, in General Ward Care, save one, which connected to a tall unit by my bed (the IV unit). It was connected to my arm intravenously so I could, principally, receive fluids and narcotics. My surgeon came by and said "let's remove this but keep the connection unit in her arm in case she needs to be connected later." So, the needle connector unit stayed in my arm, but, I got free of that tall mobile metal unit, next to my bed. It was quite a contraption. It seemed monstrous, because it was so encumbering. I asked the head nurse about it and she said it had to stay connected to me but fortunately my surgeon came by very soon after and ordered what he ordered (upon my request).

Trying to go anywhere with that 'thing' connected to me via my arm was an inconvenience. Still, it is an extremely helpful and even life-saving unit and I was glad to be hooked up to it when I needed it. I had to walk around the unit to straighten out the connector tube before I could even go anywhere, when I was connected to it. Then I had to push the unit along because it had to stay next to me because it was connected to my arm. I even had to take the unit into the bathroom with me (several times) and the bathroom wasn't all that large. The way the door opened was problematic. I'd have to maneuver the unit into place before I could do anything in the bathroom. Even brushing my teeth got to be difficult, because of this unwanted, entangling tagalong.

As it turned out, once my arm became free from having to have this metal unit connected to it, I never needed what the unit had to offer. You would have thought the nurse in charge of the area would have thought to do this earlier, before my surgeon came around and gave the order, but nurses can do very little unless a doctor orders or authorizes it first. You always want to be, and stay, on good terms with your doctor so you feel comfortable about approaching him with these kinds of things. As a patient, though, you don't have that much say around the doctors. One reason he consented to disconnect me was because I was now receiving morphine by pill form and not by IV. I took my last morphine pill the night before I left and it wasn't all that high of a dosage.

Separating the tube from the tall unit on wheels gave me good mobility, so I was thankful for the disconnecting. I could walk around the area, without having to wheel the tall unit alongside of me. I'm glad my surgeon happened to come by when he did because otherwise I would have had to have stayed connected to the unit for God knows how long, and I would have had to have pushed it around everywhere I walked. I wouldn't have walked very far or very much because of that unit—that is for sure. If it was absolutely necessary to stay connected to it, that was one thing, but if I could be free of it, earlier than later, well then that made my hospital stay easier and it got me walking around more, which helped my circulation. I'm not complaining about these units. Thank God for them. But, they do restrict your movement. Sometimes, movement must be restricted, though.

I took short walks around the ward, but I felt pain in several spots, especially in front where my cartilage had been torn. The muscle there had been so excessively pulled that the front area that was under my left breast and over the front ribs was very swollen, sore, and distressed. It was actually a damaged area. Again, in order to do the surgery, the area had to be lifted, pulled, and stretched. I, of course, had soreness and tenderness where my stitches were, and that whole area was bulgy. The morphine painkillers took away most of the pain, but not all of it. The pain wasn't extremely distracting but this was only because of the painkillers.

In the beginning, I couldn't walk much. I didn't need a cane or a walker because once I got up and started moving around I didn't get dizzy or feel as if I was going to black out. And, I wasn't that feeble. I just hurt. Every step I took was a cautionary one. I didn't want to slip or fall so I was super-cautious. I was slow, careful, and deliberate wherever I went (not that there are all that many places to go in a hospital, after you've just had surgery). I stayed in the GWC area, and there were several corridors that I could walk down.

Soon after my surgery, I got to where I noticed people who walked slow and cautiously, wherever I saw them. I never really focused in on such people and situations before. I saw them, but I didn't 'see' see them, if you know what I mean. Now, I had a great deal of empathy for slow, cautious, and even feeble walkers, wherever I would see them. I somewhat learned what a turtle must feel like, because of my walking experiences after my surgery. I soon felt more compassion for people who walked slowly and cautiously and for people who walked with canes or walkers. I suddenly felt more compassion for people in wheelchairs, too. In the GWC, there were quite a few people in wheelchairs but many of them didn't have to permanently be in a wheelchair.

At first I was quite concerned about some of the early affects or results of my surgery. I had a very sore spot in my trachea and it hurt when I swallowed. This sore spot came about because of the breathing apparatus that had been put down my throat before and during the surgery. The area there was a bit swollen and sore because the apparatus had been in my throat. The swelling made it so that some food was slow to go down. And again, I had trouble breathing, so I was concerned about that problem, too.

I had another breathing problem, besides the one of regular breathing. There were suddenly times when I had to breathe a deep breath, involuntarily. It just suddenly happened, like a spasm, and I never knew when it was going to happen. This, of course, bothered me because I thought that this could be a regular, occasional occurrence, and that it may never go away. I still don't quite understand specifically why this happened, but after a couple of weeks, it subsided, and eventually it stopped happening entirely. I found out later that it was because of the lung's effort to get back to its original shape and function. I know this now because this was my surgeon's explanation for why this was happening. He didn't go into the technicalities about it, though, which was fine with me. Sometimes 'the general' is all you need to know. Let the doctors be the doctors. Let the general public be the general public.

You can't help but wonder if these sore areas or problems are ever going to get better though, after you've had surgery. I hadn't expected these additional problems and pains from the surgery, but, they came about as part of the overall package. I was so sore in front, in the center, and on the side and in back of my upper body, where everything had been pulled and cut and stitched. You only know what you feel today, not what you're going to feel tomorrow, relative to your pain. I was consciously and unconsciously concerned that some pain would linger and always be present. I'd heard about and known about 'lingering pain' after surgery and I really didn't want to be counted in that number. I remembered the problems my mother had had, after her two surgeries, and, of course, my sister's problems, and all I could do after I had my surgery was to hope for the best.

They put me in a room with a roommate. She had just had a shoulder operation. She actually worked for the hospital. She had tried to get something from up high (a box of hospital files) and it fell down on her shoulder. I had some brief talks with her, but we did not get real close. Both of us were a little too much in a suffering mode and in our own little world to be able to extend ourselves outward and into a 'make new friends' mode. We talked about simple things, and about our surgeries. I liked her and was glad to have someone to briefly chat with. She left before I did, so for a while, I had the room all to myself. I didn't watch television much, though. There were about five local and national stations that were available to watch. I was a little surprised that that was all that was available. There was a music station, too, and you could have music on, while you read. Both the TV and the music were connected to the same remote control.

Mainly, I slept and rested, so not having a roommate meant half the traffic, or people coming in and going out. As it was, there were plenty of people coming and going anyway. (Talk about distractions.) When she left, my roommate asked to be wheeled out and down to the hospital entrance, so that her mother could pick her up outside, at the door there. She had to go down the elevator. The hospital was a huge and multi-floor one. Her stuff was set on her lap and on the wheelchair itself as she left. She was looking forward to spending Christmas with her sister, out East, and she planned to fly out there. "How nice for her that she has a sister to visit, and a mother to pick her up at the hospital," I thought, after she left. (My mother and my sister had both recently died.)

I think some people came into my room for legitimate reasons, but a few came in for what I will call 'strange' reasons. The reasons seemed a little flimsy-based or off-the-wall. I don't think so many people should come in and out of hospital rooms. It seems I was constantly interrupted for 'this' and 'that'. I just wanted to rest and sleep. And maybe read a little, although, I didn't read as much as I had thought I would.

When you are sedated, even mildly, it is hard to focus on a book's content. I think I was all wound up about my surgery, too, even though the painkillers

98

helped to take a good deal of the edge off that. I found reading to be hard to do, for some reason or other. I think it was, in part, because I got sleepy really soon, after I'd start to read. But mainly, I just couldn't focus. I kept reading the same line over and over. Entering and exiting people may have made me nervous and anxious, too. I kept expecting someone to come into the room, because this had been happening.

Hospitals should better monitor people who enter rooms of people who are recuperating from surgery. For one thing, and again, germs can float around. And for another thing, people need maximum rest and sleep. I wouldn't be at all surprised if there were several reasons why I had trouble concentrating when reading, after my surgery. I even found it hard to concentrate when I was watching TV, quite frankly. I was in this strange world, at the hospital, and it was real. It was hard to enter into the world of television, and of reading. I was likely anxious about future healing, too, and this had to factor in.

All areas of the hospital are monitored, and outside people (visitors) just can't walk around, undetected—not for very long, anyway. Strangers are always identified and asked a 'what's your purpose here' type of question. ICU is particularly guarded. The whole area is closed off to the public—sealed off even. Visitors have to clear their visit before they are waved through or escorted into the area. The Step-Down Unit was similar, and visitors were well monitored. In General Care Ward, anyone could walk into the area, and even into patient's rooms. There was a nurses' station, though, that most visitors checked in with first before going in to visit someone. Visitors had to honor visiting hours. Sometimes they had to be asked to leave.

Not every visitor checked in at General Ward Care, but most did. The station was set back from the corridor so if a visitor came in the other way and didn't have to walk by the nurses' station, they didn't always report in to one of the nurses there. A visitor could come and go and a nurse might never see them or know that they had been there. Some hospitals have a nurses' station posted in the middle of the corridor so that anyone coming into the area would usually be noticed. This hospital was not set up that way, at least in the General Ward Care section they weren't.

My visitors were all family, and of course, my surgeon. (I guess he wasn't exactly a visitor.) As I think about it, none of my relatives stood or sat within breathing range of me. My relatives were leery of hugging me, for one thing, because of my surgery wounds. Also, there was that bed rail, which served as a barrier. I really enjoyed visits from my relatives. My dad was the most faithful visitor, and the flowers he brought me when I was in ICU went with me to the Step-Down Unit and to General Ward Care. The nurses saw to that. (The flowers prettied up my three (in sequence), rather plain rooms.) One of my sons and his wife lived a couple of hours away, so they came in to see me. My dad came by, with his lady friend, Edna. I saw them several times. My dad visited by himself, too. My dad and Edna were there for me when I checked out of the hospital, thankfully, because I needed the company and I also couldn't drive, because of the pain and the pain locations, and because I was still on painkillers, although, they didn't give me any morphine tablets on my last day, which was probably just as well. I didn't ask for any, either. I was given another type of painkiller.

The night before I left the GWC I had been in some pain, and wasn't able to sleep, so I went over to the person in charge of medication and got one morphine tablet. It took the pain away and conked me out, but that was the last morphine pill I got. I found out later, that if you were in pain, you had to 'ask' for something stronger and they would decide on yes or no. They didn't just give it to you. They did bring me morphine pain pills at regular times, but they decreased the strength at one.

When I was in the GWC section, a woman came by and asked me to assess my pain from one to ten. I found this rather difficult to do because I had nothing to compare my pain with. Plus, I was on morphine so how could I really assess that? So I just said "5". That seemed like a middle-of-the-road, safe answer. She was actually trying to assess if the pain medication strength had been working, and whether or not my pain medication strength should be increased or decreased. I, of course, didn't realize this at the time.

When a person has surgery and they return home from the hospital, Morphine tablets might be prescribed, but very strictly. It can be addictive. Stronger painkillers always have considerable chance of becoming addictive. Morphine is very strong. Percocet® is relatively strong; Vicodin® is a little less strong. A patient has the right to ask the doctor what their options are, when it comes to any and all medicines. They have to actually <u>ask</u> about the different types, though, because a doctor will tend to prescribe something off the top of his head, which will work, but it is only right that you <u>know your options</u> and maybe even explore some or all of them on the Internet, if you can. Both Percocet® and Vicodin® have been limited reference sales, though, because there are deaths, every year, from taking them. They are an acetaminophen and taking too many of them can cause liver damage. Opioid narcotic analgesic drugs, because of the dangers, are only prescribed when absolutely needed. There are other names for Percocet® and Vicodin®, too, which can get very confusing for patients (and sometimes for doctors). Many medicine capsules should never be crushed or the effect will not be there. Always take prescribed pills intact. Doctors generally like to try the lower tiers of pain pills first, when they can. Sometimes the pain is so great that it can't be done. Following surgery, there's usually a great deal of pain, especially with certain kinds of surgery, and surgeons well know this.

No morphine was prescribed for me when I left. When you are released from the hospital after a surgery, it is assumed you are OK enough to not need the real strong pain medication. This depends on the situation though because some people would still need the morphine when they got home. This was the case with my sister, with her cancer. But my pain was OK, I thought, and I didn't insist on getting morphine. I possibly could have, but I didn't. I figured the fewer drugs, the better, unless they are absolutely essential to manage one's pain. Doctors are concerned that if you are given strong medication when you go home, you might take too much of it, too fast, since you are now on your own. In the hospital, they monitor each and every pill, injection, or intravenous flow—very carefully. Long story short, just mild painkillers were prescribed for me when I checked out of the hospital. A stool softener (which I'm not sure was really needed) was also prescribed.

The painkillers generally caused constipation, so the stool softener was prescribed, to minimize the constipation. All the anesthetics supposedly caused constipation, too. I don't know how they did, but this is what I was told. So, people going home after a surgery have to contend with constipation, too. It really wasn't a problem in my case, though, and I really didn't need the stool softener pills.

The painkiller I was on when I came home was only five milligrams narcotic and five hundred milligrams of an anti-inflammatory, like Acetaminophen® or Tylenol®, but I'm not sure exactly what the anti-inflammatory part was. The painkiller was weak, actually, but it did help me to relax so that I could sleep better. Actually, the body manufactures its own pain medication, of sorts, because of endorphins. Anyway, the painkillers I took were hardly habit forming, at least, I don't think they were, and, they did not take away all of my pain. Still, they were very welcome houseguests, if you know what I mean. They decreased the pain somewhat. They didn't take away all the pain, so I had to adjust and adapt to my day-to-day pain.

The meals were decent at the hospital and there were several items on each tray for every meal, which is more than you could do for yourself if you were caring for yourself at home after a surgery, if you know what I mean. Meals were served warm, not hot (does anyone remember that McDonald's lawsuit, with the spilled, ultra-hot coffee?). The dishes the hospital staff brought in were covered. The whole-wheat bread came in a baggie. Any butter, you spread yourself. In other words, care was taken to keep the food free from germs. I remember Jello®, broth, and juice, early on—i.e. the liquid diet.

Care is given to nutrition. Certain foods are avoided, and certain foods are not, simple as that. After a person has had surgery, their cells are disoriented. The last thing you want to do is eat the wrong kinds of foods. Some foods and preservatives in foods are believed to adversely affect cells. For example, you want to stay away from processed foods. After surgery, with all your cells screaming "please take good care of me," you want to eat healthy foods, preferably natural ones, and you want to cut back on sugar and salt. All this made me wonder why people complain about hospital food, when hospital staff tries very hard to meet several nutrition goals.

Three meals a day were served, without fail. Men brought the meals in, not women. Some of those trays were heavy and this may be why men brought the food around. The dishes had to be put on a table that was in each room. Then, after the food was eaten, the dishes had to be lifted off the table and on to the wheeling cart. The dishes were all heavy ones, even without their covers. One of the men had a scowl all the time, for no apparent reason. I don't think he liked his job. He was always outnumbered by women who worked in the ward. I did notice that. He definitely was in the minority. Perhaps this is the case for other male hospital workers, too.

Most of the hospital workers were pleasant, generally level, and non-contentious. One came in, a little younger than me, trying to treat everyone like they were kindergartners. As a matter of fact, I think she should have been teaching kindergarten or elementary school. I think she missed her calling. I couldn't help but think that such condescension towards recuperating people was really 'low'. Here these people are, feeling badly, likely in pain, worried, and being preoccupied with their own thoughts. They're weak, on pain medication, and they're far from being able to stand up for themselves (when someone tries to treat them like children), and yet here comes this young woman, acting like everyone who was in this weary and weakened condition were her little kindergartners. I thought "what an insensitive. She really hits them when they're down and she hits below the belt." She pushed my buttons and I stood my ground with her, start to finish. I was nice, but I stood my ground.

Some people get so preoccupied with one-upping others that they are unable to settle in and listen to content and they aren't able to intelligently hold a conversation. In a hospital setting, this is not at all good. It could even be dangerous. People's lives are at stake. Unfortunately, one-upping is something that we all have to live with, and work around. It isn't going away. There are too many people who don't want to find their way out of it. Sometimes people don't know what they are doing, but usually, they very well do know what they are doing, and they just don't care.

Actually, I experienced insensitivity and lack of concern before I even had my surgery. A couple of people who I trusted and confided in, reference my surgery, ended out being more insensitive than I expected them to be. I opened up to these people and was actually very unhappy and even depressed at the time. I expressed my concerns about the surgery and essentially poured my heart out to them, relaying numerous details about the up-and-coming surgery. About the time I was starting to trust these people, and feeling comfortable around them, they pulled a blatant, callous, and self-centered one-up on me. I wasn't trying to be competitive with these people, either—not at all. I was looking for love (in wrong places I guess). Being competitive with these people was the furthest thing from my mind. Yet these people thought so much of themselves that they could not care enough about my stress and worry about the round-the-corner surgery. They couldn't soften and be genuinely caring, and compassionate. I thought, "how sick", and I essentially lost respect for those people and I felt very sad and even lonely. I couldn't trust them ever again. I wished my husband was still alive, but cancer had taken him away, at a young age.

Well, so much for sharing my inner self....but here's some more, now that I'm on a roll. If only people would just be there for other people, when they are afraid and hurting, instead of having to one-up all the time. Some people are relentless one-uppers, to a fault and a sickness. Before surgery, and after too, try to avoid people who are bent on one-upping. Stay to yourself if you have to. Don't even tell certain people you are having surgery, if you know they are going to upset you. You are going through a great deal as it is. You don't need depression and discouragement put on you by people who really aren't in your corner. Some people are phony baloney.

Some people take delight in one-upping a person when they are most vulnerable. I've had this happen to me, in this 'surgery' context and in other contexts. Usually these people don't know how sick they really are, but many people just don't care if they hurt other people. It is really 'low' when someone is bullyish when a person is down. It is insensitive and it should be noted for future reference. It's good information to have, for a person needing to know if another person is loyal or disloyal, disciplined or undisciplined, fair or unfair. Of such rejecting people, turn away, because you probably won't be able to change them, if you've previously tried in the best way or ways that you knew to do, to make them aware of their deficiencies.

The better hospitals have a number of RN's (Registered Nurses), but some of the people who entered and exited my room, I know, were not RN's. They all wore necklace nametags (as opposed to a pin-on badge type) and I was usually too far away from them to be able to read the print on any badges. I sometimes asked what their job title was though, whenever I thought to. I wasn't exactly in the mood to be overly friendly with strangers, though I tried to be nice and courteous to everyone. Still, I didn't get to know anyone real well. I wasn't in the hospital that long and there is constant changeover of shifts for employees at hospitals.

My surgeon checked in about three times to see me, and to generally check everything out. (They are required to do this.) He had said he would be by 'routinely', and he was. Of course, if anything major had happened to me, for example, infection, the nurses knew how to get ahold of my surgeon, so in that respect, my surgeon was always accessible to me. My surgeon reviewed the pages of my chart, that the various nurses filled out, and based on his review of those pages, and based on other factors, he decided to release me more on the early side. He had originally said that my stay could range from five to ten days.

Infection source is often hard to prove. Recent one-year statistics have been as high as 75,000 to 100,000 deaths, which have resulted from infections that are related to hospital care and stays. I'm not sure if all these were proven, however. Sometimes a convalescing person can be exposed to something that could cause infection while they are at a hospital, and be able to fight it off, so no one always knows about these situations. Still, if one particular hospital gets too many complaints about this and it comes to the attention of monitoring people, they will be investigated.

In the beginning, I had been very worried about infection. I'd read that some people, who went in for even just general, uncomplicated surgeries, ended out dying from infection. This can be even more the case with the more complicated surgeries. Sometimes length of surgery is a factor, but sometimes not. Infection just sets in and takes over. It can kill a person before it is even detected. It can kill a person before proper treatment for it can take hold. As it turned out, I escaped infection, so in that respect, the surgery went well and I didn't end out dying. It eventually became a clear reality that I was still alive and that I got through the surgery after all. I was aware of my senses, and the material world around me. The consciousness of being alive made me feel very good indeed. Monitoring a patient's temperature is what detects infection. If it shoots up, there can be a problem with infection, and the multiplication of germs. Sometimes, even hospital or clinic staff gets infection and spread it amongst themselves. Washing hands between patients will reduce chances of germs being spread.

Again, I left the hospital on the sixth day, and maybe could have left on the fifth but that was a Sunday, and weekends are different at hospitals compared with weekdays. There is more overall staff on weekdays, for one thing. Of course, they're prepared for whatever hits on the weekends, but much more goes on during the weekdays. More surgeries are done and more actual scheduling takes place.

Of course, lots of things happen at hospitals on the weekends—babies are born, people have heart attacks and are in accidents, and so it goes. So, hospitals are always busy. Emergencies happen all the time. It's good that hospitals are institutions and that they're always there, all week long. What would we do without hospitals? What would we do without emergency rooms and ambulances? A large number of people would die if hospitals weren't around. We'd surely have a slower growth of population. Lives couldn't be saved, and many babies would die during childbirth. Mothers would, too. Hospitals are also disease centers. They're supposed to be equipped to take care of epidemics, but some hospitals are only prepared, in part. Still, in part is better than nothing. Some hospitals are trying to improve as disease centers.

My care was carefully monitored, noted, and supervised, in the general ward. Everyone's was. When you are in the care of hospital staff, there really is more 'order' than 'chaos'. Records are diligently kept. Everyone serves a function, performs certain duties, and works according to schedule. Some professionals get difficult shifts. There is a hierarchy in hospitals, too, and hospital employees are very aware of it and act accordingly. In nursing, for example, there are divisions that relate to amount of education, and also type of education. There are the RN's (Registered Nurses) who are on top, and next are the LPNs (Licensed Practical Nurses).

In some hospital wards or sections, there aren't very many nurses per patient. Sometimes there are no RN's at all or the only RN is used in more than one ward, or, the only RN may be off duty at certain times. In the better hospitals, there are quite a few nurses per patient. No one on staff is even allowed to admit to anyone that they are understaffed, though (and overworked), so patients have to figure this kind of thing out on their own if they can, but usually they can't. Especially before a surgery, it would be hard to figure out. While a person is at a hospital, they may be able to figure it out. Five patients per nurse is manageable, six patients per nurse is a little stress for the nurses, and seven patients per nurse is considerable stress for the nurses. This is a good on-average guide for most hospitals.

Sometimes there are more Nurse's Aides than RNs or LPNs. In the nationally-accredited hospitals, aides are not allowed to perform any duties or tasks that could endanger a patient's life. Some aides can be underqualified and they have little education or training. Some have no college at all. Aides are low in the hierarchy, needless to say. They get about half the pay as Registered Nurses get. They aren't supposed to be given more responsibility than they can handle either. Aides are not licensed. Sometimes hospitals hire too many aides, so that employee costs can be cut. Then, there are student nurses that sometimes float around. The tasks they do are very limited; they are learning by watching and hearing and only somewhat by doing. They can be in a patient's room with a more senior nurse, or in there by themselves. These workers are obviously still in a nursing program somewhere, and don't, yet, have their certificate or degree.

I had all these types of employees coming in and out of my room (and some general employees, too), but I was too preoccupied with the after-effects of my surgery to do a tally of how many of each type of professional there was in the general ward where I was receiving my care. I knew which ones were RNs, though. They somewhat stood out. They had more confidence, for one thing. Mainly, I'm happy to report, the nurses and the nurse's aides took very good care of me. They were all very busy, doing this and that. Everything went like clockwork and went well. It was probably all routine for them.

For some, working in a hospital must be stressful. Seeing pain and suffering, hearing groans and moans, standing helplessly by while people die, when they did what they could to prevent the death, and always having to be careful about bacteria and germs in general, are all loads on the backs of hospital workers. The performance of their duties is always under scrutiny, too. If they mess up in some way, it comes to light, although I'm sure the buck gets passed a lot around hospitals. Many times, the people who hospital professionals are serving are ungrateful and lacking in understanding. Their efforts go thankless, and they can be misunderstood. Many of them have probably had their feelings hurt, many a time.

The coin has two sides, though, because some hospital workers become callous, rude, and gruff. They do their jobs, but become one-uppers, towards the recuperating people, which is very sad, and also off-balance because again, usually recuperating people are too tired and weak to be able to fend for themselves. These workers lose their first love—to help and comfort people and to be there for them. They get more wrapped up in themselves. A few even become bullies, but, only if they can get away with it and not be seen by a co-worker. There are dedicated, caring workers, and there are self-absorbed, uncaring workers. The positive. And the negative. And there are those in-between. People are people are people. Naturally, this applies to the recuperating people, too. They're not always so perfect either, but it is the hospital professionals who are in the bullying position because they comprise the majority and they are the healthier, more able ones at the time. A hospital setting is not a place for bullying, but bullying goes on at hospitals all the time. It really should cease. I mean, what's so hard about being pleasant and kind and staying level.

This leads me to another point, the word 'patient'. Up to now I've used the word loosely, or I haven't used the word at all. I have my own thoughts about the word. Years ago, back in the 1950s, I can remember when people were the patients of only the doctors. They weren't patients of nurses, techs, aides, or of medical or hospital workers in general. The doctors had patients, but none of these other hospital workers did. Even through the 1960s and 1970s, this was generally the case regarding the application of the word 'patient'. Nurses never addressed a doctor's patient as their patient or acted like the doctor's patient was their patient. At most, they'd say 'the patient' but that would refer to the fact that the person was the doctor's patient, and certainly not theirs. A person may have been a patient, but not 'their' patient. The person was no one's patient but the doctor's. This is how it used to be, in all fields of medicine, which would include dentistry. Aside workers can't be doing this in the field of veterinary medicine, but they would if they could. The animals are patients of the veterinarians and not nurses, techs, aides, and office workers, however, because only the veterinarians have an actual medical degree and everything that goes along with that, to earn their D.V.M.

Today, many medical workers, other than doctors, refer to people coming in for care as if the people were 'their' patients. But, that person does not have control of the person's body, like the doctor has. Nor do they have the control of their medical destiny, like a doctor has. They don't call the shots. For this reason and in actuality, a person is only the patient of the doctor's. The doctor makes all the important decisions relative to the person's body, and relative to their medical destiny. When medical workers refer to a person as 'their' patient, or use the word 'patient' in such a way that they are meaning they (the medical worker) see the person as being 'their' patient, then they are actually usurping the doctor's authority. They are being disrespectful to the person who is coming in to see the doctor, too. And they are actually being disrespectful of the doctor. Some of them I consider to be authority vultures. They are living within a mistruth and have illusions of grandeur.

If they do not have MD after their name, I personally get annoyed if a medical worker tries to refer to me as their patient. It isn't justified. I am not their patient. I am the doctor's patient. Definitely from 1985 on, 'some' medical workers began to use the word 'patient' in a more inclusive way, as if people coming in were 'their' patients. Techs and even secretaries or bookkeepers at medical facilities do this now. How far from the truth is that. Usually it's younger professionals who do this, but not always. Sometimes the word has to be used, or is going to be used, by medical-related professionals other than doctors, but I personally always take the word 'patient' to mean 'doctor-patient' and nothing else. It's when the word is used by these professionals in such a way that people coming in to the medical facility are assumed to be their patients, too, that upsets me. I say to them, go and earn a medical degree and realistically assess what your present work really includes.

People are patients to the doctors they choose, and the word 'patient' shouldn't cross over that line. Anyone dealing with the medical world is going to come across this, though, and it can be irritating. You have to let it roll off your back, or, stand your ground, because such an attitude isn't right. You aren't coming in to the office to see them. You are coming in to the office to see the doctor. This general concept applies to other professions too, besides just the medical profession. Another word that is thrown around willy-nilly is 'client'. This word is misapplied by the wrong people more often than I can say. Often a client is really just a customer, and it isn't even their customer, per se. It's the same ole same ole, as with the word 'patient'.

Recently I heard another one of these types of words—the word 'banker'. The word was being applied to customer-service people who worked at a bank. In my day, 'banker' only referred to presidents and vice presidents of banks. It didn't refer to tellers, customer service representatives, or even lower-level managers. Semantic shifts of word meanings occur in cultures everywhere. Many do not accept these particular semantic shifts, however. The good old days aren't coming back so you have to live with these irritations. Maybe this tide will turn, but I don't expect it to, except with some (but likely not enough) people.

The doctor is at the top of the hierarchy. Again, the doctor makes all the decisions. No nurse can decide something against a doctor's decision, nor can anyone else. No one can initiate prescriptions, except for doctors. Nurses and other employees have to clear things with doctors, if they want or need something to be done or changed. Doctors are in charge of the hospitals, and of the sections in hospitals. Hospital workers march to the beat of the doctor's drums.

Doctors are very smart people. They're disciplined, too, or they couldn't have finished med school and all the related training. Their arena of learning is Medicine, which may not be yours or mine, but that is immaterial. They know their field and are constantly learning. They will always know more than you or I know about Medicine. They go four years to college, four years to medical school, have one year of internship, and then they have four or five years in residency. Some even go beyond that. Doctors learn a great deal initially and have a good foundation for continued learning by the time they go into private practice. They learn a great deal once they're in private practice, too. So I ask you, how do a nurse, an aide, a tech, or a medical worker in general, size up to the educational stature of a doctor? The truth is, they don't. So, no one is the patient of anyone but the doctor's. Take it, and be right, or leave it, and be wrong.

Don't let these other professionals pull the wool over your eyes is my admonishment. You're only the patient of your doctor. You really aren't the patient of other doctors, either, because they don't know your case. They may know parts of your case, but they don't know all that your doctor knows. Even looking at some or all of the medical records in a file does not make anyone your doctor or equal to your doctor. Your doctor has had talks with you and has kept up with your case. He is maximally in the know about you and your case. Others are only minimally in the know. Usually.

Everyone has a place in life, and they contribute in various ways to the world they find themselves in. And this is a good thing. But, without doctors, the world of Medicine could not be, or even have started up and gradually advanced as much as it has. They're at the top. They deserve to be there. And they deserve to stay there.

My release only came about because my doctor ordered it. My hospital experiences were to be no more, and my stay there was over. "My, what an education," I thought, as I slowly walked out of the hospital, with my dad and Edna. Edna helped to brace me a little, as we walked out together. She was concerned that I might get dizzy. Both my dad and Edna were concerned about getting me into the car so I wouldn't pull my stitched areas or bump anything as I went to sit down in the seat. After all I'd been through, it was nice to experience thoughtfulness and courtesy. It meant so much to me.

Of course, they were older people. Every experience I had and every day I spent at the hospital cost money. Cumulatively the bill for all of the hospital care for surgery and hospital accommodations cost around $25,000. I literally do thank God for having provided me with a coverage before I had the surgery. My surgeon's bill was separate, and it was covered, too. It was close to $4,000, which frankly, I thought was very low. It was much lower than I expected it to be. All this was because of a stupid car accident I was forced to be in, five years earlier. Thank God I had coverage. If I hadn't, and I had to go through this and pay out $29,000, my mental state would have been frazzled and shot. I thanked God for helping me through this horrible ordeal. I was glad the hospital part of it was over.

Now all I had to do was heal and get well. Healing seemed like such a long road ahead. Home was the place where it would happen.

CHAPTER 6
Healing at Home

After I checked out of the hospital, my dad, Edna, and I stopped at a local drugstore to get my prescriptions filled. The stop was on the way to my home. I was concerned about being in a car, because fender benders and crashes have been known to happen, and with recently stitched areas in and on my body, the last thing I wanted to experience was a fender bender or crash. Going over the speed bumps was bad enough. I got so that when I went over a speed bump, I'd press my head against the headrest and arch my back a little, so that the back of the car seat wasn't touching my back area, where my stitches were. It was less stress and pain that way since my stitches and surgical site didn't have to be rubbed or bumped.

When I was at the hospital, I ate well; I really did. I ate practically everything that was put in front of me. I know there are a number of people out there who believe that hospital food is tasteless and not all that good in general, but I found it to be just fine. I thought the taste was all right and it was obvious that nutrition was emphasized, by the food that was on the tray. My first meals were the liquid broth, Jell-O®, juice, and the like. Then I was given a meal having mostly liquids, like before, but, there was a slice of bread too, and a small dish having small pieces of food in it...like rice, tiny pieces of chicken, and peas. These meals were what I ate in ICU and Step-Down. After that, the meals were good-sized and complete meals. Coffee was always decaffeinated, at the hospital. (Caffeine doesn't mix too well with the anesthesia and drugs and painkillers.) Plus, they want you to sleep and rest.

I was so thankful to be eating whole meals finally, considering that for some time I had only been eating portions because of how my stomach had been positioned. Seeing those meals, and being able to eat them, was a treat for me, quite frankly. In this respect, I wasn't like other people who had had surgery. Most of them had been able to eat whole meals before they had their surgery. I hadn't been able to eat any whole meals for some time. I'd actually forgotten what it was like to eat a whole meal.

When I got home, my father bought me some food that was all healthy. This good deed was both generous and it contributed to my health. He brought it over to my home a couple of days before my surgery and had it in the refrigerator waiting for me. (I'd given him my home and mail keys so he could take care of my cats and retrieve my mail.) I had looked into a mobile meals program before my surgery. There were two or three of these programs available in my area that I knew of. One of course was Meals-on-Wheels. With this type of program, your meals are brought in by outside people. I decided to wait to see how I felt when I was released from the hospital before I joined up with a meals program.

Juices, some name-brand boxed frozen meals, fruit, and sandwich meat, were on hand when I came home, because of my father's kindness. I was especially keen on eating navel oranges, so plenty of those were on hand, too. In case I caught a cold, the oranges would help to heal it, because of all the Vitamin C in the oranges. They would prevent my even catching a cold, too. I was extra concerned about getting a cold because I had a fear of coughing. Even slight coughing hurt my stitched areas, both inside and out. (Keep in mind, I had five sets of stitches—the diaphragm, two muscles, around two ribs, and over the thickness of my skin. There could, even, have been more.) Sneezing was quite painful, too. Sneezing catches you of guard and all of a sudden you've got yourself a pain where your stitches are (and on other places, too) because your chest expands, fast and suddenly. Sneezing was a super ouch for me so I had to try to stop myself from sneezing, whenever I could. (This was, of course, easier said than done because sneezing is somewhat involuntary.)

I still had that little sore spot down in my trachea where the breathing apparatus had been and I sometimes had to cough. It really hurt when I coughed so I tried to cough as gently as possible. That is not so easy to do, either. Other areas hurt way more than my throat area did. Even blowing my nose caused a stretching and a disturbing of my stitched areas. I kept water nearby, everywhere I went, so if I felt a cough coming on, there would be the water and I'd quickly take a drink. The water soothed my throat enough to prevent my needing to cough.

I became what could be called a conservative cougher, nose blower, and sneezer. I became rigid whenever I was forced to do any of these three things (because of the stress) and I tried to suppress as much of the movement as I could whenever I had to do any one of those three things. With sneezing, I got to where I always kept facial tissue close at hand so that I could gently blow my nose whenever I felt a sneeze coming on.

Again, sneezing was stress-plus for me, and for my stitches and surgical wounds, mainly because the chest area is forced to expand so much. You don't want to have a lot of dust around your home when you come home from surgery. Your home should be completely vacuumed and dusted before you even go in to the hospital, or, right before you come home. If you have to, hire a domestic helper to clean your home before you have surgery. Or, perhaps a family member can do this, if you are unable to vacuum and dust before your surgery. In my own case, I had to be careful about kitty litter dust, although, it really is minor. I ended out buying 99% dust-free kitty litter, at least for a while, after I came home from my surgery. It costs a little more than the litter I usually bought, but that was fine with me. My dad and Edna and I went and got several bags of this litter, after my surgery, and my dad handled the bags for me because I really couldn't.

My wound care was not very much of a problem, since I didn't require a dressing. The thin material that had been sewn in with the stitches, to hold them in better, gradually fell off, in pieces. Mainly, when I showered, they fell off. I had to be careful about irritating the wound, and about bumps and scrapes, but I didn't have to make special efforts to clean the wound or to put anything topical on it. I used the anti-bacterial soap on the area only a couple of times, but I didn't really need to because the wound was doing all right. Of course, it was raw for quite a while, and swollen, too. It stayed tender and somewhat swollen past the six-month checkpoint. This was possibly because, by then, I was sleeping on the area and wearing a bra. Both situations aggravated the area but wearing clothes over the wound area, on my side and back, didn't seem to bother me at all. I could even wear a heavy sweater. But, wearing anything tight was a problem even at six months.

My wound didn't get infected at any time when I was home, but my stitches did get pulled. The scar line is thicker under my arm, because that is where movement caused the area to pull the most. Everyone has to move around after surgery. My stitched areas got pulled and stretched, but that was inevitable. Even though the stitching was well done by my surgeon, after a time, it didn't look so well done. You have to allow for some change relative to a stitched area or scar, after a surgery, because of pulling and stretching. You don't want to pull or stretch the surgical site any more than you have to. But you have to live, and do normal, everyday things. I moved around enough to keep blood flowing to the wound and that was important. Moving around actually helped the wound to heal but it put stress on the cut and the stitched area. One does what they have to do. An enlarged scar is generally expected by surgeons, because of anticipated movement.

It was good to come into my 'Home Sweet Home'. Home had everything I needed, and, there would be no interruptions. Hurray! I could eat, rest, sleep, watch TV, read, shower, prepare food, and complete small tasks, all in accordance with my own play-it-by-ear schedule. At first, my father went out and got my mail for me, so I could keep up with my correspondences and bills. Walking too far and climbing stairs, at least for a week or so, was something I avoided doing. Around this time, Christmas cards were coming in. I didn't get mine out that particular year because of my surgery. I enjoyed receiving Christmas cards, and was looking forward to Christmas. I at least got my bills paid on time, thank heavens, and I sent some letters to people who sent me Christmas cards.

When surgery is elective, you can sometimes prepare in advance for the 'time out' for the surgery. I had bought two Thanksgiving turkeys and cooked them, and cut the meat up into little pieces, for soup. I had also made a large batch of soup that I froze. For some time, I wasn't sure I was going to have the surgery because I was hoping to escape it, but subconsciously I knew I might and probably would have the surgery. I tabled it, because of fears, but as everything worsened, I faced reality. The coin had two sides. So, I got my freezer and my refrigerator in order. Then, with my dad's help, I ended out getting some other food, too, which kept me going as well, especially during my first few days at home. Again, I ate lots of navel oranges. They were the perfect snack and all you had to do was peel them, section them, and plunk them in your mouth.

My dad took care of my cats for me while I was in the hospital and he did this for me when I first got home. I had four cats at the time, all older, so it was helpful to know I didn't have to worry about my cherished kitties. I enjoyed my cats so much, when I got home from the hospital. A quote from a well-known person, Jean Cocteau, is "I love cats because I enjoy my home; and little by little, they become its visible soul." That about sums it up for me. My cats were my company, during all the days of my healing. It was a comfort to have them around, while I was healing. Cats are sedate, quiet, and loving creatures. What's not to love about cats. I genuinely enjoyed having them around, and I still do.

On the ninth day after my surgery, I stopped taking the medication that was prescribed for me, at least during the day. I only took it at night. But then, during the next two days afterwards, I was in a new kind of pain, so I had to take the pills both day and night for a little while longer. Once the swelling went down, a new kind of pain entered, known as 'tightness'. The stitches and the skin tightened up after the major swelling from the surgery went down, and this actually hurt. I hadn't been anticipating this.

The initial, major swelling stayed around longer than I expected it to, that was another thing. Since I felt pulls and tightness in various spots when the swelling finally did go down, I had to put my moving around in very slow gear. Whereas before I wasn't so fearful about moving around (and perhaps I should have been), now suddenly I decided I'd better move around more slowly.

As for lifting, I was very careful about that. I didn't lift anything all that heavy, once I got to walking around OK. This was on the after-care instructions. A list of these instructions was given to me right before I left the hospital. I didn't carry anything very heavy very far or hold something for very long, either, especially if it started to pull on my stitches or to cause any pain. Actually, I avoided lifting anything, even over just five pounds, for a long time. Better safe than sorry, as they say. I bended more carefully, too, if I bended at all. I had to bend at the knees, not forward. If I picked anything up at all I had to bend at the knees or get down on all fours. I wanted to vacuum, but I couldn't pull or push it around very well so I didn't.

Actually, I didn't vacuum my home until sixty days after my surgery, which was very frustrating because my floors needed vacuuming sooner than that. When I did vacuum, I had to be on my knees to do it. I didn't have to move the suction part as far back and then forward when I was on my knees. I couldn't bend at the waist like I would have if I was standing, so my surgical areas weren't as disturbed when I vacuumed on my knees. It was less movement in general, if I did vacuum that way. Vacuuming is strenuous work, actually. I could only do light things, and things that didn't take too much time, during the first few months of my healing. Any vacuuming took way more time than it did before. Doing dishes was no problem, nor was light housework in general.

I turned more carefully, too. In essence, I kept my body as straight as a board. I was able to take care of my dishes, my wash, my meals, and my cats, as long as I kept my body straight, and bent at the knees and not the waist. I did 'a little at a time' and I tried not to overdo it. Good thing I wasn't running any races (i.e., under pressure to meet deadlines). I worked steadily. I've always been a steady plodder, only after my surgery, I had to work slower than I like to. I kept up with everything OK, but just barely. At times I had to push myself. It isn't easy to get things done, after you've had surgery. But you don't want to complain about it and be a big baby and expect others to do things for you. You have to do things for yourself. You can't let yourself get behind or be lazy; you can't be a dawdler.

After surgery, you're tired. Your energy is being used to heal your body. I rested and relaxed, but I moved around and walked and I moved around whenever I felt good about doing mobile things. Again, movement speeds up healing. The blood gets circulating, breathing efforts increase, and muscles get back into use. You have the psychological good feeling that you are being at least somewhat productive when you keep as busy as possible, after a surgery. Doing tasks takes your mind off your pain, too, because you're focusing on something else besides your pain.

Again, even though moving around was difficult, it was a mandate for my progress. After a surgery, mild exercise—walking and general moving around—is imperative so the body can resume normal functioning. Many people who have surgery have to be in a structured program of physiotherapy. My surgery did not require this of me. However, I had to move around and do things every day, on my own. It was up to me to take the initiative. This was, on my part, an understood necessity. I couldn't just sit in a chair and watch TV or read all day, in other words. I couldn't let myself be sedentary.

One reason my surgeon wanted me to move around so much is because if you don't, your surgical site areas or scar areas will end out being too tight, and then movement will be difficult if not impossible. Movement is actually supposed to stretch the scar area, so the area at the scar site and around it will be pliable and moveable. My scar area was in an area where it got plenty of movement, fortunately. The downside, though, is that it did enlarge my scar a little.

At first I slept a lot, but then, I slowly and gradually got back into my usual sleep routine. Sleeping was a problem from the get-go, not the amount of sleep, because I was doped up and slept lots, but the position for my sleeping was a real problem. Because of the surgical work that was done because of my diaphragm and hiatal, that affected and tore the front muscle and cartilage, I was swollen and sore in front so I couldn't sleep on my front. And I was, of course, swollen and sore to my left side, because I'd been opened up there, and then over to my back. My stitches were on my left side and along the back. I couldn't sleep on my front or my left side, for sure, and I had to be a little careful if I slept on my back.

It wasn't that easy to sleep on my right side either—the other side from my surgery entrance. My body weighed down because of gravity and this pulled on my stitches and at my wounds. It pulled at my front muscle and cartilage and caused the muscle and cartilage to go the opposite way from how it was supposed to go, because of gravitational pull. The affected muscle and torn cartilage pulled in the wrong direction when I laid on my right side, but for the whole time that I was not able to sleep on my left side, which was several months, I assumed that I had to sleep on my right side and that I had no choice in the matter. The muscle and cartilage couldn't grow back quite right as a result, and so it stayed a little bulgy because it was being forced to set in the wrong direction, because I had to sleep on my right side for quite some time, after my surgery. It was likely bulgy in the first place because it had initially been so pulled during the surgery. I should have tried harder to sleep on my back, as much as was possible, but I didn't think enough about that, until it was too late. Ideally, it's good to always sleep on your back after any surgery, if you can, and when and as you can.

Cartilage heals slowly, but likely the way I was forced to sleep did not help the healing there, and perhaps it hindered it. There was nothing that could be done about it though because gravity pulled the muscle and cartilage the opposite way to how it was supposed to go. Nothing could be done about the dilemma because it was the only way I could sleep. I had to sleep on my right side for some time and so all that time, the muscle and cartilage in front were forced to set the opposite way to how they tended to set, anatomically. Needless to say, it stayed bulgy, because of the way it was forced to heal. It will probably always be a little bulgy, because it permanently healed up while being forced to go the other way because of the force of gravity. Once I was able to sleep on my back, it helped reduce the problem, but the muscle and cartilage would have healed right had I been able to sleep on my back from the get-go, or to alternate and occasionally sleep on my left side, as well. Unfortunately, it just hurt too much to sleep any other way. I hope nothing else was affected, by my having to sleep on my right side for so long a period of time after I had my surgery. I think it probably was because everything internal was forced to shift over towards the right.

When I was more heavily sedated in the hospital, I slept on my back and on my right side but that was because of the morphine. I couldn't feel a thing. I couldn't sleep on my front, because of tubes. Actually, I didn't focus in too much on what was the best position for sleeping, while I was at the hospital. I blundered through, and slept as best I could. I didn't think about it much, until I left the hospital and didn't have very strong painkillers, to numb any pain.

Later on, I found that sleeping on my back was an OK way to sleep, even though my scar was on one side of my back. It was the thinner part of the scar that I slept on, for the most part. I did not use a head pillow, so my spine stayed straight. I propped pillows beside me, so I wouldn't turn. I even put a sweater around my head because my head was by the window, and the area got cold. (Again, the last thing I wanted to come down with was a cold.) The neck side of the sweater went around my head, in front, and the rest of the sweater was bunched around my head. I looked funny, but no one saw me at home, so I was safe. I had to be sure to keep warm. It was winter, and sleeping by the window could not be avoided. I didn't catch a cold, thankfully, and I think that putting the sweater over my head was one reason why I didn't. Plus, eating all those navel oranges helped a great deal.

It was difficult getting in and out of bed because stitches pulled and pain areas got pressed against. My bed is lower than most beds are because it does not rest on a bed frame (the bed frame is in storage). Actually, I prefer a bed that is lower to the ground. The bed is two parts—box springs and mattress. I got used to a certain method or procedure relative to getting in to bed, and out of bed. Both efforts required a different approach and different skills. Then it became routine. I have a heavy-duty lamp stand next to my bed and it has an edge around the top. I used the edge to grab hold of and to grip, when both laying down and getting up. Getting into bed was just a matter of sitting down on the bed, and then laying down. No problemo. But it was difficult because of the soreness. Getting up from bed was more difficult. I had to turn over, get my knees down on the floor, raise up my upper body, and then hold onto the bed or the lampstand while I got up on my feet. It certainly did look awkward, but no one saw my struggling but me.

For some time, when I was at the hospital, I got in and out of bed a lot. This, of course, started after my catheter had been removed. My catheter never bothered me, the whole time it was in. I didn't feel anything when they pulled it out, either, but, of course, I had to use the latrine after they removed it. When I was mobile, I sat or stood up for different reasons—to sit at the side of my bed (to eat), to use the latrine, to add a sweater, to remove a sweater, and to walk. At home, I was much more mobile. I was thankful to not have to be in a wheelchair. I was saddened for the people who are wheelchair-bound.

Again, walking and moving around was an absolute necessity so that blood wouldn't be able to clot. In the hospital, they gave me periodic shots of Heparin, so that there would be no blood clotting. At home, I walked and moved around as much as I could. I couldn't walk long walks, like outside, because my stitched-up areas got to be too painful when I did. So did some other areas. I walked whenever

I needed to, but not in excess of what I had to. I'd go from room to room or up and down the hallway, doing this and that, and I really didn't want to go walking outside, not for a while.

The early days of my in-home care were difficult. The first thirty days were especially hard. If people can get through the first thirty days (after most surgeries), the difficult part is over. Taking care of yourself, your home, and your pets, if you have any, only needs to be minimal, during those first thirty days. Neither of my kids lived at home at the time, so I didn't have anyone else to take care of. Many people do, though, after a surgery, and they can become overburdened. The family has to pitch in and help. After three and a half to four months, I was doing most everything I was able to do before, as long as it wasn't something real strenuous. I was still moving more slowly, though, depending on what I was doing. I had to take my time, and also rest fairly often.

I felt pain in the back area for a long time because of the rib splitter's effects on the area. When I walked, I particularly noticed it. I often had to sit down because of the pain (or acute discomfort). I felt pain all along my incision areas too, of course. In the tender area right at the edge of my left breast and under my arm, the stitches had seemed to pull the most, in part because of the weight of my breast. There was occasional stinging there for a while, as a matter of fact. Then there was the pain in the inside middle, from the rib splitting. That pain really flared up if I walked for very long.

What really got to me was that upper front area, though, because of the pulled muscle and cartilage. Again, when the surgery was being performed, the muscle and cartilage in front was strenuously pulled and even damaged. That area stayed swollen. It bulged out and the area affected was about seven inches in width and was under my left breast, extending about five inches downward. It was over my front rib cage to the left arm/hand side. It was like having a badly sprained ankle, only the area was in front of my body. I wonder if something was supposed to be stitched down under there. It takes cartilage 'forever and a day' to heal. Muscles take a little less time. Even after a couple of months, I still couldn't wear a bra because that front area, and even where my stitches were, hurt too much. I had to wear an open backed one-piece bathing suit under my clothes if I needed to go out anywhere. This wasn't real fun and was an inconvenience, but at least I was able to have some support up there, when I went out.

The whole front area was quite sore. I don't understand why that area there, in front, ended out being so traumatized and stressed, but it was. I didn't see the operation, but something sure was done to traumatize that area. The area healed very slowly and not completely. For the longest time, there was swelling and soreness in that area. And, it was easily stressed. I couldn't sleep on my front, because of that area. It seemed to me that the work could have been done without that area even being bothered because he went in through the side and back. That front area just doesn't seem like it should have been within the range of the operation. Yet, somehow, that area got pulled and stressed. I'm sure there was a reason for it, but I don't specifically know what it was. I used a hot pad on the area, off and on, once I started sleeping on my back and while I was on my back. Heat opens up vessels so blood can flow into the area that needs the healing. This tends to help an area heal and to heal a little faster. The use of a hot pad can be considered to be a homeopathic treatment.

It was hard to laugh, because of the stress and soreness in that front area. When I laughed, that whole area was involved and affected. The muscle there got tightened when I laughed, and the cartilage got pulled. In the beginning, I actually had to avoid funny movies and situation comedies, because it hurt when I laughed. Other areas hurt when I laughed, too, but not as much as that front area did. It is, of course, a natural desire to try to not be gloomy after a surgery, but watching funny movies and sitcoms brings about laughter, which, in turn, can exert too much pressure on tender and stitched areas. I didn't read funny books or watch anything funny on television for a few weeks, actually. It was okay to smile, but laughing was actually a bit of a problem.

The time came when I ended out watching funny scenes. It came about by accident, actually. Humor or funny things come on the TV in bits and pieces and they often come on suddenly. I got blitzed by humor when I least expected it. If something is really funny, a person is going to laugh. The desire to laugh can't be stopped. I learned, because of my days at home after surgery, that it is easier

123

to control sneezing and coughing than it is to control laughter, if something is really funny.

Right around day forty after my surgery, I watched a couple of Billy Crystal movies. I laughed really hard through both movies. I got sorer, after laughing so hard, but it was worth it. The soreness level went back down, though, to how it was before, after a couple of days of not laughing at all. Laughter means you are enjoying yourself, and believe me, I hadn't been enjoying myself too much, not since I'd had the surgery.

Soon after I settled in at home, I started watching old sitcoms, which I hadn't done before, but I wanted to watch funny half-hour shows after my healing had reached a certain point and so I turned the dial to certain channels. I only occasionally watched them, before my surgery. The four older sitcoms (re-runs) I started regularly watching were *Three's Company*, *All in the Family*, *The Jeffersons*, and *Family Ties*. Even though they were re-runs, I don't recall having seen the episodes before. These shows helped me through my healing. They also helped me to get back to my old self again. They helped me to get my sense of humor back. Right before and after surgery, it is a little difficult to be relaxed enough to laugh.

At home, if things got a little too painful while walking or moving around, back to bed I'd go. Once I got through the stress and pain of getting into bed and got well covered, braced in by pillows, and had a sweater situated over and around my head (so my head would be warm), I was a happy little camper, all nestled in. Usually I would take one of my prescribed pills right before I got into bed. I had to remember to have something in my stomach when I did, however. I remembered that one nurse had admonished me to eat something first, before taking a painkiller. This ended out being a bit of a problem because eating right before bedtime caused me to have to use the bathroom fairly soon afterwards, and sometimes even in the middle of the night, so my sleep got broken up. Sleep got broken up at first, too, because of the pain and discomfort from the surgery.

If I knew I needed to sleep, I moved my cats out of my room. They had a habit of walking on my body, including my sore, stitched areas, whenever they rested or slept on my bed with me (or at least one of them did). I slept better with my cats out of the room, so out they would go. If I'd only had one cat, it may not have been a problem, but I had four cats. My cats also tend to wake me up, if I'm sleeping, so I have to keep them out of the bedroom if I'm about ready to go to sleep for a long time.

Once I started to sleep on my back, as long as I didn't move (and I usually didn't move), my sleeping on my incision that was on my back didn't get moved or pulled, so it didn't hurt to sleep on my back. It was a bit difficult getting into position—scooting or lifting my body a little to the right, to the left, or up or down—but once I got in that 'best and most comfortable position', the sandman came to visit.

Early on, when I could only sleep on my right side, I used a regular pillow, but I propped another pillow over to my left side so I could turn a little in that direction and sleep at a 45° angle towards my left side. That way, my incision area on the left was only touched by the soft pillow, and not the harder bed. So, I essentially had two positions for sleeping on my right side, which was, of course, better than one, and certainly better than none. I could sleep direct and straight up on my right side, or I could sleep with my body tipped a little over to the left, because of pillow propping. I concluded that being able to sleep in any position is a wonderful thing, and it's something that we all take for granted. At least, I did before my surgery.

There were times when I just couldn't get to sleep. So I'd watch television. I couldn't toss and turn while sleeping, that was another problem. (I'm sure I did, though.) Propped in by pillows, it was hard for me to move. It is thought that the average person tosses and turns from fifty to eighty times a night. (This might be an exaggeration, however.) This tossing and turning keeps the muscle moving, the blood circulating, and it actually helps a person sleep better, assuming they aren't awake while they are doing any of the tossing and turning.

I only had the choice of the two positions, all night long, until I was able to sleep on my back. If I moved the wrong way, I would wake up because it would hurt. I had quite a lot of trouble sleeping for a while. My sleep got interrupted during the night, especially during the first few months. Sometimes I had to wait to fall asleep, even though I was tired, because I was so uncomfortable. All in all I did OK with my sleep, though, considering the circumstances, especially as things got better.

A few times, I experienced the problem of Restless Leg Syndrome. Thankfully, I stopped experiencing this, early on, because it is horribly distracting when you are trying to sleep. This 'feeling' occurs in the legs and it is caused when the lower back tends to sway. Because my backbone alignment was now suddenly different, since my stomach was back to where it was supposed to be, this new sway or shifting of my back put pressure on the nerves going into my legs. At times, when this feeling came on, my legs felt a little like they were made of jelly and like they couldn't be used. Fortunately, it only seemed to happen when I lay down, but I'm not sure that is always the case with RLS. A muscle-relaxant pill could have, maybe, helped, but I didn't get a chance to discuss that with the doctor. He would have known if it would have been.

I was affected by RLS when I was in bed and my legs were relaxed. When this odd feeling occurs, it drives you crazy. You can use your legs. In fact, you feel like you have to use them, right then and there. It's an unpleasant and annoying sensation. It's like your legs are one big itch, and they need scratching (or movement). In other words, you have to get up and use them right away. Getting up and walking around helps, or leg movement under the covers works, too, because you can kick your legs under the covers.

I was glad when I stopped having these Restless Leg Syndrome bouts and sensations, that's for sure. I was fortunate that I didn't have to have these bouts long and that they went away. My back still had a long way to go, though, to realign and get better, because it had been out of alignment for several years. My condition had caused other problems in my spine, too, that only a sufficient period of time, after the surgery, could heal. Some of the back problems I have now may never improve much, though, and certain problems may remain. RLS is different from muscle cramps I sometimes got much later on. I got those when I'd walked a lot during the day and used my leg muscles much more than I usually did during a one-day period. Those are no fun to get, either. You'll be resting or sleeping in bed and suddenly your lower back leg muscle would clench, or your foot or toe muscles would. I call these 'bed cramps' because I am always in bed

126

when these muscle cramps plague me, but such cramping is not RLS. Still, you are usually in bed when both RLS and the leg or foot cramps hit.

Again, I am sure the Restless Leg Syndrome happened because my back suddenly curved inward more, and because there was no more pressure on the one side since my stomach was no longer there. It had been moved elsewhere. My back was suddenly forced to be straighter and better aligned, because everything inside was put back to a normal placement. Still, other things hurt, and the new shifting caused new problems. My back was sore for some time, actually, while I was convalescing and as it was being forced to resume and adjust to its new position. Over the years, it had shifted over to one side and was pressed in a little, because of the positioning of the stomach. All this shifting had been slow and gradual (possibly for as long as four and a half years), and I felt the back or spine discomfort for some time before the surgery. Now, I was feeling it after the surgery.

Early on, I was reading in my bedroom, and one of my cats (named Pearl) started to attack another one of my cats (named Iona). It suddenly happened. I quickly and instinctively threw a magazine that I was reading, near the attacking cat, to divert her from attacking. I certainly wasn't aiming for either cat—just throwing the magazine next to them. I didn't want either cat to be hurt from the cat fight. I wanted the magazine to distract the kitties from fighting. The two cats ran out of the room. The one cat got to safety from the other cat, somewhere, but I was left with quite a pain at my surgical site because I had thrown the magazine with my left arm and hand, to divert the cats from fighting.

The stitches in back were swollen to both sides of the stitches, after I had thrown the magazine. I just happened to use the muscles that had been cut open and then stitched up during my surgery, when I threw the magazine. I used more force than I should have been using, in other words, and I ended out being in pain because of the action, i.e., because I threw the magazine. I used speed and strength that I ordinarily was used to using before the surgery, but, my surgical area had not healed up well enough yet, for me to be using that amount of speed and strength. Unfortunately, I got caught off my guard, it had happened so fast and I wasn't thinking.

The swelling eventually went down, but the area in back was sore. For a while, my stitches surrounded a rounded bump along the scar and that whole area hurt. I worried that I had hurt myself too much; I was quite upset. I thought, "after all the suffering I went through before the surgery, during the surgery, and now after the surgery, what if I just did harm to the work my doctor had done." I couldn't see inside myself, to check for damage inside my body and this was the problem. Psychologically, I was upset and worried.

I would have to ride this thing out, and only after a while would I know if there had been damage. It could be that no essential damage was caused. Or, it could be that the damage was minimal, and would heal up on its own and not be a problem, once everything had enough time to heal. It could also be that minor damage had been caused, that could cause minor problems, on down the road. On the bright side, maybe the incident would do some 'unseen' good in the long run, and cause my muscle in back to be more pliable or to do something else. I doubt that this was the case, but who knows. In any event, my main hope was that no essential damage was done. My doctor had previously told me that minimum and minor moving around would not hurt my stitches. This incident, however, was more than minimum or minor moving around. You'd think that throwing or slinging a magazine would not be a problem, but when the area used is where muscles and skin had been cut and stitched, such a minor exertion can end out hurting the surgical site, to the point where something splits or some kind of problem results.

Again, there was initially a large bump of swelling all along my incision, to both sides of it. After the incident, my scar area felt even tenderer than before, and it hurt. I think that because the muscle (a rather huge muscle)—the Latissimus dorsi,—had been cut, opened up, and pulled during the surgery, that it was extremely vulnerable. Then, too, it had been stitched through. It was the stitching through the muscle that got stressed, and that ended out getting pulled when I had thrown the magazine. I hoped that my diaphragm and hiatus stitches hadn't been hurt. I slung the magazine back, and then I slung it forward. I used those back muscles when I did. I hadn't ever wanted to do such a thing, but unfortunately I did, and it became a setback.

After a person has surgery, things like this can't always be anticipated or avoided. In my case, I hadn't seen the one cat attack the other for months, so I thought the attacking was over. Accidents happen all around us—big ones, little ones, and those in-between. Sometimes people are responsible for causing them or for not preventing them, but sometimes circumstances are beyond people's control. The cat, of course, had no idea what she was causing, relative to my wounds. It was not the cat's fault. I think it was jealousy that caused her to attack the other cat. I forgave the attacking cat right away, after I'd slept all night (surprisingly well, I might add, considering there was some added pain now, and anxiety). The setback caused me to be more guarded and to be wary of potential dangers in my immediate environment. Life is not perfect. The situation could have been worse, though.

I called my doctor right away about what happened and he assured me that everything was most likely all right. He sounded pretty sincere. He said I could not have hurt my internal stitches, and that the muscles that had been aggravated would just resume their mending. He also said that if the outside stitches weren't real red or oozing any secretions, that they were probably all right, too. I, of course, immediately went over to the mirror and checked my outside stitches. They looked okay so I figured that all was well. Still, I won't be a hundred percent assured that all is okay until six months from the date of my surgery. That is a checkpoint date for my overall healing. At that time, I'm hoping I will feel no pain, anywhere. (Later on, I found out that this 'hope' had been unrealistic, but having the hope at the time helped me to keep on keeping on, if you know what I mean.)

Many things must be given time, and surgery has to be assessed at various checkpoints. Six months is a major checkpoint time. Whatever remains after that, which is negative—be it major or minor—is what may always be. Of course, one must be careful and 'never say never'. Something could still heal up after six months, but chances are not great that it will, not completely, after the six-month checkpoint has come around. It will be interesting to compare what was present at the six-month checkpoint, and what is present at the twelve-month checkpoint,

129

to see what, if anything, has changed. (This is what I ended out doing later on in the book.)

Any minor aggravation of surgery sites, if it is exertion or stress over and above what it should be, will really cause problems, because the area has already been through so much already. An unhealed surgery area is exceedingly vulnerable, and any harm that comes to it will be much more acute than if the area had first been completely healed, or, never cut into to begin with, because of surgery. This is just common sense. The slightest aggravation can mean lots more damage and pain—double, triple, or even more than that, compared with how the area was before. This is why one must take things easy, be cloistered up in a protected environment, be careful of stairs, bathtubs and showers, and be careful about lifting, handling, and pushing things. Being careful about pets, in some situations, is wise, too. Children can also cause problems, if they're young, playful, and active. Sometimes they do sudden, unexpected things that can cause damage in varying degrees to someone's surgical site or sites. Sometimes children leave things on the floor or on the stairs that can cause someone (who has just had surgery) to trip. A person who has just had surgery has to always be looking in front of them. And if they wear glasses, those glasses have to always be on, so that the chance of having an accident will be minimized.

The damage to my surgery site was minor, fortunately, but the extra pain was felt. I had to alter my sleeping position for a while. I slept on my right side for a few days, and not on my back. I got pretty good at pillow propping. I had two large pillows that I used, and my smaller head pillow that I hadn't been using because I had been sleeping on my back. I used my head pillow only when I slept on my side and I propped the big pillows next to my back if I slept on my right side so I would be forced to stay in that position when I slept. For some time I slept in that position. I read in that position too. I emphasize this point about the pillows because people who are about to have surgery need to have several pillows ready to go, when they come home from the hospital.

After surgery, pillows are welcome guests and several are almost always needed. When I lay on my back, I put a pillow to each side. When I lay on my side, both those pillows were over on the other side, preventing me from rolling over. It began to be a challenge—propping pillows—which was a new activity for me. I had two really large, firm pillows, and they worked fine. My soft, feathery pillow was my head pillow. I couldn't stand to use my head pillow when I slept on my back. I wanted my head to set as flat as possible. Whichever way I decided to sleep, I had to reorganize my pillows. Sometimes you can strain something in your sleep but if you prop yourself in with pillows, strain during sleep is less apt to occur.

Pushing or pulling something heavy, lifting, carrying, twisting, turning, etc. can cause problems. Mainly, the danger is with the handling of items of a certain weight or that are too bulky, and the danger is also with moving too quickly. You can't be too careful in the weeks and months that follow a surgery. One overdo can bring on pain that you didn't have before. It can be a noticeable, hard-to-live-with pain, which can be quite frustrating.

The pain I experienced, after my efforts to protect my cats from fighting and hurting themselves (when I threw the magazine to distract them) went away after three or four days, so I got back to square one. Except, something was also more stressed in front now, where the muscle and cartilage was. I'm not exactly sure how that area got affected, but it did. Slowly, the real bad pain from slinging the magazine did go away, but I had to move around like a turtle, and to lift very few items, for several days. I had pain and discomfort in that front area for some time, too, because of the muscle and cartilage.

That spot in front had been painful anyway. It was what I call the pain from hell. But it wasn't where one of my muscles had been cut. It was in a different spot. It was a distracting, acute kind of pain, not a nuisance, take-it-or-leave-it kind of pain. The only way it was relieved was by pain medication, or if I leaned over a certain way, or rested or slept on my left side, which I could only do much later.

Because I had been encouraged to move around a lot, I used my left arm and hand for everyday tasks. Perhaps it was my using my left arm and hand that caused some added pain in front, too. Perhaps I should have been instructed to avoid using my left arm and hand for a while? All my surgery sites were on my left side. A sneeze could have caused the added pain in front, as well, because of sneeze force. Most of the added pain came from my slinging that magazine, though, I'm pretty sure of that.

After my surgery sites had healed up generally okay, I heard about a new method of treatment for pain called laser therapy. Use of a portable laser on an injured area speeds up the healing, significantly. The main reason for using the laser is to decrease pain. It can help broken ribs heal and it has even been used to heal nerve damage, including those around the crushed spines of animals. I would have tried laser therapy on my front area where the muscle and cartilage had been so pulled, if I'd heard about it sooner than I had, and depending on the cost of the treatment or treatments, too, of course. I'd heard that the average treatment was around a hundred dollars (but it's probably gone up). Such treatment facilities are hard to find, though, because not very many professionals are trained to do this treatment.

When there is added pain, suddenly those painkillers become highly valued. I was taking painkillers more regularly, after I experienced added pain. One must be careful about taking pain medication too often, however, and take it only when and as needed. If you do not feel pain at a certain time, wait until you do to take a painkiller. You can build up a tolerance to pain medication and then need to take stronger pain medication to relieve the same amount of pain, and you want to avoid that. Some people develop a dependency on, or get addicted to, painkillers, depending on the type and strength of the painkillers. A person can become psychologically and/or physically dependent or addicted. Or both. Dependency and addiction can be mental, and then become physical, after regular, continued use.

Painkillers should only be taken when real pain is felt, not discomfort. Real pain is distracting. Your mind is on the pain when you have the pain. Discomfort is not all that distracting. You don't focus in on the discomfort. You live with it and it is more background. Pain is foreground. That is why you take the painkillers. You don't want to take too many painkillers and you don't want to compound painkillers and take more than one kind at a time. Taking two different kinds of painkillers at the same time can have a synergistic effect so that the effects on you are compounded, as opposed to being doubled. This can kill you, or put you in the hospital.

One reason the questions 'are you using any medication?' and 'what medication(s) are you using?' is on the paperwork at optical, dental, or medical clinics is so the personnel there can become aware of and ferret out people who are on medication and who may be careless about medication, in the event that they need to have surgery and insist on unnecessary or too much medication to be dispensed. Medical places don't want to be in the dark about medication and cause any kind of overmedicating. Before any surgery, the person having the surgery has to sign a form after having answered several questions and one of the questions is 'are you presently taking any medication?' This way, they won't have to be liable in the event you get overmedicated, and there is damage or death. They do not want over-prescription of medicine or medication to occur.

Picking things up was a problem for me since I had to bend at my knees and keep my back straight. Sometimes I had to get down on my knees to pick things up or to do certain thing, like, de-clump the cat litter. I'd push myself up, using furniture, counters, or whatever was nearby and stable. Reaching was difficult, too. And, I couldn't turn or twist. I had to straight-reach, so I wouldn't pull my stitches. I got to where I used my right hand and arm for reaching because that was my non-surgery side. For a while, I had been using my left hand and arm somewhat regularly, in conjunction with my right hand and arm, but it eventually dawned on me that I should try to use my right hand and arm only, unless I absolutely had to use my left hand and arm in conjunction with my right hand and arm. For example, when I had to lift or carry something bulkier or heavier than just my right hand and arm could handle, then I'd use both right and left. I was glad that my surgery was over on my left side, actually, because I am right-handed. We take so much for granted relative our mobility. When you lose some or part of it—even for a short while—you come to value and appreciate it.

In addition to telling their patient what all was going to be done relative to their surgery, a surgeon should tell the patient where to expect pain, and for how long to expect it. Some surgeons don't do this, so when the pain becomes realized by the patient, the patient has to bring up the subject at an after-surgery checkup. A couple of times I had to ask my doctor, "is this pain normal? Did other patients of yours who had the same or similar type of operation feel this pain, too, and in the same, exact place?" Under-the-surface pain needs to be explained to the patient, too, because the patient can't see anything there. For example, I didn't know what kind of pain I would feel from the rib splitting, or where it would be felt. When I had pain from it, which wasn't in the same spot I expected it to be, I asked about that particular pain and found out that, sure enough, it was from the rib splitting. This pain actually lasted for quite a while, too.

A surgeon should tell the patient how long to expect any pain they are feeling and not beat around the bush about it, or minimize it. Sometimes they don't even discuss it, because they want to be compassionate. I would rather have known more about specific expected pains than I knew. I had to learn about the several pains along the way. Some doctors may not be able to predict some of the pains, and some doctors may just forget to tell their patients because they have so many other patients. My belief is that the more the patients know, the better off they will be. Knowledge is not necessarily power, but it is comfort and it helps people to understand what is happening to them.

My father's helping me went hand-in-hand with his helping his lady friend, Edna. Edna had had blood clotting in her lungs and had been having to have her blood density monitored all the time. She was taking medicine for her condition, which will need life-long monitoring. He went through all this with her, and helped her with her insurance. After my surgery, the three of us had lots of medical things to talk about. Now, he was around to help me, and so was Edna. I don't know what I'll do when he passes on. I will be all alone. I don't have my husband, my sister, or my mother now, but when he goes, I won't have my father. I just hope I won't need any more surgeries. (Many years later, Edna died. She died before my father died.)

I'm a widow, and having someone around to help is sure better than not having someone around to help, when one goes through surgery and after one has gone through surgery. I hope that anyone reading this book will be there for other people having surgery. It isn't just during the surgery and hospital stay that people need help, it's after they leave the hospital, too. People also need others to discuss their ailments and concerns with, relative to their surgery. People even need others so they can complain about things. There is nothing wrong with complaining about legitimate aches and pains, and about situations when one is about to have or does have surgery. In my case, I wanted to get my complaints off my chest. (That's a poor excuse for a pun, considering my surgery was Thoracic.) I needed to unload, from time to time. And I did, but I was always pretty nice about it. Right before my surgery, though, I really railed. I was upset and I was angry. My father got to be the brunt of the tirade. "Why do I have to have surgery? I don't deserve this. It isn't fair. I didn't do anything wrong." These were some of my exclamations. I had to let off steam because the whole surgery experience was not going to be a picnic and I knew it.

Even if I complained, though, there was nothing much I could do about anything. Everything took its course and I was not in the driver's seat. (That may be a pun, as well—considering that my surgery was related to a car accident.) It reduces stress and takes away frustration when you can use people as sounding boards, but you have to do this within reason because the people who you are using as sounding boards are not the cause of your having to have surgery.

I think I could have handled the surgery experience by myself, though just barely, had my dad and Edna not been available. I could have driven to the hospital myself, and left my car in the parking lot. However, one pre-op instruction was that surgery would be canceled if the person having the surgery did not have a driver. I presume they meant that a driver was mandatory to have for going home, especially since the person who was to have surgery would be on medication, possibly be drowsy, have sore areas, and would probably not be able to react very fast while driving, after the surgery. If you have a driver to the hospital, you're likely to have a driver when you leave the hospital. This, I assume, was the premise. Still, I could have driven myself to the hospital, if I'd had to. I could have left my cats with lots of food and water, and several litter boxes, and when I got back, I could have cleaned out the litter boxes, and dished out more food for them and some fresh, clean water. It isn't illegal to leave pets alone for a while as long as they have what they need at hand, or rather, at paw, and as long as they're not left too long. I could have eaten what I had in stock, in my fridge and my pantry. I could have had my mail held. And so it goes. I could have gone through the experience, having no visitors. And, I actually could have paid a taxi to drive me home. Fortunately, I didn't have to go it alone.

It made things easier, more secure, and more pleasant to have my dad around, doing all these extra things to help me. It was nice having Edna around, too, because she is generally polite, thoughtful, and encouraging. When I was really down about my large scar, I said to Edna "no man is ever going to want me, because my scar is so ugly." She got this real serious look on her face and said "that is not true. A good man won't be bothered by it and will love you for you and won't care about a scar. I knew she was right but I also knew that at my age, there were fewer men around. I didn't get out much, either.

While my surgeon was no plastic surgeon, his external stitching looked pretty good but gradually the stitching areas pulled, mostly under the arm and along the side part of my back. The scar area there keloided a little, after a while. I'm sure that this was because of movement and pull on those areas. To keloid means that there has been an excessive growth of scar tissue on the skin (*Webster's New World Dictionary*). Some areas on the skin are more vulnerable to keloiding than others. Of course, a flat scar is always the ideal but sometimes you get bulges, or, thicker, more rounded scarring. You take the hand you're dealt, though. What choice do you have?

Sad to say, that at the time of my surgery Edna had been diagnosed with Alzheimer's disease, and I didn't know it then. She was in the early stages of it, but I never noticed anything. I'm adding this part in after I'd written this part. Edna finally had to be put in a special home, because of her forgetfulness. My father was there for her all along the way. She didn't have any family nearby. My father visited her practically every day, at least initially. It's been very difficult for Edna but she's in a very nice place, near where my father lives.

As it turned out, my father took care of her estate, for her loved ones out east. He bought Edna's car from them, and he ended out giving the car to me. It's as though I got a free car to replace the Oldsmobile that I'd lost because of the car accident. I was so grateful. The car I ended out with was an Oldsmobile, too, which was quite a coincidence. Edna was no longer able to drive, because of the Alzheimer's. She was put in a home but my father didn't like the first place she was in so he moved her to a better place. He eventually hooked up with a woman whose husband had died, and he married her (Ginnie). Edna worsened, and finally died. Then, Ginnie died. They took care of each other in their latter years. That is what it's all about. My father is still alive. He's in an assisted-living home.

Both my dad and Edna were concerned about me through my whole surgery experience. They were there when I came out of the anesthesia, which I really appreciated. I kept them generally apprised about everything, whenever they came to visit me. I didn't have to feel so alone, because they visited me. They brought me flowers. Because they had driven me to the hospital before the surgery, I thought "well, if I die on the operating table, they'll know to take care of my effects". No one ever knows when they will die. They can be older. They can be younger. My husband died at a young age. My sister did too, somewhat. My mother died before any of us expected her to die. She wasn't able to get real old. No one knows when or how another person is going to die.

It is a load off a person's mind to know that someone will be around for them—daily if need be—when and after they have had surgery. Specific good deeds can be done for them, that lessen their load and that can even speed their recovery. Some people need temporary caretakers over the course of their surgery and their surgery recovery. The helpers have to be workers, and not be idle. Things have to get done. They won't get done by themselves. Mental health is a part of physical health. People going into, going through, and convalescing from surgery have to be around people who <u>want</u> to help them, and who care about them. People who go through surgery and then convalesce must have a sense of well-being.

I think about men, who have to be in war situations, and who get hurt and are wounded. They may not be near a hospital. They may not have Medi-Vac nearby. They may have to suffer for hours and even days before they can get any help. Many soldiers have died on the field. Some soldiers can be in horrible pain until they finally get some pain relief, and medical treatment. The television series, *M*A*S*H*, reflective of the Vietnam War in the 1970s (but was more directly about the Korean War), covered the lives of those who served at a <u>M</u>obile <u>A</u>rmy <u>S</u>urgical <u>H</u>ospital. The wounded, usually from front-line combat, came in to them. The unit tried to save as many lives as possible. The series showed, rather definitively, how awful war injuries and situations can be and can become. Occasionally, women in the military are injured or killed, too, in war situations. What would the military do without surgeons and surgery? Actually, more are needed than are currently present.

Then too, there are injuries and deaths that result from natural disasters. Consider earthquakes. When they hit and affect a populated area, there are usually many injuries and deaths. Medical facilities may not be able to take care of injured people because, often, the medical facilities have been demolished by the earthquake. With other natural disasters, no one may get to injured people very speedily. Many may die before medical help can get to them, and this would include children, as well. There are monsoons, tornados, cyclones, hurricanes, tsunamis, floods, volcanoes, blizzards, forest fires, and again, earthquakes.

Reference any type of natural disaster, many people can end out being in need of some kind of surgery. Medical treatment can be needed under the worst of conditions. There are many unfortunates when natural disasters hit (including animals that need vet care). My little old surgery seems so minuscule, when put into this light. It's unsettling to think of the horrendous experiences that other people have had to experience and go through.

Consider the tsunami of the Christmas season, 2004-2005, when around 215,000 people died. That was what I call a traumami (a traumatic tsunami). Countries severely hit were Indonesia, Thailand, Sri Lanka, and India (parts in the south). Many islands were hit real hard, too. As far away as Africa, people experienced the tsunami. Water covered many areas and many people were hurt by large pieces of debris that were pulled around helter-skelter by the ravaging waters. Many people drowned. Some are forever lost to the sea because the waters pulled them from beaches, into the deeper water.

Hurricane Katrina, a different natural disaster, actually started on August 23, 2005, around the Bahamas and then Florida. It crossed the State of Florida and hit the Central Gulf of Mexico areas. Winds blew into various areas of Louisiana, Mississippi, and Alabama on a Category 3 storm, but with the levees bursting in New Orleans, it ended out that around 1,420 people died. There was an estimated $75 billion in damages.

When levees broke, and a high wall of water flooded New Orleans and killed many people, homelessness also resulted. Many pets and farm animals died. Disease entered, because of bad water that became chemical and bacteria-laden. And New Orleans was turned into a ghost town, almost. By February, 2006, you could still see devastation all over, even though the water had abated, and there were still many homeless people, who were unable to move back into the area. The flooding there occurred August 29, 2005.

More people had been physically hurt during the tsunami of December 26, 2004, however. More people needed surgery but many medical facilities were down. There also weren't very many workers because whole areas had been so devastated. Water and debris was everywhere, preventing mobility and response.

The crisis in our own country, in New York, on September 11, 2001, was very bad, but especially for some people. After the terrorist attacks, the neighboring hospitals were full and the hospital staffs were overburdened. There were many emergencies and much triage. (It is not always easy to decide on 'triage' cases. They sometimes make mistakes.) There were many burn cases, for example. So many people had died by being crushed by the falling buildings that there weren't as many injured as there could have been. Oh, that there were less dead, but that was not to be. The World Trade Center buildings had both been filled with a number of people (but fortunately not filled up because it was still early in the morning, when they were hit). The work day had started for some, though. The Pentagon had some injured people, and a number of them were burn victims. On 9/11, hospital and clinic personnel met the crisis head on, and then for some time afterwards. Some people ended out having several surgeries. At least, they're still alive. For many, it's been awful, though, because of the pain they had to suffer and experience, all because of the evil in a few men that took root. Doctors were on call for some time. They volunteered their time, and labor, in many cases.

Since all the disasters of the early 2000s, there have been many, many more. Hurricanes have hit the Caribbean areas a number of times, and also hit the USA, Mexico, and Central America. California had a number of terrible wildfires, and the Amazon Rain Forest and Australia got hit with wildfires, too. There's been tsunamis and earthquakes and droughts. Diseases have gone through both

139

animal and human populations. The coronavirus or COVID-19 hit the world with a super-punch and caused medical and economic chaos. It was a medical experience that became world-wide and was a time of chaos and constant stress. Terrible days kept coming. There weren't always enough hospital gowns, medical masks, ventilators, staff, and general equipment. It came in so unexpectedly. It stopped the economy from functioning. It became and <u>international</u> disaster, which started in China but because of world travel, it ended out going all around the world. People who needed surgery at different hospitals, if they possible could, had to defer their surgery because the hospitals became so full with coronavirus patients (overly so) and also, the hospitals became so contagious. Surgeries were being deferred, right and left. Medical professionals were over-loaded. Many dedicated professionals died. Some found what they had to endure excessively draining. Many saw death all around them. As of mid-Summer of 2021, there had been 600,000 deaths in the USA. Vaccines came in a little slow, all in all, and some people were leery of them. Still, the vaccines worked to slow the virus down, considerably. Some people had natural immunity to it, but there were a few strains of it that developed (God only really knows how they did) so there were new dangers. Again, surgeries were deferred, whenever possible and whenever necessary.

World health and medical authorities and professionals have, at times, been stretched to the max. Some countries cannot take very good care of their people. Health and medical is always one of the political-platform issues. Barack Obama got through a nationalized health-care program, which continued, with modifications, after he left office. Nationalized health and medical works well in quite a few countries, even in democracies. What's a person to do if they need medical care and don't have enough money? Well, if a government has put some of everyone's money into a huge pot, the medical care can be affordable as long as people don't abuse the program. Frankly, a few people become hypochondriacs when medical is free. They abuse the system with claim after claim after claim, and some of the medical care wasn't needed. Still, there are others who rarely, if ever, go see a physician. Neither extreme is good.

My surgeon confirmed that, sure enough, my stomach had been up in my chest for several years. He was able to confirm this because of what he observed during my surgery. There were several adhesions (or connections or bonds that had formed) up in the chest area. The stomach was partly adhering to the esophagus, to the heart, and to a lung. My surgeon had to gently pull at these areas and cut them apart ever so carefully before he could put my stomach back into place. My surgeon was on my side, in more ways than one. (That's a pun for sure, considering that he cut me open on my side and worked on my side.)

Actually, my surgeon had been on my side all along, and he was there for me after the surgery, too—caring about me, answering questions, encouraging me, and doing what he could to relieve my pain. I was fortunate to have such a good man as my surgeon. I found out later that my surgeon was Mormon, and a dedicated one at that. I might have known it. He didn't drink or smoke and he adhered to and upheld some good values. I was particularly glad to find out, absolutely, that he wasn't a drinker. Some surgeons are. You don't want a surgeon nursing a hangover on the day of your surgery. You don't want him (or her) having the shakes.

I had to take time out to interview my doctor, and to pin him down so he would answer my questions. During my whole surgery experience, it was a good opportunity for me to get answers about medical issues and about surgery in general. My questions were all pretty pointed. Many of them were answers in themselves, if you get the picture. I had to be this way. There was a lot at stake. Unless you have surgery, doctors aren't too available to answer medical questions. You can't get through to them by telephone because the phone receptionist blocks calls, unless they're for an important reason. I asked many questions before my surgery, and then when I saw him at the hospital. I had several follow-up visits with my surgeon when I left the hospital, and I certainly used those visits to my advantage and asked him even more questions. If my surgeon had not been accessible, I wouldn't have had the peace of mind that I had. He must have known that, too. He eventually left the area and moved to the State of Idaho.

Over the course of the overall experience, start to finish, there were times when I experienced different emotions. Somehow I worked through these emotions and issues and I wasn't miserable. The surgery was a difficult experience, but God was with me. He walked with me and carried me. Many incorporate the spiritual when they go through surgery.

I'm trapped in this body, until it completely heals, and after it heals too (if it does, completely). It's been a day-by-day walk, and I assume that healing will continue to be gradual. For one thing, my healing has been so slow and gradual that it's hardly been noticed and it doesn't even seem like it is happening. But it is happening. There is day-to-day progress, but it does seem to be going at a snail's pace sometimes.

For a while, I was homebound and couldn't drive. For one thing, I couldn't drive while being under pain medication, for obvious reasons. For another thing, my surgical sites were still too raw and vulnerable and so driving was chancy. My reactions weren't that great, and I didn't want to cause an accident. Also, the areas were sore and when one drives one has to turn one's body at times so that surgical sites can be stressed and even harmed. It was difficult for me to turn my body to look to either side when I drove. I had to make sure that all my car mirrors were lined up really well, before I went anywhere. It is believed that after major surgery, a person should wait at least two to four weeks to drive, depending on the type of surgery they had. Even then, they're taking a chance because areas are not yet healed.

A doctor should let the patient know if they can drive, but actually, doctors don't like to say, one way or another. They don't want to be responsible—directly or indirectly—in case there is an accident. So, the recuperating person has to decide when it is all right for them to drive. If there is an accident, the surgical areas could be vulnerable to tearing, even if the accident is minor. A person who can't turn well, while driving, can cause an accident, or run into property, an animal, or a pedestrian. One must wait to drive, until their turning ability is normal and reacting ability is acceptable.

I stayed home most of the time. My father and Edna came and picked me up and took me places, so I didn't have to drive. They took me to the doctor's for my appointments, and they took me to the supermarket, so I could get groceries and some personal or household supplies. I like my home. It meets all my needs and I've worked hard to fix it up, maintain it, furnish and decorate it, and put everything I need in to it. So I enjoyed being home after my surgery. Healing at home was a joy and a privilege.

CHAPTER 7
On the road to maximum healing

When I had the surgery, I was in good shape and had good health, especially for my age. I was a non-smoker, and most of the time, a non-drinker. I ate pretty good food, and I usually slept well, except that I often cut an over-the-counter sleeping pill in half to take before bedtime, so I could sleep better all through the night. I think that some of the sleep problems I had before my surgery had been caused by the symptoms that were related to my stomach. For one thing, I usually couldn't sleep on my right side. The food, my stomach, or both would shift over and put too much pressure on the area where the problem was (remember, my stomach was bent or curving around and over to one side). So, it became uncomfortable to sleep at times.

I think that some of my symptoms and the overall condition had to have been affecting my ability to sleep but wasn't conscious of it in the beginning. Eventually, I become conscious of it and could only sleep in certain positions. Being unconsciously and/or consciously concerned about my symptoms, caused me to be uneasy, so I had problems sleeping for that reason, too. A half a commercial sleeping pill relaxed me enough so that I could go to sleep. I didn't take a whole one because when I woke up, I'd be a little groggy. I figured that if a half a one works, well then, that is all I needed to take.

I bring up the subject of sleeping because good sleep is essential to healing. Once I stopped taking the prescribed painkillers, that not only curbed pain but also helped me sleep, I resumed taking my half a commercial sleeping pill so I would have better success at sleeping through the night. I knew I needed to sleep throughout the whole night. When your body is at rest, when and as it needs to be at rest, healing comes about more quickly. A worn-down, tired body is stressed and doesn't heal so well or fast.

Again, I had been told by my surgeon that it was possible that if I didn't have the surgery, the remaining part of my stomach could go up in my chest. I couldn't see how it could come up any more than it had already, but that's what the doctor told me. If more stomach went up into my chest, at that point, my intestines would likely start to come up and would then be dislodged from their usual place. It is easy for intestines to turn, too, so this could have been dangerous. I was told that if at any time anything should start to rearrange within my digestive system, something could twist. This would cause a restriction of blood flow and people have died from such a situation. If something twisted, I could end out in the emergency room and would then be <u>forced</u> to have a surgery that would be more difficult than the surgery was that he had been proposing (because of the emergency complications). As one of my friends put it, "The doctor is trying to save your life."

Before I had the surgery, I realized what was involved, but not as in-depth as I now know. I learned as much or more after I had the surgery than I had learned before I had the surgery. Learning is cumulative, and experiential. Precept is built upon precept, when one learns. All the facts, data, and information get filled in to what has already been learned.

I learned from my own experience that <u>there are twelve stages, at least in general, that people go through, both before the surgery and after the surgery. From start to finish it is a process.</u> I decided to list my stages and steps here. They are rather basic. The stages that are listed don't necessarily happen in the exact order I am listing, and they can be going on concurrent with one or more of the other listed stages. The twelve pre and post-surgery stages are:

1.   experiencing and noting the symptoms
2.   realizing the medical disorder that is causing the symptoms
3.   realizing that surgery is a possibility or probability
4.   making efforts to avoid and escape surgery
5.   acquiring knowledge about the medical disorder and about various aspects of the possibly pending surgery
6.   resigning oneself to accepting having surgery, and setting the date
7.   preparing to have the surgery, and having the surgery
8.   receiving necessary hospital care following the surgery

9. acquiring knowledge about after-care and convalescence
10. coming home, and learning about and applying in-home care
11. resigning oneself to accept the slow and gradual process of healing
12. experiencing more and more healing to the point of being able to function satisfactorily

This last point only happens within a normal range of time, if the surgery went well and if the person who had the surgery didn't turn wrong, fall, or hurt themselves in some way while they were recuperating. As healing comes, there is more psychological relief.

I wish I could say I had been brave all the way through the surgery process. Actually, I wasn't real brave and courageous until the weekend before my surgery. The surgery was on a Monday morning. I was only brave and courageous (to a degree) because of the knowledge I had acquired along the way. The accumulated knowledge helped to put my mind more at ease. Once you decide to have surgery, you have no choice but to be brave and courageous. You have to accept your fate, have the surgery, go on with life, and do your best while you convalesce. The coin has two sides. I wasn't a coward, but I wasn't exactly courageous because I had to do what I had to do and that was that. I may as well be honest.

Whereas right before my surgery I became generally courageous, once I had the surgery, I had no choice but to be brave, if you want to call it bravery. The cuts and the stitching had been done. All the repairs had been made. I woke up from the surgery, and I was stuck with what had been done and with what I had to face, which was slow and gradual healing, along with some pain. You just go on with life. You sail along, and go with the flow. You have no choice since done is done. Know what I mean?

Two to three weeks after my surgery, I began to feel pretty good. But I still moved around real slowly. I had learned, experientially, to take it very slow. Also, around the same time, I felt better psychologically. I felt like things were going to be OK, even though healing was obviously going to be slow. I knew that healing was going slowly but surely, and that was really all that I needed to know. The worse part of the pain was gone after about thirty days, so some of the burden had been lifted. Certainly by forty days, the worse part of the pain was gone. Things lifted for me enough though, after thirty days.

I felt that the stitching part of the surgery was well bonded, right around that thirty-day milestone. I had pain from the rib splitting, and around that front muscle and cartilage, and sometimes I got a pinched nerve, because of the way I slept. Also, I had a minor but distracting pain in my left shoulder, and my doctor said that this was probably because of transfer pain, that was being felt in my shoulder because of pain from my diaphragm, due to the stitching. This would be another example of pain in one area being felt in another area. Go figure. Some of the pains I had were short-term; some were of a long duration.

Thirty days is the milestone for most surgeries, I believe, at least on average. I thought at the time, "I feel like I'm out of the woods now," and, I really believed I was. The extra pain that came on me, when I threw a magazine near my cats to divert them from being hurt from being in a cat fight, and when I used my left hand too often and I used it to lift too many items, as, the phone book, laundry, certain kitchen items, and heavier bags of food, set me back a little from regular progression of healing. Sneezing could have added to this, too, at least, a little, because I did sneeze from time to time. By the fortieth day, though, I was not experiencing distracting pain when I moved about, doing whatever it was that I had to do. I experienced some pain, but I wasn't too affected by it. However, standing-up and sitting-up pain was quite different from laying-down pain.

An optimism set in around the forty-day mark. I entered in to what I call a discomfort stage, as I felt the pain stage go. The worse part of the pain and most of the pain was gone, but, I was not totally comfortable when I moved around. I was still not secure with my movements. I still had aches—several of them—and in bed, when trying to get comfortable, I experienced pain. The pain I experienced from the pressure whenever I laid flat on my body was obviously going to be more felt than when I was sitting or standing. Still and all, I began to think that things were mending internally, like they should, by day forty. I knew I still needed to give the healing more time, though. I knew I still had a ways to go. It wasn't yet time to jump up and click my heels. All along the way, I thought that healing would take much less time than it did. Don't ask me why. I don't really know why myself. My guess would be that in the past, whenever I had anything that needed healing, it always healed up pretty fast. Of course, I never had anything this major that needed healing.

One thing I learned along the way was that while I was healing, it helped to be around other people. When I was around other people, I talked a great deal and so my mind was taken off my pain and discomfort. Even when I discussed my surgery and my condition with other people, I wasn't thinking about pain and discomfort. I was thinking more about what I was saying, and about the dialogue and conversation in general. Most of the time I talked about things extraneous to my surgery, when I was around other people. Sometimes I talked about my surgery, but I wanted to have a life outside of and apart from my surgery.

Keeping busy was important, too. Focusing on work, activities, and projects helped to keep my mind off any pain or discomfort I was feeling. Light work, activities, and projects helped me because time passed so much more quickly when I was busy. I was continuing to write, and my writing included writing this book. Writing helped me to keep my mind off the negative. I was forced to concentrate on writing and not on the pain or discomfort. Plus, I was able to sit, and sitting was easier on me than standing or lying down was.

Before anyone has surgery, I'd like to make some recommendations. When you come home after the surgery, you want to have things to do besides just cooking and housework. Make sure there are materials around for working on hobbies or crafts, for one thing. Visit a craft and hobby store before you have the surgery, and pick up supplies so you can work on something that you've done before, or some supplies for even a new craft or hobby, that you think you'd like to try. No one can do this for you. You have to do it for yourself. (Plan ahead.) Make sure your computer is in good working order, too, with some interesting programs in it, assuming you have a computer. Have some good books stacked up before you have the surgery, and if you have in-home deskwork to do, all the better, actually. You can even prepare the year's Christmas cards, in advance. Some people enjoy card games and Bingo, and these can be diversions as well. Taking a correspondence class by mail is also an idea. And, of course, there are so many other constructive things you can choose to do to stay busy and be pre-occupied.

Find <u>constructive</u> ways to keep yourself busy, besides just doing day-to-day survival things and the regular activities that you have to do to keep your home, and yourself, organized and presentable. Keeping busy is what I did, and time passed pretty fast for me. Mainly, because I was being productive, I felt good about how I was spending my time so I felt good about myself.

Of course, you can sit around and watch television all the time, but I found that I noticed my pain and discomfort more when I was watching television than when I was busy working on activities and projects and doing light housework. I had the TV on, whenever I worked, but it was background not foreground, relative to my focus and attention. Besides, 'variety is the spice of life', and keeping a balance is good. Be free to move from one thing to another while you are convalescing, if you can and when and as you can. Again, set 'doing projects' up <u>before</u> your surgery. Do some coin or stamp-collecting work, organize your photo albums, reorganize some files or records, do some spring cleaning, alter some of your clothes, or mend them, etc.. Doing some hems is a good project, too. Reorganize your closets, drawers, or cupboards. The list can go on. None of these activities should be too strenuous, though. Be very careful about that. If something becomes that way, set it aside and do something else.

Be busy and stay busy after your surgery; only engage in light activities and don't overdo it. Men will want to arrange different projects or activities for themselves than what women generally do, but some projects or activities could be the same or similar. There's certainly much to do on the computer, for anyone. Men will probably do different projects than women will do because they tend to have different interests. But the principle of preparing for one's surgery applies to both men and women. Both men and women should set up a program of projects and activities well before the actual surgery date, assuming they are able to do this, because some people end out having sudden or emergency surgery. Planning, organizing, preparing—these are three key words.

From day one, I couldn't wear a bra. I had to wait for the incision area to settle down a little, and to bond well and scab up. All I could wear for a while was that darn bathing suit, which was better than nothing. Whenever I left home, I wore the one-piece bathing suit under my dress. Thank God I had it. It was loose fitting, somewhat, and had built in bra support but no band that went around to the back like bras have. My incision area was quite sensitive but mainly, it was that front muscle and cartilage area that hurt and made it impossible for me to wear a bra. Wearing anything tight or restrictive over the hurt areas made the areas hurt all the more, so, of course I couldn't do that. Some aspects of the surgery were inconvenient and this was one of them.

Men are fortunate that they don't need to worry about wearing bras, if they ever get cut into for surgery, in certain specific areas. Women who have had the kind of surgery I had have to buy special kinds of bras for when the time comes that they can wear a bra. The bras have to be cut and made a certain way. Once I started wearing a bra again, my back straightened up more, which it very much needed to do, to reduce the back pain and discomfort I was having. A bra gives a woman support and helps her to sit and strand up straighter. Being somewhat 'top heavy' I even wear a bra to sleep in, so my back will be straighter for more hours of the day. I have to wash my bras more often, but I don't care.

My back was experiencing change. The spine had been forced to realign and straighten, after it had been in a different position for a while—years in fact. With the osteoporosis and dextroscoliosis that had been there, causing the spine areas to degenerate, the affected areas around my spine were even more aggravated now, because of the realigning. When I was sitting, I constantly had to readjust my position so my back wouldn't hurt. Working on activities and projects and doing light housework kept my spine or backbone moving, and this was good for it. Sleeping on my back was good for it too, because it forced my back to flatten and be straight while I was sleeping. The time came when I decided to sleep on my back as often as possible—during day-time naps and all night long—whenever I remembered to.

After several weeks had gone by following my surgery, my father and Edna took me to the closest mall to shop. (I wanted to look for a couple of sports bras.) Before my surgery, I didn't know I would need special bras. Before the surgery, I wasn't sure where my incision would be, at least, not exactly. I generally knew, but as it turned out, my incision was along one side and the back, where a bra strap goes. Unfortunately, the sports bras I found (but didn't buy) ended out being way too tight, along my sore areas. None of them were loose, which I should have realized. Sports bras have a tight band at the bottom. That front cartilage area was just way too sensitive and sore to have something tight on it, for one thing. Plus, my scar was too much in the way. After my excursion to the mall to find sports bras (and with no success), I couldn't help but wonder if that area would ever heal up to the max. Several months into my healing, I saw an ad for sleep bras (different from sport's bras) and I sent for several of them. These were more comfortable to wear than regular bras were, so I was glad to have them. I had to push any bra band up on the side and above my scar, though, and wear it riding high, even though it felt odd. Still, these bras were better for me then than regular bras were.

Again, one reason the already distressed muscle and cartilage area in front was even more distressed for a while is because when I was forced to sleep on my right side for so long, the pull on that area was against the grain of the natural inclination and direction of how the muscle and cartilage tended to grow. Gravity pulled it down to the one side. The already-distressed muscle naturally went one way, but when I slept on my right side, it forced the muscle to pull the opposite way. This is another reason why I was especially happy when I was finally able to sleep on my back.

When I was able to sleep on my back, the muscle and the cartilage (in the front) laid flat and so it was able to heal in its more normal position. It was a long time before I could lie on my left side. Even at the twelve-month checkpoint, I couldn't do this, because the whole area under my arm was still tender and vulnerable. Still, sleeping on my back, as often as I thought to do it, was best, because my back needed realigning and straightening. I didn't want to have to go into a back brace, which some people have to do to keep their back straight, for whatever the reason. For example, the politician, Ted Kennedy, wore a back brace for a long time, because he had been in a car accident and had perhaps pulled his back and had a resulting disc problem. In any case, he had some kind of back trouble and pain for years and years. John F. Kennedy wore a back brace for a time, as well.

I reflected back to earlier days, when I was younger. Once, I played basketball, and ice-skated, and snow-skied, and water-skied. I played volleyball, badminton, without even thinking about it, and tennis, and I did many other active things. I realized I'd never have that youthful body and resilience again and that I'd always be a little rigid. I'll always have at least a little concern about re-tearing my diaphragm in the future but I'm not going to let this fear deter me from living a full and busy life. Still, I'll always be more cautious about doing certain strenuous things. Mainly, my back just isn't what it used to be. Some strenuous things, I just won't be doing anymore but where one door closes, another one always opens so I don't feel as if I'm deprived. Again, I think of people who are permanently in wheelchairs, and so I can't complain about any restrictions. At least I can walk, move about, and get done what I need to get done. I can do some strenuous things.

I know I'll always have a large scar. I am not real happy about it, but what can I do? Scars are permanent. I'll just try to pretend it's not there and I'll ignore it. Scars are not pretty. Well, there I go again, being negative. I need to condition my thinking to be positive. So what if I have a scar. Everything will be fine. Oh, the power of positive thinking. The problem with positive thinking, though, at least at times, is that it can keep a person from being realistic. One must use wisdom, when applying positive thinking to anything. Frankly, sometimes positive thinking shouldn't be applied. One must live in the real world. But I hardly think that a rather large scar, along someone's side and back, is going to be too much of a handicap. All I have to do, if my scar ever starts to bother me, is remember what some burn victims look like and how their burns must feel or have felt at one time. Some burn victims have such a positive attitude that it's nothing short of miraculous. And so do some people in wheelchairs have a positive attitude. They all get their strength from somewhere.

The days kept going by and gradually things got easier. As some healing came, my motion and mobility sped up. I tried driving a month or so after my surgery, but I only went to a couple of places that I absolutely had to go to. I kept my driving to a strict minimum. I probably should have waited to drive, but there were some things I had to take care of. Frankly, driving even short distances made me nervous, so I stopped driving for a while. At first, my father and Edna had taken me grocery shopping but the day came when I drove myself to the supermarket. I had to be careful about grocery shopping. I asked for more bags or sacks than usual, with less items placed inside them. I didn't buy any watermelons when I grocery shopped, if you know what I mean. I only bought items that weren't too heavy and that were manageable.

Of course, I didn't drive at all if I'd recently taken a painkiller. When I drove short distances a couple of times, I was only taking painkillers at night, before I went to bed. One time, early on, I drove twenty or so miles, one way, so forty or so miles, both ways. This was too much driving for me. My surgical areas that were still sore got a little too pulled, from the driving. I also got a little too tired. I again resolved to only drive real short distances after that. On that longer trip, I tried not to change lanes unless I had to. Changing lanes adds to a person's chances of having an accident, plus it caused my muscles, the ones that had been cut and stitched through, to be pulled and stressed. Sitting upright didn't bother me, so I was able to drive, but driving was tiring. Mainly, it was muscle use and certain movements that I had to be careful about. Again, I didn't drive very far for some time.

My doctor told me that I would always have to be careful about driving, and being on the road. He said that if I was in another accident, the diaphragm would be more vulnerable to ripping, because I had had the surgery. I was already being more careful driving, though, but mainly I was more careful about watching other drivers when they were driving. I will always have to be extra guarded so that the diaphragm will never be re-traumatized. If I'm lucky, I'll have another twenty, or even thirty more years of life. Every year that I'm alive, I'll have to be on the alert for possible and potential accidents. I have to 'hope' for the best, because accidents can happen despite one's best efforts. Don't I know that!

About the time the pain had subsided to a tolerance level, some very negative emotions kicked in. All of a sudden I got angry about the whole situation. Certain questions came to my mind, like, "why did this have to happen to me?", "why do I have to suffer through this ordeal?", "why do I have to be alone?", and "how am I going to have the patience to see this through another week, let alone another month?" I got depressed. I'm surprised depression didn't hit me sooner. I felt sorry for myself, and was discouraged. I was in a type of trap or pit, so to speak, and I didn't like being there. Outside circumstances and things that were not my doing had put me where I was. I moved in and out of these emotions and moods, but it wasn't a pleasant time for me, at all. I was in a wrestling match with my thoughts. The experience of having had surgery became a psychological ordeal, with accompanying stress.

Sometimes thoughts and moods come on a person, and the person has little or no control over them, at least at first. Somehow the person has to overcome these negative thoughts and moods. Rest and sleep helps the person to be able to do this. In my case, there wasn't much I could do about my situation. It was what it was. It was what I had had to go through with and that was that. It was reality, and I had to accept that reality and live within its grip. At one point, I wished my mother was still alive and with me but that, too, became stark reality because my mother couldn't be with me, since she was dead. "At least", I thought, "I had my father and Edna through this, and my faith in God, that stayed steady in spite of the realities that I was being forced to face."

To summarize, when the three-month checkpoint came around, this was glory day for me, if you know what I mean. By this time, I felt very little actual pain. I did most everything I had done before, with somewhat reduced speed and ease. I was using most of my muscles. I could even bend at the waist, although I was still bending at the knees most of the time. I particularly became aware that I was doing everything I'd done before and not getting too tired. I was getting more done, too. I was venturing out and driving whenever I needed to as long as my destination wasn't real far away. And, I was cooking off and on. I still couldn't twist or turn real well, but I was twisting and turning better than before so that was a good sign. I still had to be careful about lifting things, even items that weren't all that heavy.

Also at three months, the area in front didn't hurt quite as badly as before, but it still hurt plenty, especially when I laughed. It was still slightly bulgy. I found some bras to wear that didn't affect my scar area too badly. They had a really thin band in front so they didn't press down on that front area that was so sore. I had to pull a bra up as high as it would go in front so the band was higher than the sore area was. In other words, I had to wear a bra differently than I had before. I had to pull it up over my scar area, too, in as much as I could. It took me a while to get used to the overall feel. I'd been off painkillers for some time but was still taking half of an over-the-counter sleeping pill, right before bedtime. I was generally sleeping all right through the whole night. I was still feeling a tightness where my rib had been split, if I exerted myself too much. I still felt my incision areas, at the back and side. How could I not, when you think about it.

Furthermore, after three months, I could pick up slightly heavier items, but I still had to be careful to not overstress the areas that had been stitched together. I wanted to do even more than I was doing, but I knew I still couldn't do some things. I wanted to plant some plants, but I knew I shouldn't dig out dirt with a shovel. I wanted to wash and wax my car, but I knew the waxing part would be a little too much for me. The same applied to my repainting my stairs. I would have had to have bent and maneuvered too much. I had to be patient. I couldn't lift heavy or bulky things and I wanted to get into some things I had in the shed so I could have a garage sale, but I knew I shouldn't lift boxes, so I didn't. I couldn't lift boxes before my surgery, either, because the weight of the boxes caused me to feel pressure, over to the one side.

When people have surgery, there is a point, at the end of the healing trail, when a person is as maximally healed as they're going to be. In other words, they are healed as much as their body will heal. Each surgery has a different maximum healing date, or date range. No one really knows when that exact date will be, for themselves or for others, but that day does finally come. You may, of course, not recognize it, if you are the person. After three months, I wasn't maximally healed, but I sure felt better, and was better. I was back to my old self. I knew I still needed time, however, before there would be even more near-maximum healing.

Even after six months I wasn't maximally healed but there was marked and measured improvement. The area where my ribs had been split felt much, much better. My surgical wound—the incision area along my left side and back—was still tender, but I could wear a regular bra. What a milestone. Sometimes the bra irritated the area, because of pressure, but it wasn't that much of a problem because I continually pushed the band up, above my scar. The front area was still sore and bulgy, but less so than before. I could even lay on my front, if I was on my bed. Sometimes I read lying down on my front, with the book in front of me and my back bent a little. When I got up, I felt some pain in my back because my back was not yet used to that kind of pressure. Still, varied movement was good for me to do.

My back was still sore, after six months. If I laid down flat on a floor, and then got up, I'd feel pain in the center of my back. Even just sitting and I'd feel stress there. I may always have extra stress there, because of the initial damage and degeneration. As the back is being forced to be in a new position now, even more damage could be occurring, who knows. I hope not, though. I hope the back is going back to its original position and being corrected. Only time will tell, how my back is going to end out. I am able to live with the back problem, but now I have to be more careful about my back, and I especially have to be careful not to overstress it. All in all, after six months, I was doing almost everything I was doing before, but I was still limited about doing some things. And I was still doing things more carefully, deliberately, and slowly. After six months, I felt greatly relieved because I was alive, mobile, and certainly eating whole meals. I was able to eat whole meals right after the surgery, actually.

I wrote a poem that relates to hope and to healing, and to the relief that comes from healing in general. This poem is the first poem I ever wrote and I wrote it some time ago. (I went on to write many more poems for several poems and short works books.) Something inside me causes me to want to keep writing poems. Maybe it's because I live alone and, therefore, have a need to communicate. As time went by, I decided to put my poems and short works into separate books. It dawned on me that this particular poem, *Sweet Spring*, could fit in here. It ties in with the overall surgery experience. Since this was the very first poem I wrote, it is rather short; I wrote it in the early 1980s. It has an abcc rhyme scheme, which tends to be used less often than other rhyme schemes. It is a universal poem and so it has universal and multi-application, but it fits in here and could fit into a number of medical situations. I rediscovered the poem when I was writing this book and it took on a new application, relative to my surgery. I hope you get something out of the poem and don't find it too lofty. Elevating perhaps, but not lofty.

Sweet Spring—the Poem

Sweet Spring, sweet Spring, it's your turn now.
The death of cold has been pronounced.
Life and growth is your tomorrow–
Color, sun, and an end to sorrow.

Sweet Spring, I say, hold your realm close
And I'll reach out and embrace you.
All that's lovely will be around.
Beauty in nature will be quickly found.

Sweet Spring, bring flowers to my soul,
And then let butterflies dance around.
Unfriendly weather had caused a low,
But time brought Spring and cold must go.

My having had surgery and my having gone through the process of surgery and its related recovery has given me a new lease on life. I look around, and I see people who are worse off than I am. In fact, I'm way better off now because I had the surgery. But, I'm sore and I'm still healing. And, I still have some anger I'm trying to deal with. You have anger because you can't help but think 'why me?' You, maybe don't share that with others in your sphere, but it will sometimes surface. Frustration is added to the anger because what the hello can you do about it? Nothing, is the answer to that. But, I'm on the mend and progressing. I'm very grateful I was able to have the surgery. I'm very grateful that I can eat whole meals, too. Before, I only had about twenty percent use of my stomach. I don't have to worry about my stomach being up in my chest now, and be concerned about what dangers that condition could bring, since, I did have the surgery.

My maximum healing is around the corner. It's not quite here yet, but it will soon be. I don't yet know if I'll have lasting discomfort or problems, once my maximum healing comes around. I believe that most of the pain will eventually go away, but some minor discomfort and problems will probably stay around.

This is often the case with people who have surgery. Doctors don't like to tell their patients this and will try to sidestep doing so. But, permanent and lingering aggravations and discomfort can stay around, and sometimes pain can, too. Doing somewhat strenuous things, and feeling aggravation or discomfort anywhere at all when strenuous things are being done, will not be a good sign, after twelve months have gone by, but I suspect that this will be the case to some degree.

I ended out having one more in-home accident while I was healing. This one was even worse than the cats and the magazine incident. I tripped on a doorstop that was out too far into the doorway area. I had been walking sideways, because I had turned to pick something up on some shelves by my door, and the doorstop caused me to trip and fall, as I was sidestepping. There was nothing around to protect my fall, either. Any tripping and falling is always a danger after a surgery.

The bad news was that I fell. The good news was that I fell sideways and landed on my left arm, which ended out cushioning my surgical wound (on the same side, under the arm). At least it cushioned that area somewhat. The area there ended out being more sore and swollen for several days, though, after I fell. The incident set me back a little, and it caused me some worry.

I fell pretty hard and I was mainly worried about my diaphragm re-tearing, even just a little. I knew I wouldn't feel it if it had torn. I called my doctor and told him about the fall. He listened intently and then assured me that such a fall, at the stage of healing that I was at, would not result in the tearing of anything, including my diaphragm. The fall had been on a carpet. It was a short distance, and again, my arm had cushioned and buffered the fall.

The fall traumatized me, though. It had happened so fast. When I fell, I just laid there for a long time, afraid to move. Strange as it may seem, I may have been in a mild state of shock, because of all the factors. I was more upset than I would have been had I fallen and not have just had surgery. The fall occurred right around the fifth week of healing. When I fell, I hit my side buttock pretty badly, which further cushioned me. It was the impact of the fall that I was worried about. I was really quite fearful, when I called my doctor about it.

Just as I was beginning to feel pretty good, and safe and secure, I had tripped and fallen. I was in my own home, too. I wasn't driving my car. I was frustrated and upset, and I remember thinking "if this operation doesn't take, it surely won't be the doctor's fault." The doctor had felt pretty good about the surgery that he had performed, and, I got a sense that he was being sincere when he was speaking about that. I was embarrassed that I fell, quite frankly. I mean, I should have been watching where I was going. I trusted my doctor and I wasn't afraid to discuss anything with him, even something that was on the embarrassing or humiliating side.

As I contemplated the fact that it was a good thing to trust one's doctor, I thought about some articles I had been reading. A couple of them were in *Reader's Digest®*. The articles were about doctors that had not been so worthy of trust, like my doctor had been. In the past, there have been doctors who removed the wrong organs, amputated wrong limbs, missed removing cancer areas, and, who misdiagnosed, just to note some examples. One doctor actually murdered a number of patients, by putting a toxic substance into the patient's intravenous unit. (Nurses have done this, too.) This has happened in America. Another doctor 'purposely' didn't de-bacteria his hands before surgeries, so the patients ended out having infected areas. In fact, some patients died because of this negligence. Another doctor, this time in England, purposely killed a number of his patients. And yet another doctor practiced medicine for some time but without a license. He obtained a license using another doctor's name so he was an absolute fraud. He never even went to med school. He was apprehended and put in prison for a while, but when he got out, he did the same thing, all over again. My doctor was a good one, and he was a conscientious and legitimate one, as well. I had much to be thankful for. He wasn't a rogue doctor by any stretch of the imagination. He was just the opposite.

Because of my fears, and not my doctor's, I wanted to have a chest X-ray of the diaphragm area, after my in-home fall. I had an appointment with the doctor anyway, so, he ordered a chest X-ray for me and I had it done the same day as my appointment. When the results came back, everything was fine. I felt better, and breathed a sigh of relief. I had only been set back in my healing by a few days because of my fall, so I was fortunate. It certainly could have been worse. I could have fallen down some stairs, for example.

There is a point to be made about pain in general. People who haven't had surgery misperceive all pain as being of the same magnitude and having the same intensity. Therefore, if they hear about surgery, they think all pain from all surgeries will be the same. This is not the case. Many surgeries are actually very light, and the accompanying pain is not that bad. I now realize this, experientially, because I've had light surgeries, and now I've had this heavier one. This surgery had a lot of pain to it. I can attest to that. I wish it hadn't been so, but it was. Still, other surgeries can be and are worse, relative to pain. I'm not complaining about my pain. I'm only trying to make clear that not all surgeries are the same. I used to lump or muddle them all in together, but now I realize that surgeries are not all the same. They don't all heal up the same, either.

Some people who have been in really terrible accidents can suddenly be in horrible pain, and require lengthy surgery and sometimes several surgeries, before they are patched up. I was fortunate I wasn't hurt badly when I was in my car accident. I was hurt internally, but never felt the pain and never knew it. The impact was awful, but because it was on the passenger-seat side of my car, and because I happened to be in a heavy-duty muscle car and had a seatbelt on, I was spared from being mangled. The other vehicle, a pick-up truck, was only hurt on the bumper, and the front side somewhat, and the bumper partly came off. Otherwise, that vehicle was OK and the other driver (and the toddler in the car) hadn't been hurt at all. I was glad about that. He was probably happy that I wasn't hurt. But, I really had been hurt. My diaphragm had been torn, unbeknownst to me.

When I went into my surgery, I hadn't yet conceptualized that muscles would be cut. I just hadn't thought about it, which was probably good. I didn't know that the front muscle and cartilage would be pulled and stretched so much either. <u>The surgery ended out being more involved than what I first perceived</u>. It would have been a less difficult one, had my surgeon gone in from the front, but again, I had been told that it couldn't be done that way. My doctor had discussed this with other doctors and they all felt that side entry was not only the best way but also the only way, for entry. Being outnumbered and overpowered on this matter, I had to comply, and I trusted in the expertise of the doctors. This was their final say, and I had no say on the subject. It was their call. I really couldn't even object, if you know what I mean.

The healing went slower than had the entry been frontal. I wanted to heal up as quickly as possible because no one wants to be in pain, or inconvenienced for very long. One wants to minimize pain and inconvenience. But, being anxious is the opposite of being patient, so one must put aside anxiety. Actually, being cut in the front wouldn't have been too much fun, either. The cut would have been as bad as the cut I ended out with but also, the surgical area may have made it hard for me to sit down and to do as much writing as I ended out doing, since you tend to bend a little when you're sitting, and that bend area would have been right where the incision area and surgical wound was.

Along the way, it dawned on me that when I learned and knew as much as I could about my surgery and my healing, the knowledge I acquired helped my mind to heal. When you have surgery, your mind becomes a big bundle of fragmented thoughts. Many of these thoughts are unconscious. They slowly and at times come out, and get tied in with new or other, older thoughts, that also get put back into your unconscious. It's all a process—an extraordinary one. The mind is aMAZEing. It's quite a maze. Before you acquire enough knowledge about the surgery, you're not really disturbed, although you may think you are, but you are disadvantaged, and you lack mental empowering.

When I did my gardening, it felt great to get out in the sun and to work in the yard so it would look more presentable. I love to garden. Time passes fast, when I garden. I have flowers, plants, bushes, and trees all over my yard. I have cacti in different places. (Some cacti are actually succulents.) I have a blend of pine, leaf, and spiny-thorn landscaping. Variety is the spice of life. My garden or yard is an extension of my home. I love to work in my yard, adding new plants, creating new beds, putting in rocks, stones, and pavers, maintaining what's already there, and then looking at and enjoying the fruit of my labor. I've been a gardener for years. All around my yard, it's pleasant to look at. I even wrote a book on the subject of gardening and landscaping.

I wouldn't call gardening therapy, though. That word is thrown around too much and is often used in wrong contexts. I would actually call gardening 'work', with resulting accomplishments. Just as you fix up and decorate the inside of your home, you do this with the outside of your home so you can enjoy your home inside and out and at every bend and turn. Work is work. Whatever takes strategy and effort is work.

Working in the garden, for several days in a row, helped me to get back into shape, a little, although, I only worked one-half to two-thirds the workday because I would get tired and sore. I was very careful about bending, turning, twisting, and carrying anything. I took breaks, too. I just couldn't do everything to the same capacity that I did before. Of course, I felt tired and had sore muscles the next day, but that was OK because no pain, no gain. Truly, I was progressing and that is what was important. I especially tired out more because I had been forced to take things easy for several months, so I was out of shape. I was careful, though. Gardening got me out and got me doing physical work, which was different from the mental work I had been doing, with my writing. Endorphins get charged up when you do physical work. Endorphins contribute to physical healing. They can even help to improve mental alertness because thinking, and thinking better, is generated because of endorphin stimulation. One is not mentally dull when endorphins get moving and charged up.

I also continued to work towards a museum I'd been working towards establishing—one that is for families and for children, but that is another subject altogether. But, in a nutshell, for years I've been preparing and collecting items for a display museum, of that type. I have thousands of items for this museum. Plus, I've been collecting books so there can be a family and children's book store next to it. My writing, and the museum and book store work has kept me busy.

I continued working in the yard, every so often. Fortunately, I have a low-maintenance garden—at least in some ways. Even just going out and watering certain areas around my home got me out in the sun and moving around. With no children around to take care of anymore, I have myself, my home, my yard, and my pets to take care of, which is enough. Plus I have my writing, which is something I tried my hand at and discovered later in life. I had done some writing before then, but it was mostly hobby writing and not serious writing.

Writing isn't just a diversion for me. Instead, it's of primary importance now. I'm not a musician, an artist, or a dancer, and I don't have a skill, like plumbing, carpentry, masonry, electrical/electronic work, or photography. But I learned that I could write, and when I did, I began to soar, like a bird in flight that had finally been freed from a cage. I try to go wherever my writing takes me. I can impart huge chunks from my soul to others, when I write. Some things that have hurt me in the past can be reflected in and through my writings—directly or indirectly. I can get things out that ordinarily have to stay inside. I can write that which may be of help to others. I can make an effort to bring comfort and even peace to others, through my writing. I can transfer knowledge to others, because of what I write. When I went through the Teacher Ed program, at University, and when I taught school, I acquired that teacher spark in the classroom and as a teacher, and this has all stayed with me ever since, and it hasn't been extinguished. I thrive on teaching people whatever I can, whenever I can. I love learning on a continual basis myself.

There are people who have conditions far worse than any of mine have been, and that are debilitating. There are leukemia and cancer-ridden people, who fight the disease daily. There are people who have degenerative diseases that continually worsen and are not going to go away because of their usual trend and tendency. There are people, too, who have lost mobility of limbs, or who have lost limbs. Some people have to be hospitalized or institutionalized, because of their disease, illness, or loss. Some people are dependent on having a caretaker around all the time, if they are in their home. Life is not easy for any and all of these people. Who can ever forget the late Christopher Reeve, who faced paralysis so bravely? He was heroic (and there's been so many others like him).

I thank God that I'm able to get around and live a relatively normal life. I want to use what time I have left on this planet to do good things with my life, and for others. I direct loving prayers towards those who are suffering from conditions that they have no control over. The person in the wheelchair, or at the hospital, or the nursing home, and the house-bound person—none must be forgotten or overlooked. They all deserve sensitivity and compassion.

Even when I was a young girl, all I ever wanted to do was help people. At one time, I'd even wanted to be a nurse. When I was a young adolescent, I read several Cherry Ames books and they greatly impacted me. (My sister read Nancy Drew mysteries; I read Cherry Ames.) All in all, twenty-seven Cherry Ames books were written. I have first edition copies of the first two Cherry Ames books—*Cherry Ames, Student Nurse* (1943) and *Cherry Ames, Senior Nurse* (1944). Early ones were written by Helen Wells 1910-1986), then another author wrote a number of them—Julie Campbell Tatham (1908-1999)—but then Helen Wells re-entered and wrote the rest of the books in the series, that ended in 1968. These girl's books are mystery books, usually set in hospitals but within different perspectives and at different places and even countries. During World War II, the series nudged girls into becoming nurses because of the War effort. Young girls wanted to do what nurses did. I am a war baby, or baby boomer. I read the books a little later on. Cherry Ames had many adventures along the way of the series progression. Some company should bring these books back because they've been out of print for some time.

For myself, for a week or so after my surgery, I had a little outside help. Then I got to where I was able to do some things on my own, even though I had to move slowly. I was thankful that I didn't need physiotherapy, like so many people have to have, for different reasons. At times I had to push myself, and then take time out to rest, but, I got the essential things done (though just barely) for my day-to-day existence and survival. Some people are so debilitated that they can't even do essential day-to-day things. And some people are not on the mend and will never be on the mend. Their lives will most likely continue like they've been, or their lives will become even more difficult. Some people have conditions that are gradually worsening, and they have unimaginable stress. There are varying degrees of pain, too, and some people have had to cope with more pain than I ever had. I thank God that I was under pain management by trained hospital workers and professionals. From day one of my surgery, if it hadn't been for pain management, life would have been difficult, stressful, and in some cases, impossible. I am but one of many who have been helped by pain management.

Pain has always been, and pain will always be. In third world countries, it's often not managed well or at all.

I have a broadened perspective of life now, because of my collection of experiences relative to my surgery. I have always been going up the learning ladder, and this time, I went up several rungs. I'm thankful I was able to have the surgery, and that I did have the surgery. I'm thankful that the medical profession, overall, has advanced as much as it has.

Usually, operations make your standard of living better, if the surgery goes well. Whatever is wrong is corrected and 'ideally' there is no more pain, discomfort, or aggravation. For several months, some things that were bothersome lingered, after my operation, but they weren't debilitating. They really weren't major aggravations but they did cause me to slow down, to be careful about certain movements, and to be careful to not overdo it. I noticed the problems and lived with them. They were a different kind of aggravation compared with the symptoms I experienced when my stomach was up in my chest.

I'm still learning from my surgery experiences. One very important point that got ingrained was how hard my life would be if I had to continue to be slowed down, like I was right after my surgery. If I had to live like that and be like that all the time, my life would constantly be inconvenienced and difficult. I walked and moved very slowly, and I hurt in several places. There are people all over the world who have to live like this every day and all the time. They have medical problems related to birth defects, degenerative diseases, accidents, and even addictions.

I acquired a real and genuine sensitivity towards those who must live their lives in a substandard and inconvenienced way, because of one or more medical problems. Before, I felt badly for people who were in these situations, but now I have acquired a pathos for them to a greater extent than I had before. I can never totally share in all of their suffering, however, because my life improved, and my medical problems were remedied. It was a slow, uphill climb, but at least it was a climb. For many people it is slow and level, or slow and downward. Once my medical problem was diagnosed, the chain of events took their course. Now, it is all behind me and fading out as I move along and encounter new events and experiences.

I'm thankful that America has such a high level of medical care for its people. In America, there is one doctor for four hundred and twenty people. In many countries, there is one doctor for every thousand, or even more than every thousand. The approximate range around the world is one doctor for every three hundred people to one doctor for every three thousand people.

Some countries have it really bad though, relative to doctor/patient ratio. Sri Lanka and Bangladesh have one doctor for every seven thousand people. Nepal is bad—with one doctor available for every seventeen thousand people, which is about the same as for the people of South Africa, but Cambodia beats these, at one doctor for every twenty-five thousand people. Mexico's ratio is one doctor for approximately every two thousand people. African countries have it the worst. I can give you stats for three more African countries, besides the stat I already gave for South Africa. Zimbabwe is one doctor for every sixty-two thousand. Mozambique is one for every fifty thousand, and Kenya is one for every seventy-five thousand. Clearly, life is not good in many countries around the world. Kazakhstan, Uzbekistan, Turkmenistan, and Kyrgyzstan have the best ratios and they range from one for every two-hundred and fifty to one for every two-hundred and eighty. Israel's ratio is one doctor for every three-hundred and fifty people. It's very close to America's ratio and is slightly better. All of these stat facts I was able to find in the book, *Geography of the World* (DK Publishing-New York).

Criteria for what constitutes 'doctor' was not noted in these statistics. Nor were requirements for training noted. Availability of medicine and medical advancements are issues relating to all these countries, too. If a country has a good number of doctors, but they have little medicine and aren't up on or able to use medical advancements, then the country is still medically impoverished. Also, medical facilities may not be hygienic, in some of these countries.

Just because more doctors are available to a larger number of people in a certain area does not mean that people can afford the medical care. If a country does not have socialized medicine, hopefully there are insurance plans available for people needing medical care. But, often, there aren't any medical plans. Everything is just random. Sometimes, even records aren't kept very well. Some countries run low on medicine. In America, we have an abundance of medicine, for the most part. Maybe we have too much of it. Or, too much of some and not enough of other. We have to pay high prices for some medicines, too. So, who will get the money—the doctor, the clinic or hospital, or the medicine and pharmaceutical companies? Some people just run out of money, and they can't pay medical bills or buy medicine, even in America. Socialized medicine is on its way and has been slowly infiltrating America. It's in other countries around the world. It will be entrenched in the United States, and stay entrenched.

I was off painkillers within a reasonable period of time, according to my surgeon. I purposely didn't reorder more, after the last prescription was ordered. Painkiller dependency is a known problem. In my case, it would have been a mental dependency, but I wouldn't and didn't let that happen. After all, I was healing. I wasn't in chronic and continued pain. That is when people become dependent and even addicted to painkillers. People can overdose on painkillers by taking too many of them. This can cause heart failure. I didn't even use up all the painkillers I had in the last refill of pills that was prescribed for me. I scaled down to zero and had some left over. All I took was a half an over-the-counter sleeping pill every night that was really very harmless. I still take that half of a sleeping pill every so often (if I happen to remember to do so), and I probably always will, on occasion. It's kind of my Snoopy® blanket so I guess I'm mentally dependent on them at times. I don't see this as a problem, though. In fact, I consider it to be a help.

I could have easily gone in and sued the owner of the vehicle that hit me—big time—but 'you can't get blood out of a turnip'. Again, the actual owner of the car was an older woman who had not taken out insurance. The driver who had borrowed the car from the owner didn't have insurance, either. So, an insurance company was not available to pay me anything, relative to a settlement. I could have sued them medically, which is a completely different lawsuit.

Medically, later on, the Statute of Limitations was extended to begin from the time of my first chest X-ray results, because my condition was actually diagnosed because of the chest X-ray done in the spring of 2001. Also, the doctors (more than one) documented that the ruptured diaphragm related to the car accident because symptoms began showing up soon after the date of the accident and because the kind of ruptured diaphragm that was diagnosed was a trauma-related one—one that occurs after the abdominal area is subjected to a great force, like a car accident. Regardless of all my strong evidence, and my extended length of time for the Statute of Limitations, I decided to bury it all and not sue. Had I not had coverage for medical, I would have been forced to sue. The owner, and the driver, were not even close to being well-to-do so I decided to leave the matter be. Call it a donation to the poor, so may God reward me in the afterlife. I'm okay now, and I lived through the ordeal.

This book would not have come about had I not gone through all I did and lived through the ordeal. This book is a silver lining, of sorts. I never would have learned all I did had I not been in the car accident in the first place and not had my diaphragm and hiatus ruptured or torn. I never would have learned everything that I did from writing this book and I never would have been able to pass everything I learned along to others. Not only is my surgery journey noted in the book, but there is considerable trivia throughout—knowledge tidbits, in other words. I hope the content of this book will serve to help others, in whatever ways it can. In the end, that is what is important.

CHAPTER 8
Twelve months after the surgery

If anything in this book seems a little incongruent, it's probably because, for a while, as I was writing the book, I was on painkillers. I revised what I could, from an already established base. I am not unhappy with the way the book turned out. If I left anything out, I surely didn't mean to. I think I got most of it in. If I repeated myself, it was material put in by way of a different context (to enable me to bring in new information), and also it was an effort, on my part, to emphasize new and entering points and information. I didn't repeat myself much, though.

When I report my progress, I have to touch on all the problems I had after my surgery, so this might seem like repetition, but it really isn't. I have to touch on the problems with any report and at every stage, all along the way. So, for example, the problems I had at six months have to be touched on in this twelve-month report, and this therefore becomes intentional repetition. I plan to do a three-year report next, and it will seem repetitive then, too.

Since my surgery, I've gradually been changing or supplanting foods. I've eliminated certain foods, and replaced them with new ones. In general, I'm eating fewer carbohydrates and less sugar (which is actually a carbohydrate, too) and I'm staying away from certain processed foods, but not all processed foods. During and after surgery, there is cellular disarray. If good food does not come in to the body, those cells don't get fed very well and they react accordingly. They also react if bad food goes in to the body. They can't talk and say "stop doing that." They can't put up a red flag. You have to consciously know and be aware of what you are doing or not doing, relative to the foods you choose to eat.

Think of your cells as being millions of little children. What do you want to give those children? I always knew about eating good foods, and I ate OK, most of the time, but I became more conscience of my cell's needs after my surgery. I am the caretaker of those cells, just like I'm the caretaker of my thoughts, my home, my pets, and to some degree, my children (since they are now grown) and also to my overall family, whenever and if ever they might want and/or need my help.

Your health belongs to you. You own your health. How well will you take care of it? You <u>can</u> take good care of it, with the help of God or your Higher Power. I like to refer to God as the cosmic force. It can be a struggle to only buy healthy foods when you go to the grocery store or the supermarket. Sometimes you forget and buy wrong foods, and sometimes you are tempted to buy wrong foods. Much of the time you buy what I refer to as borderline foods. These are foods that are not best foods but might seem like best foods, for some reason or other. So, you must take time to read food labels on cans and packages. You have to prepare your mental state when you leave to buy groceries and before you even enter the grocery store or supermarket. Some people make a list, and stick to that list. Some people are tempted to buy wrong foods because the foods are on sale, and this is not good. Doing this is quite common, though, in our free-enterprise and competitive society. The solution to this problem is that people should budget their money so they can afford to spend a little more money on the better foods. Make better-foods buying a top priority, as soon as you can. Buy some good books on foods and nutrition, too. And read them. Even just reading portions of these kinds of books is better than not reading anything at all.

Another point to be made about foods is to let the raw form of the food stand on its own, whenever possible, and don't add all kinds of negatives to the food, to enhance its native or virgin flavor. You can add in flavorful positives, but not negatives. A pitfall—and we've all fallen into this one, many times—is that we eat some good foods alongside with bad foods. We subconsciously think, 'well, I'm eating these good foods so it won't hurt too much to also eat these bad foods.' We also subconsciously think, 'Well, I've eaten these good foods so now I deserve a reward and I'm going to eat these other foods that are not so good for me.' We need to get away from both lines of thought because they aren't wise. They're partial truths or deceptions, really.

One good point is that people should be investigators of new foods, with the aspiration of finding better foods. This takes time and effort, and perhaps some study. Try new foods on occasion, if you know they are good for you. You don't have to stay in a rut. The other day I bought some root vegetables I had never bought before. Because of the way I prepared them, they tasted good.

Every bite that goes into your body has to pass your inspection, and that inspection should be fairly strict. Think of yourself as a customs officer, at a border crossing. If people don't have the right paperwork at a border crossing, they can't come in. If they're in possession of contraband, they can't come in, either. Be a customs officer of the foods you let into your body. Think of your mouth, as the border crossing.

Not only did I improve on my intake of foods, and on a regular basis, but I began to think more about death, in general. Life is precious and every day is a gift. Even just being able to breathe is a gift. I began to appreciate being able to live. I became more aware of what all was around me—material items, the earth, sky, the universe, people and each person's uniqueness, animals, and natural foods. I became more aware of my own body. I was aware of all this before, but now my awareness had significantly increased. I became 'aware' aware, if you get the drift. I decided that life was worth trying to live for as long as I could live it. Of course, I'd still have to be careful about the people I chose to spend time with. Certain people can really drag you down, and they aren't really in your corner and certainly don't have your back.

I became more thankful for the material items I had, and for the food and shelter that I was blessed to have. I felt ashamed of any excesses I had, relative to personal possessions, and I thought 'it is time to start eliminating and parting with items I'm not using.' I still wanted to keep certain of my treasures and 'artsy' items, because they bring me pleasure and I enjoy looking at them. But, I decided to at least thin out such items from my possessions. Any of my actual collections of items, I did not want to part with, because I'd worked hard to organize and compile them, but all else was to be sold or given away, if the items were of no specific, current use. I certainly didn't want to part with any of my items for the museum, or the books I'd prepared and had ready for the book store.

I wanted to enjoy the few personal items I had, and not be burdened by excess. I thought, 'I'll try to get some money for unneeded items and use that money to take a dream trip, because I'd rather have memories from a dream trip, than have items I don't need or use.' I decided to part with whatever came close to the 'unneeded' classification. I also decided to give a portion of what I had to people who could make good use of the items. I'd been doing this from time to time, and would now do this again, only more so.

As far as exercising goes, I've always been a walker. I walk a great deal. Fortunately, the surgery took place in my upper body so my legs and my walking were not affected. However, I cannot walk very far right now, because a few areas in my upper body get sore. I do get in several short-distance walks throughout the day, though, and they all add up. I'm usually active enough throughout the day because one must survive. I have to do KP work and cook, and I have household tasks I must complete. I have a walker or skiing-type of exercise unit that I use, a little, too, for a more total-body workout, but I have to be careful about pulling my scar area when I use it. Twisting is absolutely out of the question. Reaching too much is, too. I was able to adjust the amount of resistance on my walker unit while I was recuperating from my surgery. At first, I used the less-resistance gauge. Speed of use was somewhat up to me. I increased the resistance, slightly, over a period of time. Again, speed of use was somewhat up to me. I also used hand-grip 3.3 pound weights (or 1.5 kilogram)—mostly for my arms. (That's about all they can be used for.) This is rather a minimal weight, actually. I was careful not to harm my surgical site areas, when I exercised. I monitored that closely. Mainly my left side needed to be guarded.

Again, I also gardened, being careful about bending whenever I did. I have a little over a hundred plantings on my lot. They need tending to on a regular basis, especially in the summer, when it's hot. Some of my cacti need watering and sometimes special shading. I have to trim back bushes and clean out beds because of dried-up blossoms, leaves, pine needles, and pods. I have to rake two sides of my home, periodically. Often, I have to pick up such items by hand. There's always something to do, even weed pulling. This can all be light work, or heavy work, depending on how it is approached and how it is done. Often, I do this work on my hands and knees. I move slowly and am careful to avoid certain movements. I only do a little at a time. And I don't garden two days in a row, for now.

With gardening, you are working with the living—plants and trees, that is—and after going through surgery, I appreciated anything that was living, more than I did before. I'm constantly puttering around my yard and garden. Sometimes, I like to just go out and enjoy the beauty that is out there. Everything looks so immaculate and I've organized everything just the way I want it to be and like it to be. Being out in the sun from time to time helps me to absorb Vitamin D, and this has been very good for healing, after my surgery.

I didn't get 'overly' depressed about the surgery itself, and its effects on me. That's because I tried to stay focused on work, projects, and all that must be done to survive. I did get sad and discouraged, at times, about other things, that concerned people in my life and circumstances that were affecting my life. But I kept busy enough to overcome those thoughts. Besides, I have a simple faith that God is in control of everything and that He will judge all and so I can't let worry and being occasionally downtrodden get to me. I get discouraged at times, because the healing has been slow, but I don't get overcome by depression, most of the time. It's okay to be a little beset by depression on occasion, but never let it overcome you. I say to people "no, I don't get depressed, but I do get to the place where I must think and rest, periodically." Isn't that what depression is—thinking and resting. Well, that's what I do, but, I don't wallow in it, or get beset by it.

What some people call depression I call my 'rest and think' time. If I'm resting on the couch, for example, I'm thinking through whatever happens to be affecting me at the time. I am not depressed. I'm just sifting through things, in my mind, and making an effort to decide something or to choose a specific path. It may just be little things that are going through my mind. I don't let things press down on me because I work through things, in my mind. That is what the mind is for. I don't think too much about what is affecting me unless I have to, and I don't linger on past events too often, unless something current is relating to something that was past and unless something must soon be decided.

I try to avoid using the word 'depressed' because if I do, it becomes suggestive, and we all know about the power of suggestion. I use the words 'saddened', 'disheartened', 'discouraged', and 'concerned' instead of 'depressed' and 'worried'.

I try to avoid using the word 'unhappy', too. People should remove certain words from their vocabulary, just like they should remove certain foods from their diet. Mental health is important, just like physical health is. Protect your mind. Protect your body.

I was also careful about what I watched on television. I'm still careful about what I watch on television. I always have been. Not that I put my head in the sand like an ostrich, to avoid reality. I keep up on news events—be they positive, neutral, or negative. But I try to limit negative exposures, especially when there is redundancy. And I watch, listen to, or read something more neutral or uplifting whenever I can. After my surgery, I tried to stay in control of what came into my mind and what I allowed myself to watch and to be exposed to. As my healing improved, I found that I could handle the more negative news. Some of it has been awfully discouraging, though. I try to think that things are getting better and that things will get better, so that optimism shines a light on the darkened negativity; however, one must keep a realistic perspective, too. Some things will get worse, without fail. News events around the world are always going to be happening and some of it is always going to be unpleasant, sad, or revolting.

After I mended pretty well, I started to think about moving. I thought, "I don't have all that many years left on Earth, law of average, so where is it that I would like to spend my latter years." Furthermore, I thought, "I don't have all that many years left, to make a strenuous, cross-state move and get settled in, before aging really begins to take me over." I mulled all this over in my mind and thought about the areas where I would like to spend my final years—West Virginia, New Mexico, Arizona, Colorado, Montana, Nevada, California, Florida, and even Canada (where I once lived), and possibly England. I ended out shelving the decision, indefinitely. Any one of these places would work just fine for me, though, if a door would open up enough for me to go through it. Maybe I just need to push one of those doors open, and then go on through. Maybe there's a door out there that I don't yet know about. Whatever the case, I'm giving it all over to Father Time. I have to keep in mind my museum plans, for sure, and any move would relate to that. People who have surgery tend to think about relocating, though. It's only natural that the thought at least enters their mind.

As for any physical problems, that lingered around a year after my surgery had been performed, there were some that I had to continue to live with. The two areas that were bothersome all along are the culprits—the area where I was cut open, at the side and to the back, and the area in front, where the muscle and cartilage had been pulled. Both areas were sore, especially if I did something to aggravate them. They were still tender. I knew that if I were to bump either spot, it would hurt way more than were I to bump other areas of my body. My bra band still had to be worn high, so it couldn't press against the scar area. Again, it was still tender around there. Sometimes it got inflamed, especially if a bra band accidentally went over the area or if I lay down on that side, which I tried to avoid. If I did anything that used the back muscle, or the muscle in the front area, the areas would get strained and feel sore. They didn't dramatically hurt. They just felt sore.

These two areas had come a long way, though. At twelve months, they were more background than foreground. The areas were sensitive, and I felt them when I tossed and turned at night, but they weren't overly distracting anymore, to where I was overwhelmingly affected by them throughout the day, and even at night. I still had to be careful, about lifting heavy items and doing anything that involved my using those muscle and cartilage areas. Nothing was going to rip the stitches out or tear anything, but stress or strain to those areas caused soreness and there was nothing I could do about it if stress or strain happened. I will have to live with this situation, perhaps until I die. Lifting anything too heavy caused a pain in my back area, where the ribs had been split open. That area sometimes felt painful to the point where I would have to stop what I was doing. Carrying some lighter-weight items sometimes caused stress. Carrying often involves lifting. Like lifting, carrying causes certain muscles to be used. In general, though, the soreness or discomfort was background, and I was able to live with it as long as I was careful about doing strenuous things.

Perhaps all the soreness will still go away, after a longer period of time. I just know that after one year, some things were not at all like they had been, before I had had the surgery. One doctor had told me that I'd be fine in a year, but that was only partly true because while on the one hand, I was mobile and could do minimum tasks minimally, and thereby function; on the other hand, I continued to feel pain or aggravation in several areas. My surgeon told me later on that it would be closer to a year and a half before I would really be back to normal. 'Great,' I thought at the time, 'just great.' I had thought things would be much better much sooner.

A major problem I was having to live with was the mid-back problem. Fortunately, I had no lower, or lumbar-spine problem, like so many people have. Once, I hurt that area when I tried to pry a nail out of a stair. I put too much pressure on that lower back area, because I was in the wrong position to do what I did. I remember how painful that was, and how concerned I was that I had permanently damaged the area. It healed in a week or two (very slowly) and I was quite relieved, in more ways than one because such a back pain can be debilitating and distracting. There's just something about those nerves down there. You don't want to strain that area.

The problem I had was mid-spine stress and discomfort. Again, this was partly because of back problems I had had before the surgery, because of misalignment of my spine, and partly because of back problems I was having after the surgery, because of re-alignment of my spine. Again, that my stomach had been up in my chest area for as many years as it was, caused my spine to re-adjust to the location of internal parts and organs. But, there was a new problem that crept in—one that I wasn't expecting. It came out of left field. Because I had to sleep on my right side, as everything was healing up, everything inside that had been affected by the surgery shifted over to the right. Now, the weight around my stomach appears to be over to the right side of my stomach, and it isn't real even or well distributed over to both sides. This unevenness doesn't hamper any functioning, and it really doesn't look all that bad. It's just something that I happened to notice and it's an aftereffect of the surgery. It's something I have to live with. I hope, that over time, my stomach area will even out and I'm sleeping on my back as much as I can, to correct the problem. We shall see what we shall see. Probably, I'll always have some problems along my spine.

The other problem I had relative to my back, and that I first thought was linked to my problem of spinal misalignment, was that the spot in back where my ribs connected to my spine was sore in one area because my two ribs had been split apart. Splitting the ribs put pressure there, so the area of the two ribs, at the spinal connecting point, was sore. At the twelve-month checkpoint, it was still sore because I noticed this if I laid flat on the floor. (Sometimes, I do this when I watch TV). I especially felt it when I went to get up after laying flat on a couch, a bed, or the floor. I'd get up and all of a sudden that spot would hurt. I also noticed it when I walked too far, lifted anything too heavy, or twisted around the area, for example, when I stood and did the dishes. You have to do some reaching and turning, when you do dishes.

When I lay down flat on my back and then get up, I am very aware of this acute pain in my back area, but the pain goes away, soon after I'm upright. I'm pretty rickety getting up because I feel the pain pretty strongly. I don't notice the pain and discomfort until I go to get up. Clearly, my back isn't used to being flat and straight, because of the problems that have developed there over the years; it isn't just because of the pressure that occurred there because of the rib splitting. Quite a few people have spine problems. Over the years, I'm going to have to monitor my back problems closely.

Getting up after having laid flat on the floor is so painful that I have to turn to my side, get over on all fours, and slowly struggle to get up to a standing position. I always let out a loud 'oh' or 'ow' when I do this. Getting up from the couch or bed if I've been lying on my back is but a quick-to-feel, less acute pain, and then it's gone. Possibly because my backbone can curve out a little on my couch and bed because my couch and bed are soft is why getting up after being flat on my back on either of them isn't as much of a problem compared with how my back feels when I've had my back flat on a hard floor and then try to get up. Anyway, this was one of those extra problems that I hadn't expected to have, after my surgery. I really couldn't lay flat on a hard floor because getting up caused pain. There are several unexpected problems that came with my surgery package. As far as my back problems are concerned, I guess you could say I got thrown a curve.

Another lingering problem, that became evident later on, was that I couldn't stand up for very long. If I did, after not too long a period of time, I'd feel discomfort and minor pain in my back area, and also in front. It was fine if I sat down for long periods of time, but standing seemed to cause stress in a couple of places in my body, which I attribute to the force of gravity, and weight and pressure put on certain areas. I'd have to be standing for a while, though. Then I would feel the stress. Movement, of course, was the main contributor. I didn't notice it when I stood for short periods of time. If I stood in one place, using my upper body to work (for example, to do kitchen work), I'd begin to feel pressure and stress, somewhat because of the movement, but also because standing, after a while also caused some pressure on two internal areas (versus along my back). I already mentioned that twisting too much was a problem, but frankly, just standing too long caused discomfort, because of weight and gravity.

I also had a problem with occasional food jamming, which was a problem I didn't have before but some who have hiatal hernias do have. When a person has a hiatal hernia, the esophagus can turn or get bent, because of the stomach's placement, and so there can be some vomiting. Depending on how the stomach gets turned can cause some vomiting, too. Strangely, for a time after my surgery, I occasionally vomited up some food. I had a problem with my esophagus, which was in-between the hiatal that had been repaired so the esophagus couldn't have been bent. If I ate even average-sized bites of certain types of food, at a certain spot in my esophagus the food jammed and took a long time to unjam. It moved down slowly and even drinking liquid didn't help because the jammed area, after several bites in a row, became clogged. So, I'd have to sit or stand and suffer until the food slowly got through. A couple of times, I vomited up some of the food that wasn't able to get through fast enough. I had thought that this problem would go away but after a year, it hadn't. It didn't happen a lot but it sometimes happened. So I learned to be careful about food jams and the minute I sensed one coming on, I had to stop eating. Eventually and later, this ceased to be a problem, but it was a minor problem for some time after my surgery, strangely.

There were quite a few unexpected problems. And also, I hadn't expected everything to take so long to heal. At times I became anxious, until I realized that having anxiety only affected me negatively. Truth be told, I had no choice but to be patient. Patience was put on me. It wasn't necessarily something I had. Eventually, though, I just gave in to it and patience had its way with me.

This somewhat relates to forgiveness, too, which is something I wrestled with for a long time. At first, I didn't want to forgive the young man who ran into me. He wasn't sorry, after all, and he had a lot of ugly pride and arrogance, and probably fears. He wasn't even supposed to be driving, and, he lied about his speed, because of his arrogance and fears. Finally, though, I decided to forgive him and just let it go. It's something I had to do so I could go on with my life and move on. God will judge him, and all his other deeds.

Today, I'm not exactly turning hand-flips, but I'm mobile. I have aches and aggravations that I can live with. At least I don't have to worry about dying anymore because my intestines might twist or get entangled (because my stomach would end out being in my chest). My surgeon assured me that the stitching was good and would hold and he gave me the strong impression it would hold for good. He actually told me that odds were essentially nil that the stitching and mending would not hold. In so many words, that is what he said, and so I felt safe—probably too safe.

I'm not able to participate in some of the sports I was once able to participate in, but I can do general routine things that relate to everyday living. I have some limitations, and I probably always will have, but they're limitations I can live with and work around. I'm not so young anymore, anyway. Some things just don't matter that much.

Eventually, I went through a resentment phase. I was resentful because my body had been so hurt. I was resentful about the fact that it was hurt because of the car accident and because of the five years that no one was able to detect what had been going on in my chest area, but I was particularly resentful about the fact that my body had been cut into, split open, and maneuvered so much. It had been damaged, by the surgery. The cutting, the moving around, the several sets of stitches—all of this actually did damage my body, even though it healed.

I suppressed the resentment feelings for a long time, but they eventually came to the front and when they did, I suddenly felt very territorial about my body. I became angry. Partly, I wanted to be angry at my surgeon because he is the one who performed the surgery. I was going through a kind of grief, because of my loss of a once better-functioning and stronger body. I had been focusing on the healing and on other things up until then, but suddenly it hit me full force that I had a damaged body, because of the surgery, and that it would never again be like it used to be. I, of course, wasn't really mad or resentful at my surgeon, down deep. I was really grateful. But I went through this stage, this time of strangeness.

I felt sore in back, on the side, in the front, and inside, because of the damage to my body. All surgeries do damage to the body, but people don't usually think about that. It isn't the usual perspective. Their focus, instead, is that surgery will relieve the problems they are having. But there are these two sides to surgery, and not just the one. The day comes when you're suddenly hit with the realization that you have been damaged—truly damaged.

These thoughts entered my mind like a huge wave, but after about a month, they just went away. I didn't even have to think much about the resentments or work through them, either. The phase just seemed to end on its own. I guess I finally entered into the acceptance phase and that's pretty much where I am today. And, of course, I wasn't angry at my surgeon for very long because it just wasn't logical to be angry. He was trying to do well, when he performed the surgery. And he did do well. How can anyone stay mad about someone like that?

One must play the hand they are dealt, before and after a surgery. So be it. At least I'm alive. I'm eating whole meals. I'm no longer suffering because of my stomach being jammed up in my chest and turned to an angle. I'm breathing better, because my one lung isn't being pressed. I learned enough to write a book, even if I did put in some occasional, minor repetition because the effect of the painkillers, there for a while, caused my thoughts to be a little disoriented. But again, the repetition was always put in different contexts. Living through this ordeal was a great deal of repetition for me anyway, though. Every day was same ole same ole and I couldn't get away from it. I've sure learned a lot from all the every-day experiences. I hope I never have to go through anything like this again, though, because once was enough. But stay tuned. For now, this was the route I had to take, to learn certain things. What I learned has become a part of me.

From start to finish, it's been an odyssey. All in all, I would rather have had the experiences than to not have had them. I'm more aware and am a better person now, because of all the experiences. Isn't that what life is all about.

I'll give the healing more time and let everything settle in more. Everything is going to get better, I'm sure, after this twelve-month milestone. By three years, I ought to be able to turn handstands.

CHAPTER 9
Three years after the surgery

Again, please understand that some of what may seem like repetition, may not be. I have to cover all the problems I have had after my surgery in this three-year reporting too, just like I did for the six-month and the one-year reporting. After three years, I'm aware that my suspicions were right all along. It's looking like I'll have to keep on living with certain specific problems, but I'm all right with that. By now, I've learned how to improvise, and adapt, and, the problems are very minor now.

I never complain about the lingering problems I have, and about any pain. I don't like to whine and complain. If someone asks, I might tell them. Compared with some of the slams and hits professional boxers and wrestlers take, over and over and over, my overall experiences have been minor. I have various areas that are still sore and I guess that's the way it's going to be and maybe stay. Such is life. Maybe they'll completely go away.

I'm writing this after-note three years after my surgery and though healing has come, it really isn't total. Mainly, any lingering pain is all around the scar area, the front area over my left rib, and there's a sharp discomfort spot in my back area if I do certain kinds of work or projects for very long, like washing dishes. I tire easily and if I do too much physical work that involves a lot of movement, as gardening, I get sore and suffer that night. Also, I have to be careful about my back. It still gets sore and so I have to lie down and rest. I can eat whole meals, though, and my intestines can't strangle.

I wanted to skip this part and keep things positive and optimistic, but there really are lingering problems so obviously I've had to take the good with the bad. If I happen to bump my side area and to the back, where my scar is, it's a little painful because that area is still tender. (It's so much better, though.) If I happen to bend and twist a certain way, a pain goes through me like I can't describe. It's enough to cause me to moan. So I try to remember to not turn that way and if I

185

do, and it starts, I quickly shoot up, real straight. This situation relates to that pulled and displaced muscle in front, and that compromised cartilage area. If I happen to use the muscle there, in a certain way, the force seems to lift up that muscle, away from where it's supposed to be, or it does something strange to it and it hurts until the muscle goes back into its normal position. It may take a short while for it to go back into place. In the meantime, it's painful. It may be somewhat similar to the dislocation of a bone at a joint, only it's a muscle that is dislocated. That's the best way I can describe it. The muscle gets moved over— dislocated—and it's pain plus.

Again, I didn't want to end the book on a negative note, and I'm really not, except for this 'honest' after-note. But once again, the good news is that I can function. I'm able to write and so I have been writing. (I've been doing a lot of writing.) I can do household chores because none of them are too strenuous. I have to be very careful about vacuuming, though, because first-off, that one muscle sometimes gets dislocated, and second-off, bending over so much seems to bother something in my body because I have breathing problems afterwards and sometimes wonder if my one lung is as normal as it was before the surgery. I learned to vacuum on my hands and knees so I don't have to bend very much.

I garden, but with caution and at a slower pace than I gardened before. I can lift heavy items and boxes as long as they aren't too heavy or bulky and I use both hands and arms. If I lift too heavy or bulky an item and it pulls around my scar area, the whole area still swells up and becomes sore. It may take a day or two for it to not feel stressed. I just have to be careful, no matter what I do. Doing things cautiously is probably a good thing.

I want to emphasize that the good result of the car accident, surgery, and after-effects of the surgery, is that I haven't put the pen down now for a number of years, and don't plan to. I've enjoyed my time as a writer. Writing has helped to keep my mind off my problems, which are manageable and I'm thankful for that. I tend to put a great deal in to my writings. I actually like being at home. I still have a few clients from my counseling business, but most have been phased out so I can write.

One person told me I shouldn't put so many facts and details in to my writings . . . so much knowledge and information. The person said that less would be better and that keeping it simpler would be better, too. Why do you want to give so much out to others, was this person's perspective, or why do you want to do so much for other people, was what they were thinking. I've been inclined to do for others for as long as I can remember. I don't really know where it comes from—probably from many places—but also, I've been pretty downtrodden all my life and I empathize with downtrodden people and I want to help them. I want to be of service to others.

Even though I've had a number of advantages, I've still been constantly downtrodden, and I've actually been a very sad, unhappy person, for practically all my life. I don't stand up for myself enough. Many times, it's just not worth taking the time and effort to stand up for myself. Time is very valuable. Sometimes you have to walk away or turn the other cheek, especially when defending yourself in an intelligent way doesn't work. I've learned to cope with life but I don't really enjoy life. I know that some do. I do like being alive and I try to stay positive because life goes along better if you do.

Writing has been my pain reliever. Writing definitely helped me to not notice the physical pain so much, as I was healing from my surgery. Researching, organizing, creating, and doing the actual work of writing and revising kept me going, and going, and going. All total, I've written thousands and thousands of pages (obviously, not all of them are in this particular book). I've worked like a beaver, and an ant. Two or three of my books ended out being quite long. Writing was great to be doing during COVID, too, though a number of books had been finished . . . but some weren't.

I'm not afraid to drive a car now and this is good. I just get in the car and go where I need to go. Life went on, after I lost my beautiful 1970 Oldsmobile Cutlass Supreme. Again, I now have another Oldsmobile, and it was given to me so I see it as a replacement for my previously-demolished Oldsmobile, which was almost a total loss. Presently, I can run general errands around town but I still can't drive for too long a period of time. I can drive, max, for about half a day. Then I have to stop and rest for the remainder of the day. I can drive around town for longer so long as I stop to run in to do errands periodically and stop to sit and rest and eat a meal.

I can cook—no problem. I can do some repair and maintenance jobs around the home, but not certain ones, so I have to hire out for those jobs. Some things are just too strenuous for me, or they put too much pressure on areas that are still vulnerable and sore or that get sore fairly easily. I keep busy because that is the key to life. I do whatever I can do, whenever I can.

I try not to think about the negative or about the lingering aggravations or problems. When you keep busy, you are focusing on doing a project or finishing up a project so everything has to take a back seat to that. I hope to keep going like this until I no longer can. I just keep on going at the best pace I can—doing this and doing that. I could have died from the car accident, before the surgery, or during the surgery. I'm still here—pressing on, trying to do what I can for other people, and also for animals. (I've written a very long cat (and animal rights) book.)

I really don't know how long I have to live, so I work towards my goals as best I can. The world has changed, and so many of the changes I don't like, but what can you do. I hope my writings will help to buffer some of the not-so-good changes or efforts at change. People have to hold on to core values and ethics, and not let them slip away or be taken away. But this has been and is still happening, and frankly, this whole world needs surgery. Society needs surgery. Some parts are still good but some parts are not. Of course, one person can only do so much, and in my case, I'm somewhat handicapped, though not entirely.

I enjoyed writing a book about my own surgery. I don't think that such a book has been written but I'm not positive about that. I've never come across one, though. I was surprised that I was able to remember as much as I did while I was writing this book, especially since I was on painkillers for some of the time. (I also wrote a book about my Shingles experience, which was no fun to go through either, and was a step-by-step process.) During the course of my ordeal, I asked many questions. I've always been an observer. I also have a good memory. All the medical professional people were helpful along the way, especially my doctor—the man in charge of my surgery. I'm grateful for all their help and support. The book could not have been written had they not helped me along the way. I hope they know who they are. I don't know all their names. Many people have helped me along the way. Most have been Good Samaritans.

I picked the book back up when the surgery was at a five-year checkpoint, and there has been no significant improvement of that front area over the ribs on the left side, nor around my scar area, i.e., the surgery-opening and cutting area. So I was right about my prediction—that those areas would not improve. My scar area is still sore and tender, and I have to be careful not to bump it. It's still swollen a bit, sometimes. I noticed some swelling the other day. That left side area is rounded out, to both sides of the scar. I guess I'm not surprised, because so much cutting had been done there, and the cutting was deep. The scar is not so pretty. Women always want to be and look pretty. I'm glad the scar is always covered up.

Also, one side of my body (around the stomach area) has a different shape from the other side and the whole lower area (under my ribs) is not symmetrical. This has to do with how I had to rest and sleep, right after the surgery. Because I had to rest and sleep on the right side for some time after the surgery, what all had been loose inside me after the internal surgical separations and overall the surgery, tended to shift over and bond to the right side more than it should have. Had I slept on my back, everything would have ended out being better distributed (as everything was growing back together). No one, I say no one, told me that this could happen and that I should try very hard to rest and sleep on my back, early on. I had to learn, too late and after the fact, that I should have forced myself to rest and sleep on my back, right after or very soon after my surgery. Because of that lack of awareness and knowledge, I must now suffer from lack of body symmetry of my waist and abdomen areas and from too much weight being over on the right side. I relay this now in an effort to caution and help others.

I am embarrassed about my figure now, somewhat, but I'd rather be embarrassed and be open about it, if that will help others. Whatever had been loose inside, after the surgery, ended out bonding more over to the right, because that is how I rested and slept for some time. Had I known this would happen, I would have done everything I could to rest and sleep on my back. It's a good idea to sleep on your back anyway, as often as you can, even if you toss and turn during sleep. Sleeping on your back helps to straighten your back, over the years. (You don't need a pillow when you sleep on your back.) Most people probably don't even notice this lack of symmetry about my body, but, of course, they might now, because they are now aware of the lack of symmetry there. I could perhaps have plastic surgery for it, but I doubt it because everything is bonded. It is not fat that liposuction could take care of; it's everything that is internal, slightly over to the right side. It's not a handicap, just minor disfigurement that is not real detectable because I wear slightly full dresses. Like my scar, though, it can bother me psychologically at times if I let it. It can bother me physically at times, too, because there is pressure there.

As an after-note, I could rest and sleep over on my left side fairly easily several years after my surgery. This, of course, means that if I rest and sleep on the left side, and not on the right side, that better lower-area symmetry may still come about. However, it probably won't because all my organs have already bonded (grown together) and are where they'll likely stay. If everything stays as it is, it won't be the end of the world. It's just an aggravation./

CHAPTER 10

A Second Occurrence of Symptoms

I don't exactly know how to start this chapter. I'd thought the book was finished, but there is more to write now. I've definitely been flattened. "Help, I can't get up." I have to have this surgery again because my stomach is up in my chest again. My last surgery had been done thirteen years earlier. I recently learned that hiatal hernia repairs don't last indefinitely. I'd thought they did. I learned that they can go for from five to ten years. Mine has gone for thirteen years, but I don't know when my stomach became internally affected, or if one particular incident occurred to make it start to happen. I wasn't in another car accident, but I perhaps lifted too many heavy things. It's been a part of my lifestyle to lift heavy things. I move boxes around because I'm working towards establishing a museum. Most of those boxes are lightweight but some are bulky. I'm also working towards establishing a family book store to go along with the museum, but those boxes are never very large. Some have been heavy, though. Yard work requires moving heavy items around, too, like rocks, bricks, and boxes of leaves, branches, cactus, and anything else related to removal of cuttings, clippings, and that which is dead.

My previous surgeon had made me feel that the surgery site was invincible after he'd done the surgery. His selected statements and the way he emphasized what he said caused me to think that all would be A-OK for probably forever. He said the stitching was good and holding and he specifically said "it would take something of great impact, like another car accident or heavy punches in the gut, for the work that I did to not hold." He left me thinking I was essentially invincible and so I lifted some heavy boxes and did strenuous yard work. I didn't work out at a gym, but I walked a great deal, did daily housework (that is exercise), and I did way more yard work than most people do. I even wrote a book on landscaping because I'd learned so much from doing my own landscaping and gardening. I loved doing yard work from day one and kept my lot up and continually improved

191

my yard and lot. The book title is *Landscaping a Small Lot*. Perhaps I should have hired out for some of the heavier work I ended out doing but I didn't even think to do that. It was my poor judgment to do any heavy work. I should have thought through the overall subject better than I did. I should have tried to find help for some of the landscaping and yard work done (but I am always try to save money).

I've had trouble eating whole meals for some time now, actually, but I didn't think anything of it (but probably should have). I just thought that my stomach had perhaps turned a bit so my stomach capacity was less because of constriction and the angle of the stomach. I believed my diaphragm and the hiatus were fine and that all was still in place. That's what I'd been telling myself, over the course of time. That's what I believed. So in conclusion, since I was eating somewhat smaller meals for a couple of years but wasn't significantly bothered by it and felt no pain or discomfort (unless I ate way too much, for the stomach capacity), I didn't even think to look into it. That may seem strange, but it is, nevertheless, true. I thought everything was generally okay. It's when you are in pain or too much discomfort that you go see the doctor. I was not in pain, plus I firmly believed that the first surgery was still holding.

Well, around September 25, 2014, pain decided to visit me—big time. I suddenly had some horrible pain all through my torso—it surrounded the thoracic and abdominal area, back to front and side to side. I assumed it could have something to do with my stomach being tipped and from eating too much, which was not very good thinking. At this point, I wasn't thinking the hiatus and diaphragm area had split anywhere and that my stomach was up in my chest. Again, I just thought the stomach had somehow been tipped or turned up, because of normal wear and tear down there, since the surgery. I had no clue the hiatus and diaphragm had ripped and that the stomach had been gradually going back up in my chest. Both the hiatus and the diaphragm hold the stomach down, especially the diaphragm. The hiatus makes it so the esophagus goes down and stays straight. If the stomach presses up, the positioning of the esophagus can be compromised, one way or another, depending on how the stomach tips. The stomach moves up too, and can bend or turn. But, this medical scenario was secondary to my major problem in late September of 2014 (and thereafter). My main problem was something else—something I hadn't been expecting, at all.

That day, after a while, that all-consuming, very distracting pain went away, after leaving me totally wrung out. When I had the pain, I had a high temperature and was perspiring considerably. This had never happened to near that extent when I had eaten too much and my stomach couldn't take any more food and there was pressure from that. That was somewhat painful and I had to ride it out until digestion got everything back to normal, but it wasn't acute and severe pain, like this pain was. How I had first thought it was related to that pain is beyond me now because there is no comparison, relative to the two pains. The first tends to be distracting and very uncomfortable; the second made me want to jump out of my own skin with one quick jump. But I was stuck with the pain for a few hours. Weird as you might think it to be, at the time, I'd believed that subsequent digestion would make the pain go away in the usual amount of time, but it didn't. In retrospect, I realized the pain was way more severe for that to be the case. I was almost ready to go to the hospital. I rode it out a little longer and the pain did go away and didn't continue. (It was to return soon after). I still thought it was the one problem, though, not an entirely different problem.

Pain is stressful and it is hard to concentrate on anything when pain is present. There is a Misery Index, relative to pain, discomfort, inconvenience, and even unhappiness because who is all that happy if they register high with pain? It would depend on someone's definition of happiness, though. Still and all, misery is essentially the opposite of happiness. If a person has pain, there might be other aspects of their life that they are happy with or about and that would give them a higher number on the Happiness Index, but probably not on the Misery Index because pain causes misery. Painkillers will decrease misery because they reduce or eliminate pain.

I surely do wish I'd had at least one painkiller on hand, when that one noted pain overtook me. Very soon after, I was inspired to write the poem, *Pain*, which I am including here. The experience of having that much unmanaged pain put many new thoughts into my consciousness, and relatively fast, too. Had I not experienced that pain, the poem, *Pain*, would not have been written. I wouldn't

Kathy S. Thompson, M.A.

have thought of those particular ideas and concepts that are in the poem. It's one of the poems that I didn't have to do much to after it flowed out. This is probably because everything got so set in, because of the recent experience. Here is the poem. You have to read it with the right inflections and accents on certain syllables. What happened again to me—the return of that same medical condition and pain, follows the poem.

Pain

Pain will quickly wake you up,
Even from a real deep sleep.
It can be so distracting
And can be an awful strain.
It can also come and go.
Its affects can enslave you.
Pain will surely leave you weak,
And become a dismal drain.

Pain can fully engulf you.
It can cause you much worry.
It can make someone feel hot
And can bring about a sweat.
Pain can create a panic.
And can bring on agony.
It can cause those near the pained
To be stressed, and fret and fret.

Pain can make you immobile
Because it can hurt too much.
It can make you walk around
Because you cannot stay still.
Pain has to be well managed.
It will surely need relief.

194

Bad pain is hard to live with.
It can make you write a Will.

Constant pain ruins your life.
It can change priorities.
There's disorientation.
There can be meandering.
Pain can be all over you,
Or be present in one spot.
Bad pain makes some want to die,
And can be real frightening.

Somebody, call 9-1-1
If a pain seems to be high.
Pain can range from 10 to 1
And go from acute to slight.
Pain makes you change your diet.
It makes people moan and groan,
Pain can make you tighten up.
Sometimes, it, you cannot fight.

You will have to get some help
When you know pain's here to stay.
You will want to be pain free,
And then live your life, daily.
You might need medication
Of one type—or more than one.
You might need to change habits.
You might need some surgery.

There is pain, and there is pain;
Pain's a matter of degree.
If you've ever almost died,

You'll see life a brand new way.
When there is just too much pain,
Everything will go on hold,
When you find there's suffering,
Pray that bad pain will not stay.

Know about your own body.
Learn what might seem different.
Know about anatomy,
And about current health trends.
Realize one body part
Can be adjoined to others.
When pain's in one area,
If it's fixed, the body mends.

We have amazing bodies
That are so wondrously made.
Even with the best of care,
Bodies give out, and will die.
Take good care of your body
So you can circumvent pain.
Eat well and get exercise
So you'll fare as time goes by.

Once you've encountered real pain,
You won't forget how it felt.
You'll remember that bad time.
Suffering will come with it.
When pain's gone, life's different.
You'll breathe a sigh of relief.
Live a good life while you can,
But know, one day, death will hit.

Several days went by and I had no bouts with that same pain. I'd assumed everything was OK and was so totally oblivious to what was really going on. They say you should never allow yourself to get too complacent. So often, as soon as you do, something of magnitude will hit, and hit it did—it hit hard. That same pain came upon me, again. It was so all encompassing that I was barely mobile. I'd try walking, but that didn't relieve the pain. I'd try lying down. No dice. I'd try sitting at my desk. Still no dice. I'd even try leaning over my desk or the kitchen counter, and yet again, no dice. The pain went on and on. I'd cry, but that didn't do any good at all. It brought no results. Plus, no one was around to comfort me. Even if someone had been around, they couldn't have comforted me. This pain was huge. It was the same pain as before, and all over the upper torso (and I do mean all over). It was worse than childbirth because at least with childbirth you know contractions are off and on and temporary and will stop because a child will be born. With this pain, you don't think it is going to end and you are seriously panicked. It is a pain similar to that of contractions, though.

The pain first hit me late at night, probably around the midnight hour. I tried watching TV but was so very distracted. I tried to ride it out and kept thinking it was going to go away, but it didn't and by 4 a.m., I decided to drive to the hospital. I was actually capable of driving, even with the pain. I thought this strange because I was in genuine pain, but my alertness was strong and my reflexes were okay. My concentration was 'the road' and that helped me to not think of the pain. There were few cars on the road but I was able to concentrate on the road and on stopping at the stoplights and I just wanted to get to the emergency room as fast as I could (but I did not speed). Reorganizing of roads had taken place over the last couple of years and I ended out getting lost on my way to the hospital (and it was dark). That was very stressful, but I found my way. I do not recommend that anyone ever drive themselves when they're in pain. I'm sorry, now, that I did. I did not think that I had a choice, at the time. I was all by myself and did not want to bother anyone at that hour.

I eventually got there and parked near the emergency room and that big sliding door wasn't opening so I knocked on it, while being in agony. A young man came to the door and seemed upset that I was knocking on that big glass door. He reluctantly opened it and condescendingly said "in the future, don't come through this door, come through the door over to the side" . . . and I barely heard what he said because I was thinking of my pain and needing pain relief, and I was somewhat thinking that this young insensitive knew I was in considerable pain yet he was criticizing me for going to the two big glass doors. It's all I had known to do and he knew that. He was not being nice. He was critical at the worst possible time. Talk about lack of sensitivity and caring. He wore a white uniform. I think he should have been wearing very dark gray. I've never punched anyone in the nose but that young man deserved a punch in the nose. I wonder, now, if this young man was an intern. In any event, I thought hospital people were supposed to demonstrate compassion and mercy and truly be of help to you. He didn't. He wasn't. I saw none of any of that. Far from it...in fact.

When I got in, the staff was quick to do the paperwork. Oh yes, they always are. And they were somewhat quick to get a nurse in to ask me questions. (It was a male nurse.) But then, it seemed they just dropped me. The male nurse just disappeared, never to be seen again. The staff, including the male nurse, had said the doctor would be by very soon. I'd told them all, and more than once, that I was in considerable pain and even asked if I could have some kind of pain relief as soon as possible. They'd stuck me in a room all by myself and I kept standing at the door, hoping to see the doctor. I asked anyone who walked by if they could hurry things along and if they knew how long it would be and no one had a clue. I was in such pain. I could hardly stand it. I was getting more and more agitated. My lipase was going up more and more, I learned better. I could have died.

A janitor came by and said they may be short of doctors at this hour. (By now it was about 5:30 a.m.) What he said was enough for me to really panic because I thought 'am I going to die, here, before a doctor comes by, and is something going to rupture?' I was so panicked that something inside me went into motion and I scurried out of that room, that corridor, that staff section, and out the door and into the parking lot. I hopped in my car, and with adrenaline and a survivor instinct kicking in, I headed over to another hospital. It was so early in the morning that there was still no traffic to speak of. It was even still somewhat dark outside. There were quite a few hospitals in the overall city but I only knew how to get to a few of them. So, I drove to the one I knew how to get to the fastest. It's amazing what you can do when you are by yourself and alone. Adrenaline kicked in and that is what really drove me. I had to wait for lights to change, but there, literally, was no other traffic besides me. Another time of day would have been a different matter. Had I had a cellphone, I would have called for an ambulance. At that hour, there was no place to stop to make a phone call. (There's no neighborhood phone booths any more). I took the most direct route I could. No businesses or offices were open. Except, that hospital.

When I got to the second hospital, I had no trouble finding a parking spot. It was way before even 8 a.m. I parked close to the emergency entrance but I went through a front entrance this time. It was around the way from the emergency entrance. I didn't want to go over to those glass double doors again by the neon emergency sign, lest I encounter disgruntlement again (which I probably wouldn't have). I should have said to that rude young man at the first hospital "well, pardon me for living". Perhaps that would have stopped him in his tracks because maybe I could have died, right there and then. He would have just harshly gone on his way if I did, not caring one whit. When I got to the emergency desk at the second hospital, I encountered efficiency and no negativity. Thank God. That was such a good sign. 'By gosh', I thought, 'I think I'm at the right place'. Of course, I really didn't want to be at any hospital but since I had to be at one, this one would certainly do. Meanwhile, and during this whole time, I'd been experiencing considerable pain.

The young woman at emergency admissions was a smidge aloof but I detected a little concern on her part, for me, but more important to me (at the time) was the attitude of the security guard who was over a couple of feet from her, sitting in a chair. He became quite alert when I told him about my pain and that I needed to see a doctor right away and he was responsive in a positive way. He obviously cared about me and one thing he said was that they usually got to emergency patients right away, which encouraged me no end.

Either the admissions clerk or the security officer said "sit down, won't you, while you wait" but by that time I could not sit. It was too uncomfortable. I had to stand. I had barely gone over to the chairs when a young man came for me to take me back to the emergency room. This all went fast. This room was large and had partitioned sections with long navy blue curtains or drapes around each of the beds, that were at different angles and near the other beds. The curtains or drapes separated the patients. You could hear people talking nearby, and what they were saying if you tuned in, but other noises were going on so most all the words got muddled. They drew blood right away and took my blood pressure and they took my urine (from a cup I'd filled in the bathroom) and they very quickly, thereafter, came in and put me on a morphine drip, thank God. A doctor was in the large shared room, going from one patient to another. I'm sure he saw my test readings or they wouldn't have given me morphine. He knew rather quickly what my problem was. I'd described my symptoms, too. Again, my problem and pain had been a complete surprise to me.

The admitting doctor told me I had pancreatitis. My lipase level was up to 9000 because of it and it is supposed to be at 100 or even less. It's a good thing I got to the hospital when I did. Apparently, a gallstone had left my gallbladder and then jammed at the pancreas area. That is the best way I can describe it at the present time. It stayed jammed there for a number of hours, apparently. (Sometimes they go through faster.) The stone passed through on its own while I was at the hospital, fortunately or perhaps even before and while I was en route. Because I'd, at first, thought it was linked with digestion and that the pain had related to a past hiatal hernia surgery and that the diaphragm may have broken or stretched, they put that in their notes so it could be checked, which I asked them to do and they did, and that is how I found out for positive sure about the torn and stretched areas of the hiatus and diaphragm. I mentioned to them, early on, that the hiatal hernia could be back and that another test might be needed to check for that. If it is logical, hospital doctors want to run as many tests as they can. The more tests you run, the more apt you are to detect one or more medical problems and see what is needed to be seen.

Having gallstones, and passing them, is something I would never have even thought of, relative to a diagnosis. I knew a little about kidney stones, but nothing about gallstones. I guess they start forming and then increase in size when you're a little older. A reduced-fat diet reduces the chance of getting them, or will at least slow their formation down and keep the numbers down. They can easily pass, and often do, but one can cause a blockage, for a short time, a long time, or permanently so there absolutely has to be surgical removal. It is hard to know how many gallstones are formed in the gallbladder. A person with gallstones can have no problems, an occasional problem, or something serious can happen. I don't know if there is anything you can drink to get gallstones to loosen and pass. Somebody ought to patent something that can, but you probably couldn't guarantee something like that.

Along with the blood and blood pressure and urine test results, there was an MRI test result. Before they put me in a private room, which they did soon after they knew I was going to stay, they wheeled me over to a room where they did the MRI. I was instructed to breath in and out in a certain way at certain times because as the scanner moves, you're not supposed to be breathing. Any movement can distort the images, in other words. Magnetic Resonance Imaging is done by a large machine. You lay down and it scans and photographs internal images. Medical people were mainly interested in checking my pancreas and gallbladder but a doctor would also be able to check other organs in my chest and abdomen. Doctors look for diseases and abnormalities. The MRI is helpful for bringing many different medical problems to light.

You absolutely can't have anything metal on you when you go in the MRI machines, including jewelry, and even hairpins. Metal interferes with the magnetic field of the unit. Anything metal or electronic can't even be in the same room. The machine is handled by a Radiologist. Anything metal in or on your body you must tell the Radiologist about. A heavy cover goes over the body before the machine is started.

This imaging method is not at all like X-ray exams or Computerized Tomography scans (CTs). You are in an actual magnet, and radio waves redirect alignment of hydrogen atoms in the body but no chemical changes occur in the body's tissues at the time. Energy is emitted as it scans and takes a picture of what is being scanned. An electric current goes through wire coils in the MRI unit, thus producing a magnetic field. Signals get sent out and a computer processes the signals and images result. It's all very technical—way more technical than I am able to relay.

Some problems can be better detected by way of MRI than by CT and Ultrasound. MRI results deliver soft tissue imaging. CT scan results deliver bone imaging and some other imaging, but again, MRI is mainly for soft tissue. You cannot be exposed to radiation if you have an MRI because it is not a radiation (X-ray) method. I was not shown specific images and results of my MRI, except to see shadows in my gallbladder, which meant that there were quite a few stones there, but the test did not reveal size, amount, or if the stones were stacked up in layers inside the gallbladder. But, the doctors who came by my bedside (and certain ones were required to at least come by once a day), affirmed that I should have my gallbladder surgically removed—so there would be no more gallstones slipping out and resting on my pancreas and causing pancreatitis, for one thing.

MRIs are often used to diagnose heart problems. I'd, of course, heard of MRIs, but I only vaguely knew what they were. I still don't know that much about them, technically. I have the general gist about how they work but there's so much more to them. They are a modern-day marvel, though. There must be many stories behind getting all those many patents filed along the way even before such a machine was able to be put together. Someone could write a whole book just about that, if they were the right kind of scientist.

As far as the results go, the doctor gets to see all the images and often the patient only gets a critique or write-up about the results and what's been seen. This happens with other kinds of medical tests, too. The doctor is at liberty to show patients the actual images of any type of examination, or not. Frankly, some doctors would just as soon avoid it. Some patients insist on it, and, they want to hear the diagnosis with the images serving as back-up facts. Every picture tells a story, as long as certain things (in the picture) can be pointed out or explained.

Ultrasounds aren't as expensive as MRIs, and ultrasonic imaging or sonography can be used to detect certain medical problems. Ultrasound screenings have the ability to actually 'see' inside arteries, along with their other abilities. With Ultrasound, inaudible sound waves are able to produce a resolution or picture. Here again, this is very technical. Frequencies, reflection, and diffraction of sound waves relate to the technicality. The scanning times and power settings have to be low, and are. A CT scan involves actual radiation, like X-rays do. Patients fear radiation of any amount, but medical professionals are trained in precautionary procedures.

A CT scan is a group of X-rays taken from different angles of one particular medical problem. A computer is also used (so what else is new). It is X-ray computed tomography (initials, CT). The scan can detect many problems inside the body. There are different types of CT scanners, and they keep on improving them as to efficiency. A CT scan is what I'll need to have, again, right before the surgery. Doctors have to know about and keep up with all these kinds of medical diagnostic units, and their improvements. They have to know when to use what and what type of unit or units would be best to diagnose certain, specific medical problems. If you trust the doctor who diagnoses and interprets these tests, you may not mind not actually seeing the test imaging for yourself. Sometimes more than one type of test is needed to zone in on a particular medical problem. Sometimes one test type has to be done more than once, too.

CT tests can examine bones and aspects of soft tissues. They do better than regular X-rays do, and Ultrasound. Often, CT scan results are needed to further examine something seen or questioned on an X-ray or Ultrasound screen. Cancer is often picked up on a CT scan. Blood tests help to do that, too. A nurse told me that I didn't have cancer. She was looking at my blood test results. It seems they continually tested my blood. I know they tested my urine and took my blood pressure more than once, too. I don't know how she could conclude I didn't have cancer, though, because several blood tests from one blood test would be needed to know that, for sure, and I don't believe all the different tests were run. She could have been right, though. I'm not sure what particular test or how many tests they did with my blood sample.

I decided that I only ever wanted to have a minimum of CT scans, because the machine is a radiation one (whereas an Ultrasound and an MRI aren't). There have been errors with CT scans—some with setting the machine. One problem with MRI machines is that they are, essentially, a giant magnet. Its magnet will draw in to it anything loose that can be magnetized...and it has done that on occasion, hurting the patient lying down. One time, a hospital worker had a large metal oxygen tank and she foolishly entered the room and the tank flew out of her hands at such a rapid speed that it hit the patient and killed him. This is also why no jewelry and watches are allowed to be worn by the patient. Even gold and silver jewelry can have metal underneath it, or metal clasps.

I was at the hospital from very early morning October 4, 1014 to mid-day, October 7, 2014. It was miraculous that my pancreas level went down as fast as it did. I was on an IV that had morphine at first, and definitely antibiotics, and then just antibiotics. I was also given glucose at one point because my body was low on sugar, and also potassium, because I was low on that. At first, the potassium wasn't diluted enough and the IV drip caused my arm to be red and irritated so they diluted the potassium. The drip took longer to administer but by their diluting the potassium, my arm got back to feeling normal, except that, is any arm really normal when there are needles stuck in it, that are being used to connect the arm to an IV, by way of tubes? Why I was so low on glucose or sugar may have tied in with my pancreas problem. My pancreas was quite inflamed and therefore, was not functioning up to par. The pancreas is obviously used in digestion and one of its functions is to metabolize or process sugar and salt. The pancreas produces insulin, which is a hormone needed to metabolize or process carbohydrates and control the sugar and salt that goes into the blood and urine. How well the pancreas functions is of paramount importance. No one ever wants to lose their pancreas. The pancreas maintains blood glucose balance. It produces both hormones and enzymes that are needed. It is only six inches long and sets between the stomach and spine. With my stomach being up in my chest, I like to hope that my pancreas is not affected by that shift of position, since it is so important.

The hospital I ended out at was a private one, and is quite large. It has a good reputation. Nurses kept changing shifts; that is one thing I really notices. There were always two nurses. One was the main nurse (very possibly an RN); another was considered a tech nurse that was around to do the more mundane tasks, quite frankly. The main nurse operated the IV and did any testing. She did what was more technical. She took charge and made the nurse-related decisions. Either would check on me if I pressed the buzzer button. It would depend on who was around. Both wrote their names on a board on a wall in my room. When new nurses came in for a change of shift, new names went on the board.

I slept so much of the time when I was there—both day and night. Because my body had been so traumatized, I needed to sleep. Subliminally, sleep helps you forget the pain; it can bring about speedier healing.

I didn't eat anything at first. They wouldn't even let me drink any water. I received lots of fluids, intravenously, but could not drink water. They wanted to keep track of my urine amount to see how that amount related to the fluids they were giving me, for one thing. They'd put an attachment part on top of the toilet seat so they could measure my urine amount. It wasn't always easy to aim into that unit because it was forward on the seat (in the other direction of the toilet tank). Again, I was so very thirsty. I secretly snuck in just enough water to get one or two swallows in so my mouth could be moistened; it was so dry and parched around my whole mouth. They'd given me a type of Q-tip® and small glass of water and I could use the Q-tip® after wetting it to coat the inside of my mouth but that didn't work very well so I snuck in water from the bathroom tap and wet my whole mouth area because I was so parched. I drank one gulp, too. I had to.

When I was first in the hospital emergency room, I had one bladder-control accident (because of the morphine, and because the nearest bathroom was a ways away (and it shouldn't have been). There was no bathroom in that 'shared', partitioned emergency room. I had a bladder accident right there in the hallway. Young men were around at the station desk; so were young women. It was so embarrassing. I hope someone quickly and well cleaned it up. The nurse who accompanied me was supposed to. I never found out if she did. You'd think they would have had a bedpan or two around that emergency room since they didn't have a bathroom nearby. The bathroom was more like a block away, quite frankly and so many people were around it. I complained about this later. I don't know if it did any good.

Several doctors came by after I was given my own room—the Admitting Provider, the Referring doctor, and two Consulting doctors. One consulting physician practiced Gastro-enterology and the other one was a general surgeon—the man who, most likely (at least at the time), was going to do my two surgeries, which were the gallbladder removal and the hiatal hernia re-repair. A Gastro-enterologist specializes in the digestive system and any disorder related to it. It is an Internal Medicine field. There can be gastro-intestinal bleeding and cancers. I had neither going on, thank God.

As for follow-up, the only doctor I really needed to continue seeing was the general surgeon, who was relatively young but he'd done quite a few gallbladder removals and diaphragm and hernia repairs (and re-set everything back in like it should be). All the doctors had wanted both surgeries to be done while I was in the hospital. I about hit the roof with that one because I had no bag packed, was not prepared for either, and had cats to take care of at home.

As it was, I was already very worried about my indoor cats, and all the stray cats I fed. I'd suddenly and unexpectedly had to leave them, and had no clue when I would be released. Fortunately, my indoor cats had enough food and water for the days I was gone because I always leave lots of food out, and the strays didn't starve (because they were around when I returned). The strays had been waiting for me, and it had about killed me to not be able to leave earlier so I could get food to them. Perhaps they all found food elsewhere for my days away but to this day, I don't know that. It's entirely possible they at least found some food.

Competition out there is keen for stray kitties. Not very many people put out dry commercial cat food for stray cats. You'd think people would but they really don't (and they should because so many stray cats go hungry and even starve). I even put their food in a dish set in a large pie tin I fill with water so those carnsarned ants can't get into their food. They drown trying. I want to make sure the strays can eat the food I put out. When it gets cold enough, the ants go underground, but they're above ground many months of the year and you have to go the extra mile to protect the food you put out for stray cats or they cannot eat it.

It's one thing to be able to make plans to go to the hospital. You can find someone to feed the animals. But, if you suddenly have to go to the hospital and they will not let you leave and you have to stay there many days, then woe to the animals.

I was told that if I did leave early, the insurance I had would not be paid or covered. I could not even leave and return. The insurance group would only cover me if I was formally released by a doctor. This caused me considerable concern because I wondered what would happen when the first hospital I went to and was checked in to put their claim for costs in to the insurance people, since I left there without being formally released. Would the insurance group deny the claim for money so the hospital would, then, try to get the money from me? I knew I would just have to wait and see, and be willing to do battle if it came to that. In the meantime, I had to set it all on the shelf. I really didn't even know it if the insurance people would cover all the costs related to the second hospital—the one I stayed at. It was going to be interesting. I worried that they might not cover the surgeries, too. The surgeries were 'around the corner' for me, and I was new to this insurance business. I had no idea what, and how much of what might be covered. It's a bit nerve-racking. I had a 'provider', and a 'secondary provider', but what would both do? Will everything be covered, or will it not? What about that first hospital? Will insurance pay for that debacle? All I could do was stay tuned.

By this time (2014), I was on Medicare and had a secondary provider to Medicare, like everyone does. I was a Senior Citizen. People choose their own secondary provider. It can be private, or tied in with the Military, like AARP, Tricare, and USAA. What Medicare doesn't pick up on the bill, the secondary provider might. Note I use the word 'might'. Because the ObamaCare government health program has been implemented over the course of the last few years and has been bringing about different changes to the health care system, every year, people on Medicare are nervous when putting in claims now because they wonder, 'are there any affecting changes we don't know about' and 'is there going to be more money taken out of our own pockets'?

My hiatal hernia surgery will be a more involved one, and there will be deep cutting so I'll require hospital care for several days. The gallbladder removal will be a snap surgery and ordinarily would be done by laparoscopy at this hospital. Mine would be different, though—it would be done because I had to be opened up anyway for the other surgery. It would be done by incision. My surgeon's office was essentially across the street from the hospital but a laparoscopy is still done at the hospital. It's quick, and cause minimal scarring. I could still go with a laparoscopy, should I choose to delay the hiatal hernia surgery. It seems more practical for the surgeon to remove my gallbladder by way of open surgery (which, before laparoscopy, was the original method of gallbladder removal) because he would have to open me up anyway because of the disorganization in my thoracic and abdominal parts. My gallbladder surgery would be a single-sight entry versus a multi-port entry (as with laparoscopy). There is also the da Vinci surgery to remove gallbladders, which requires going through the bellybutton and using special instruments. But the da Vinci procedure won't be done on me.

I could get pancreatitis any time before the gallbladder surgery is done because a stone could, again, leave the gallbladder and come to lodge on my pancreas. If this were to happen, I'd have to go to the hospital right away, to be safe. True, it might dislodge and pass through soon after, but I won't know what the gallstone will do, and that will be the problem. With the surgery, the gallbladder connecting tube has to be cut and clipped and I want to assume the clip will always hold?

Both times I had a stone that lodged on my pancreas—the first time for several hours and the second time for even more hours so I had to go in to emergency—I had been either resting or sleeping on my stomach. I later assumed (after I'd learned that the hiatus and diaphragm were no longer holding down my stomach), that pressure going from my stomach to the liver, and therefore the gallbladder had perhaps pressed the stone out of the gallbladder, because I had been laying on my stomach, which may have caused pressure and squeezing. This is total conjecture on my part, though. Still, I decided to never sleep or even lay down on my stomach again—not until it is completely safe to do so.

The gallbladder is right under the larger side of the liver and the stomach is over to the smaller side of the liver. The stomach sets in right next to the liver and then it curves around and under and narrows and when it does, becomes the duodenum. Right behind the duodenum is the pancreas. The gallbladder is right next to both the liver and the pancreas. I am still wondering if resting or sleeping on my stomach had something to do with the pancreatitis, but my surgeon said 'no' to that question, but I don't know how he had time to give adequate thought to it because he said 'no' so fast. I think there could be something to that so I now refuse to sleep on my stomach, for now.

When I had my appointment with the surgeon—Dr. Charles A. Atkinson— after I'd been released from the hospital, I had around eight pages of questions for him to answer (all written in longhand), but he didn't have the time to answer all my questions so I directed only some of the important questions his way instead. I felt a little unrequited but I understood. This surgeon is a very busy man. On my own, I went through my questions afterwards and did what research I could to acquire some answers and then I re-wrote another list that only had the most important and key questions written down for next time. This is what a patient must sometimes do. Don't leave it all to chance.

I also, during that office visit, didn't have the surgeon all to myself because a resident-in-training flanked him; she was with him at the visits he made (to me) during my hospital stay, too. She seemed pleasant enough but only listened and did not talk. I couldn't help but think of her as being his shadow for some reason. One day, she, too, will have a shadow—a resident will walk in her shadow.

I have always had very good blood pressure. The top range is supposed to be 90 to 140 and the bottom range should be 60-90. To be normal, though, it should be less than 120/80. A 140/90 reading means you have high blood pressure and need to see a doctor. When I first came in to the hospital, it had a high, unacceptable reading. It was fine when I left. It was 114/78. Your temperature should always be around 98° F. If mine gets to be 100.4, I'm supposed to be on alert, particularly if I have any of the same symptoms. The doctor told me to go on a low-fat diet, since fat and cholesterol are what cause the stones. I had thought my diet wasn't all that bad. Well, there are low-fat diets and there are low-fat diets, but I assume less is better but some fat is needed in everyone's diet.

There is good fat and bad fat and some saturated fat is okay. Fat is noted on packages by grams, and, percentage. I should still cut back on saturated fats, and also trans-fats, which are margarines and store-bought cookies, crackers, and cakes. Trans-fats raise LDL (low-density lipoprotein or bad cholesterol) and lower HDL (high-density lipoprotein or good cholesterol). The saturated fats raise total cholesterol. Too low levels of LDL can increase your chances of cancer. High total cholesterol can increase your chances of coronary artery disease.

Mathematically, you can periodically figure out your cholesterol ratio. If you know your total cholesterol (for example, 200 milligrams per deciliter or mg/dl) and if you know your HDL (for example 50 mg/dl), you have a cholesterol ratio of 4 to 1 (by dividing the 50 into the 200). You can get the ratio down even more, for example, to 3.5 to 1. You have to keep good track of facts and figures when you keep records on cholesterol and intake. Some people have to do this if they want to keep on living. Real low HDL or high LDL puts people at risk. LDL must be reduced, for one thing. Foods must be studied. If calculation isn't done on a regular basis, then, simply put, some foods must be avoided, some should be eaten, and some can, perhaps, be eaten every so often. It is not good for LDL cholesterol to collect in the arteries and jam blood flow anywhere. Again, you have to have some cholesterol and your body needs it.

Both types of lipoproteins are needed. The lipoproteins carry cholesterol through the body. They are made of fat (lipid) on the inside and proteins on the outside. High LDL builds up cholesterol in arteries, some of which carry blood to the heart. A high HDL carries cholesterol from other body areas to your liver, and your liver removes cholesterol from your body. Plaque builds up in arteries and restricts blood flow. Arteries can be blocked by plaque and by any blood clot that can form on the plaque, if the plaque breaks open. For sure, coronary arteries can get blocked. The next thing the person knows is they are having symptoms of heart trouble.

There are three types of Unsaturated Fats posted on food packages and containers—Trans Fat, Polyunsaturated Fat, and Monounsaturated Fat. Trans Fats can be found naturally in some foods but they usually come about by way of food processing (i.e. partial hydrogenation). These Fats are not good for heart health. Trans Fat and Saturated Fat tend to be solid after being at room temperature for a while so these are called solid fats. Food of Monosaturated Fat and Polysyllabic Fat tends to be liquid at room temperature. Some Omega numbering in foods can be included, like Omega 3, 6, 7, and 9. Then there are Saturated Fats, which have no essential divisions like Unsaturated Fats have. You get into chemistry and molecular biology when trying to explain these fats and some of the science is advanced, but, melting point of the fats has a lot to do with their classifying. How well the hydrocarbon chains bond is also important.

Unsaturated Fat tends to be healthier than Saturated Fat. The Monounsaturated and Polyunsaturated Fats are actually good for you as long as the diet is a balanced one. Monounsaturated fats are found in certain foods and oils. There are health benefits to eating foods with both types, and also, the Omega Fatty Acids, which is a type of Polyunsaturated Fat. It is separated from the Polyunsaturated ones because the Omegas tend to relate to fish, whereas the other Polyunsaturates are found in plant foods and oils. There are plant sources of Omega Fatty Acids, however, and this would include certain nuts. Saturated Fat comes from animals sources, like red meat, poultry, and 'whole' dairy products; 'whole' refers to full-fat, not partial fat. They raise total blood cholesterol levels and the LDL cholesterol levels and this can cause heart problems.

Nutritional aspects and food value ties in with these fat types. There is no need to eat the bad fat types, only the good fat types. Cancer can relate to eating foods having little to no food value or nutritional aspect or having negative food value or nutritional aspect. Lipidology is a nutrition science, and a field all to itself. It ought to be offered in both high school and college/university. We live in a biologic world. What it always comes back to, though, is that everyone should eat the good and better foods. Be careful about what foods are coated, mixed, and dressed with, though, and be very careful about additives. It is sometimes very difficult to know when foods are processed, and about additives and food values. Most people don't think enough about those things, and they end out eating the good with the bad and they end out with health problems. All food intake should be good, not just some food intake. Sauces, dressings, gravies, additives, enhancers, et al. have to be carefully analyzed. It can be difficult to find useful information about these 'extras' so inquiring minds must go on a hunt. I refer to them as 'extras' because you don't really need sauces, dressings, gravies, additives, enhancers, et al. They are extraneous to the actual food. They can be made to be healthy, or healthier, by choosing healthy, or healthier ingredients. All spices are okay if they are natural and not mixed with anything synthetic or unnatural. Find healthy recipes, too, because recipe choice is important.

I'm probably going to have to start up a notebook for keeping a record of best foods, in a learn-as-I-go process. When the doctor instructs 'go on a low-fat diet', you take it seriously. Acquiring knowledge about fats and foods is how one must begin a low-fat diet. If there is no actual knowledge, everything will be hit and miss. Fat tends to be high in calories, too. Even small amounts of it can add up very fast. You can often tell who the people are who eat a genuine low-fat diet because they will be thinner, yet still have that healthy look. Being thinner can sometimes be deceiving, though, because the person might not eat well at all. The person could even be some type of addict who puts money into drugs and not good food.

So many things can go wrong with a body if a person's diet isn't managed and health isn't their priority. We must all be reminded of this from time to time. It's so easy to get off on a tangent. We can all get off the healthy path—temporarily, or for some time. Going to the hospital has certainly been a powerful reminder for me to continually focus in on buying and eating only the better, healthier foods. It's a struggle sometimes, though. It's easy to forget the healthy path—when you are buying food, and when you are preparing it. You have to stay on the healthy path every day.

At first, I'd thought it was the occasional wine I drank that may have created the gallstones. The Bible says 'have a little wine for your stomach's sake', which I'm paraphrasing but the gist of it is, a little wine is good for your health. Wine actually breaks fat down. It somewhat destroys some fat, actually. Wine also kills germs and can keep some kinds of food poisoning at bay. It can even kill some parasites (though not all kinds of parasites). The doctor told me that 'no, it wasn't the wine' and that it was okay to keep drinking wine, within limits, which I was already doing. I am in control of my intake. I'd learned over the years that if I drank alcohol, at all, that I should do so very sparingly and also only drink low alcoholic content. I got to where I did not like the taste of beer so I stopped drinking beer mainly because I preferred the taste of wine, but since wine had slightly higher alcohol content, I drank less of it than I had the beer. After a time,

I would only drink a half glass of wine so the alcohol would kill any bacteria in my stomach. It can help if someone gets food poisoning bacteria, but it doesn't kill most viruses and possibly all viruses, but I wouldn't know about that—it has no effect on the coronavirus (COVID-19 and its variants).

I drink a little wine with some dinners (and only at night) but I space it out and I try to only drink wine, on average, every three to four nights, and even then, I never have all that much. I'm very strict with myself. It's either, be this strict or don't drink wine at all. I have always stayed away from hard liquor because even when I was young, wisdom told me to avoid it. I drank hard liquor in college, however, definitely on weekends. It's what college kids did and still do. When I got older, I gradually phased it out, but I did drink beer for quite a few years. There was a time, with the beer, that I wasn't so strict with myself. I wasn't exactly a beeraholic but the amount I drank wasn't wise. At some point, I turned to God and gradually learned to be very strict with myself, relative to drinking. Now, I drink no beer and very little wine, all total. Many people have their own story about such things. I always kept all drugs out, too, including prescription drugs. I have always essentially shunned drugs because they scare me. Because wine breaks down fat, I'll continue to buy at least 'some'. Again, it kills bacteria if you happen to get a little bacterial food poisoning (of a certain type). It is good to keep a little beer or wine around, for that very reason. Both are low in alcohol content.

One book I've had for some time and that I've found very useful is *Food Additives, Nutrients, and Supplements, A-to-Z, A Shopper's Guide* by Eileen Renders, N.D., but I probably need to keep it close and on my desk now in that I'm making my diet more maximally low fat. All three of what's noted in the title have their own chapter and list what's noted in these chapters alphabetically; the next three chapters cover dietary sources, supplements, and herbs, respectively. It's a very organized book. Her glossary at the back is helpful. Her information about what's safe and what's dangerous and about refined and processed foods is important to study. Some books merit studying and this is one of them. Anyone who wants or needs to modify their diet should do a study of all these subjects—both initially and along the way. Print articles off the Internet if need be, and frequent the library.

Once again, surgery to have the hiatal hernia and diaphragm area repaired was elective or optional—at least up to a point. I could keep on living by eating partial or small amounts and not whole meals. For how much longer I could do that, I did not know. I lived five years before I had it done last time, but I think that during some of that time my stomach had not been way up in my chest, just somewhat up in my chest. Once it went way up in my chest (and I actually remembered when that happened later on), the condition worsened. (I felt the movement in my chest area—an upward movement—when I was walking quickly to get somewhere. It stopped me in my tracks, but I went on, and soon forgot about it because there'd been no pain.) An Upper GI test was scheduled, just like it had been last time. Once the results go to the surgeon, he will go over the results with me and help me to decide what to do. It will be the same ole same ole.

For the test, I'll drink the barium drink. It may or may not taste like marshmallows like the previous one did, but it will go all through and settle in my digestive tract and organs so the machine can do its part and the results will reveal the placements of everything. How much and far my stomach is up in my chest and how it is placed will be revealed. I'm very curious to know the placement of my liver, and where both it and my gallbladder are positioned. (The Upper GI will reveal that, though.) Is my stomach somewhat being pressed in by my liver, I wonder. Not that it's probably going to matter about that, per se, because it's looking like I'm going to have to have my gallbladder out anyway, when he does the other, more complicated surgery.

I'm hoping the more complicated surgery can be done through the stomach and not through the ribs, but this is why I have to have the Upper GI test done— so the surgeon can know how to best proceed. I hope it tells him everything he needs to know. It may not. The last time, it was done through the ribs and it took quite some time to heal and I had some residual pains in certain places. I do not want to experience that ordeal again. Deciding to have surgery is a dilemma, regardless of someone's age, so you want to learn all you can from every professional you encounter.

The surgeon from the hospital I was just at doesn't do the through-the-ribs surgery. Not many surgeons do. I will have to transfer to another surgeon, who might end out being older (is my guess). But, the surgeon I'm with right now has a good reputation. The other doctors from the hospital told me he was an excellent surgeon and that were they me, they would want him to do the surgery. So, there were some good statements made about his work. He is young, but he's done a number of surgeries, including hiatal hernia and diaphragm repairs, but he's only done those ones from the front (i.e. through the stomach and abdomen area). I wonder exactly where the scar would end out being, and how big it would be. I have to let Father Time figure that one out for me. Father Time figures out a lot of things for me.

Between appointments with a surgeon, a patient should have time to research what they need to research, talk things over with friends and relatives, and think about all related issues. There is usually time to think more clearly about the surgery and about having it. That's if the person isn't having pain and if something isn't actually damaging the person.

Quite often, when someone goes to a hospital with an emergency, they aren't able to leave because of their particular condition and they must have surgery right there and then. Some of the doctors at the hospital I ended out at had wanted me to stay and have at least one and perhaps both of the surgeries right there and then, but I was so stressed out about the cats—both in and outside of my house—that I could not consent to that. They had no choice but to release me when my levels went down to normal range, and so they did. Therefore, I was able to buy some time, but I suspect it is all going to close in on me very soon. It could even be scheduled before Christmas. I suppose it would be a 'good' Christmas present. However, I'm not presently in pain, so I could defer the surgeries. I surely don't want to write off my gallbladder just yet, though. It's instinctive to want to keep your body parts.

The surgeon ordered the Upper GI (Gastro-Intestinal) for me, right after my first office visit with him following my hospital stay. He was concerned that someone might have to go in through the ribs, when doing the surgery, especially after he learned that that was how the previous hiatal hernia repair surgery had been done. Most of these kinds of surgeries are done through the stomach area but every so often, it's best if one is done through the ribs. The Upper GI had to be done at the hospital and obviously couldn't be done at his office. It's another one of those expensive big machine tests.

Generally, those big machines are only found at hospitals, and so MRIs, CT scans, Ultrasounds, and Upper GI tests are done at hospitals. You won't usually find these expensive machines at doctors' offices, clinics, or Urgent Care facilities. Urgent Care facilities are neighborhood clinics where you can go for health care needs and even emergencies, but they're limited as to what they can do at these clinics. They can do quite a lot at these places and will likely even have X-ray available, but the majority of them will not have these larger, more complicated machines available. You do not want to go to Urgent Care with pancreatitis, for example, because it will be a waste of precious time and they will refer you or send you to a local hospital.

The Radiology Department at the hospital was quite large. There are many machine rooms there. I got lost there trying to find my way to the main desk. I didn't have to wait long once I got there, so I wondered 'are they just not busy, just a little busy, or did I just hit it right and was lucky to get in that fast?'. Before I was put under the machine, I had to put aside everything metal. I was first given a drink of a carbonated-type of drink. It was thin in consistency and had bubbles in it. I drank it before I drank the barium drink. It cleared out some internal coating build-up so the barium mix would better coat the internal areas being filmed. I had to lie down and turn around several times as I was drinking the barium liquid, which frankly, tasted somewhat like Kaopectate®. The time I'd had the barium drink before, for the first surgery, it had tasted like marshmallow so that one had a better flavor. I had to drink two cups of the barium drink. My turning so much as the images were being taken and put on record caused everything gastro-intestinal to be coated, but I'm sure it did not have time to get into all the intestines (and anywhere else). They mainly needed to check the esophagus and stomach, but the location of intestines and bowels placement was also important.

The room I was in was called the Fluoro room because the images of the GI tract became fluorescent because of the barium and the effect of the actual machine. All these big machines are extremely scientific and technical and they're only around because of scientific evolution. They are now tied in with computers but for a while, they weren't. Earlier on, everything took longer before the results were realized by a Radiologist and medical techs.

The Radiologist had his M.D., which means he had completed med school, had done his residency, and he had completed a one-year Fellowship (in Rhode Island), in addition (which had been optional). Radiologists are paid handsomely for their work, in large part because they manage and maneuver these large machines that nobody else knows anything about. (Anyone who repairs these machines gets paid handsomely, too.) Nobody else knows how to read the screens in the Fluoro room, either (except a trained tech). There were two screens in the room and one was on top of the other. They were approximately 20" by 20" but that is just a guess. On those two screens, there was a good deal of what I call gobbledygook as a layperson because I could neither make heads nor tails out of it. There were symbols, numbers, words, etc. that I could not read or interpret. As the machine was in use, the Radiologist guided me along, with general instructions, but I wouldn't say he explained much to me. At least one of the screens was used as a monitor, while I was under the machine and the machine was producing images. One of the screens was used to show me image photos of my upper internal areas after I was removed from the lay-down part. (All these big machines have a lay-down part to them.)

The Radiologist didn't stay in the room for very long and he wasn't the one who showed me the images. He did manage to say, before he exited to go to the next patient, that "your stomach is completely above your diaphragm", which I somewhat knew before, but I hadn't realized that it was completely above my diaphragm. He passed along to the female lab tech an order to show me the films, which she did. She was, perhaps, a little too brief in what she said and I was left unable to draw at least some definitive conclusions and so I knew I had to go back to see the surgeon after he had seen the UGI images. Since he had ordered them, they were sent to him as soon as the Radiologist's report had been done. You always have to have a medical person interpret images that are produced by these machines because most people don't usually know where everything is, or what everything is. Most people don't know when something is irregular or not right.

217

While I was at the hospital Radiology Department, I had a staff member at the desk pull my other Radiology reports for me—the ones that had been done during my recent emergency stay at the hospital. There were three of them—the MRI, Ultrasound, and CT scan. I'm sure there's other reports the hospital has related to my care, but I don't have those yet. I don't even know where they all are, but any other records have to be centralized in one area, I would think. I will get them soon. There's also some at the surgeon's office. At least I was able to retrieve the Radiology ones. The three had information in them I had not known. The fourth one—the Upper GI—I'd asked to be mailed. It is a patient's right to obtain any and all of their records.

Once someone has an Upper GI done and it picks up something specific that will need surgery (like a hiatal hernia), the patient pretty much has to have the surgery relatively soon, not only because the condition warrants it, but because the Upper GI has to be done right before the surgery and if the surgery is delayed by too many days, the Upper GI will have to be done again, later on, should surgery be sought. Again, these tests are expensive. Some people who end out having hiatal hernia surgery will put it off. Some people who have gallstones will put gallbladder removal off, too. However, people can die from hiatal hernias and they can die from gallstones (from pancreatitis and also, deterioration of the gallbladder).

I'm being pushed along (to have the surgeries) like food inside a gastro-intestinal tract gets pushed along. Surgery is looking imminent. It's frightening (I have to admit) because I know what I'm in for. I wrote a whole book about it. (Well, I guess I'm still writing it.) Still, every surgery is different. Maybe some of the problems I had after the last surgery won't happen again, after this next surgery. I don't exactly know what to think or what to expect. I'm not a very happy camper right now. I hope I live through the surgery—so I can finish writing this book, for one thing.

These machines don't come cheap when a patient has to be put under one or more of them. They cost more if a patient comes in to the hospital by way of an emergency situation than if they come in by non-emergency general care. Bills that relate to having tests done that require these big machines are not affordable so insurance coverage is absolutely needed.

Under ObamaCare, more people are covered for these kinds of medical expenses. Because I'm a Senior Citizen, Medicare covers eighty percent of them but what happens is that hospitals often bill so high that Medicare will only cover a certain amount (and less than what is billed). People on Medicare always have a secondary provider, but secondary providers will not cover what they consider overbilling, either. They will only cover up to a certain amount. Sometimes, they may not cover certain parts of a bill. If something was done they don't think needed to be done, then it will be on the patient to pay that part. If something was done that was self-initiated and not doctor ordered, the patient may have to pay that part, too. Everything should be doctor ordered—that's the gist and the reality of it. Health and medical coverage should be on and for everybody—from the fetus to the very elderly (senior Senior Citizens).

My symptoms aren't yet debilitating or overly difficult to manage but anything can happen to me at any time. Different sudden occurrences could cause me pain and trauma and put me back in the hospital.

CHAPTER 11
A second diagnosis and a second surgery concern

The one surgeon I'd seen (who was a Thoracic surgeon), and who had ordered the Upper GI test, decided to, temporarily, bow out and not do my surgery. That is because my symptoms were not that bad. He only goes in through the stomach area to repair hiatal hernias. If he absolutely had to, he would go through the ribs but that would only be after he first went through the stomach and then realized he had to, also, follow up and go through the ribs. My stomach is way up, not more down, so it involves the thoracic area, which will probably call for a different kind of surgeon—a Cardio-Thoracic one, or a Thoracic one. They're more used to going in much higher and often do actual heart surgery. Most of my stomach, again, is above my diaphragm and can be pressing against the heart, and the lungs, too. Again, the Thoracic area is higher up. My stomach hardly belongs up there and it should be put back into place but I'm holding out. (I get older by the year.) So far, though, my symptoms aren't all that bad. I could go the rest of my life without them worsening. Also, it may not be what I end out dying from.

The surgeon who said 'no' to doing the surgery noted that if he did go in through the stomach area, and my stomach was attached to my esophagus (and other), up above my diaphragm, that if he tried to pull it down and there had been adherence and resistance, I could die if it would rupture or tear from being pulled down. He wouldn't be in a position to see to separate it by cutting it, to separate the two if the incision was from the front, and all this should certainly happen. If there was any scar tissue up there, which there could be from the last surgery, the stomach or the esophagus would be even more vulnerable to tearing if it was thinner in areas (and I could, then, die). So, they would then have to go in up higher, and once again, split the ribs. Two large incisions would have to be made, then—one through the stomach and then one through the ribs. Even if there were just one entry, it could still be a little dangerous, since I had the operation before and also, because I am now older. They went in through the ribs the first time for

221

essentially the same reason—i.e. because you cannot see and maneuver so well via a front incision compared with a side incision. In any event, I think I'm up the creek without a paddle and all I can do is float in the boat.

When the stomach has been up in the chest for a while, it can somewhat attach to the esophagus. It's not all that attached together but some of it could be, and therefore it would be hard to separate. There could be some adhering and bonding. It would take an eagle eye and much precision to cut the two apart, perfectly. Going in through the ribs would provide the best vantage point for surgery. At least, that is what I assume to date. Other organs might need separating, too. When there is a touching of organs, after a time there can be bonding. Separation of organs can be a part of a person's surgery. It can be a bit dodgy.

How I wish I could watch my own surgery. Doctors would be too afraid of lawsuits, though, so this could never happen. Doctors and residents watch surgery theaters of other doctors and discuss what is going on, or had been going on if they watch the filming afterwards. They watch babies being born. When I was having my second child, I recall looking up and seeing a large number of faces peering down at me as I was giving birth. I hadn't known this was going to be done. I hadn't given my consent. I was a celebrity in a medical theater. This was in the early 1980s. You'd think they would have asked me first; they were way up high, behind glass, and I was not too lucid or with it, at all, but I remember this happening.

I suppose I could have shaken my fist at the people with the peering eyes, but I somewhat didn't care because they didn't know who I was and I didn't know who they were. I wonder how much of this odd kind of voyeurism goes on in and around med schools without permission of the patients who are being observed. Do they even do it anymore? (Yes, I think they often do, for teaching purposes.) Patients should first be given the option of signing a waiver or a release to this kind of voyeurism, which is exactly what it is.

With my hernia issue, the one surgeon referred me to the other surgeon (the Thoracic one) so now I have to go see him. I called the new surgeon's office and saw to it that they got all my records from my recent hospitalization. Then, I went to the hospital where I'd had the first surgery and got those records, of which there were thirty-five pages. I compiled all the records that were compiled before my last hospital surgery and after it, as well. The surgeon who had done the surgery—the attending physician—worked out of a clinic a good distance away from the hospital (but obviously did the surgery at the hospital). There were records from two places, in other words—his clinic, and, the hospital where the surgery was to take place. Records are usually in more than one place. You have to go in, in person, to get them because you have to show an i.d. and sign for them. They were happy to get my previous surgery records because it had been done at a military hospital and they very much wanted those records, since military hospitals do things differently than civilian hospitals do. They wanted to compare and contrast and perhaps do what the military hospital tended to do and to use what the big military hospital tended to use, relative to supplies and medications. Who can blame them? Everyone wants to improve and do better. Everyone wants there to be improvements, at hospitals and in the different medical fields. I even took it upon myself to go to the local copier place and I personally did copies for them and for myself (and I paid for both sets). There were quite a few pages of the cumulative records, all in all.

Some people don't bother retrieving their own records after a surgery but once they have been written up, they are available. Patients should get whatever records they can. It's their right. Patients should go through all their records and perhaps more than once. Some things may need to be researched, too.

The surgeon I was now to see (a Thoracic surgeon) needed my records before he could decide on 'yes' or 'no' to even doing the surgery, or so his assistant told me over the phone. Yet, one worker there told me (over the phone) that they didn't do hiatal hernias through the ribs there and she seemed to be fairly certain about that. His assistant didn't let that on and tell me they do not go through the ribs and she should know so I assumed they at least might. So, here comes another doctor visit, at yet another fee, and, a visit to an office of a surgeon costs twice as much as a visit to a regular doctor does, on average. The primary care doctors cost the least for an office visit, specialist doctors are next in cost (so they're higher), but surgeons have the highest cost per office visit, on average. Their bills can be jaw-dropping, plus they don't give patients all that much time per visit. Some of them hop around from patient to patient rather quickly. If they need to spend some time talking with a patient, though, they will.

I hesitated giving this next office all my records if they didn't do the surgery from the ribs, which is what I probably need, especially since they probably already knew they didn't do that kind of surgery. Some offices want as many records as they can get, just for the education. This surgeon may have once done this kind of surgery but doesn't do it anymore. Many no longer do through-the-ribs surgery. I'm not sure anyone in town does the operation through the ribs anymore. I may have to go to a larger city for the operation. I cannot go to the hospital I previously went to, even though they still do the operation there, because I no longer have the coverage they accept and I am not able to change the coverage. There is no window of opportunity there, now, like there was before. It's possible I'll have to go to a bigger city, but, of course, I could die in the meantime. Every day that goes by, I'm concerned about something happening, but also, every day that goes by, I'm relieved more and believe I'm safe.

Something that I had thought was happening to me because of the hiatal hernia is Acid Reflux Disease. If the stomach contents are close to the esophagus and therefore the throat, a person can get heartburn. Stomach acid can, to one degree or another, irritate the esophagus. GERD is Gastro Esophageal Reflux Disease. It is a more acute condition than general heartburn, which is something that most everyone gets from time to time because of spicy and acidic foods that they eat. GERD can happen if there is any twisting and food cannot go down as fast as it should (which can also cause vomiting). There is also a part in the area that opens and closes and it can become problematic. Food can back up or remains in one spot and causes heartburn and choking. When these problems are present, a person may cough more because the acid can be irritating the throat. In my case, the sphincter that opens and closes in the lower esophagus works all right (I believe) so I do not have too much acid indigestion, at least presently I don't. I really don't even have heartburn. But this could change if anything turns or, especially, twists. The stomach is up 75-80% above the diaphragm and it could go up even more but it probably won't but who can say?

I went to see the second surgeon (since the first one bowed out and doesn't do that kind of surgery) and it seems he will be able to do the surgery but he thinks he'll have to first try the front-stomach area entrance and if he, then, finds he has to open me up at the ribs on the left side, he'll have to do that, too. So, I will possibly end out with two long cuts. It would be one surgery time, but two large openings. The possibility of this happening does not set well with me but if they can do it from the front and do everything needed and do everything right and then not have to go in through the ribs, too, then I would be very happy. I dread another through-the-ribs surgery, and I have no choice but to gamble, or do I? At this point, all I can do is delay the surgery and take life one day at a time.

If this Thoracic surgeon can pull at the stomach and esophagus and they come down all right, and everything else that is up there comes down all right, then the stomach-area entrance would have worked. If it doesn't pull down and too much cutting apart has to be done, especially since there is possible scarring from before (scarring causes a hardening of tissue), then he'll suddenly have to shift gears and go in from the ribs, as a secondary effort. The pressure would be on, to relay the very least. So, he would be working from the open front, the side, and possibly the two areas simultaneously. He would have to work feverishly to get everything separated, repaired, and closed up within the time constraints. When I would wake up, I would suffer grievously from my wounds. This I know that I know. Whether there are one or two opened-up areas, the surgery isn't going to be a picnic in the park. Of course, there will be internal wounds too, just like before. If there are two big cuts, there would be even more internal wounds. May God help the surgeon, and may God help me.

Because the Thoracic surgeon wanted to wait several weeks so my pancreas could get better (since it was so compromised because of the gallstone setting on it for so long and since that had been a fairly recent occurrence), another appointment was set for the next month. He indicated to me that by now there would have been strangulation if it was going to happen but he didn't swear by that because he couldn't. He felt my gallbladder would be all right before any scheduled surgery for the hiatal hernia. If I pass another stone and it sets anywhere, then I can either wait it out or go in to emergency; I do not think it would kill me but a lodge gallstone has killed people. You can wait out a gallstone's passing, but you can't wait too long! And so, when to have hiatal hernia surgery is a waiting game for me. It's a one-day-at-a-time waiting game. In the meantime, the Thoracic surgeon is going to go over all my tests and records and then call me if he believes anything could, more specifically, be life-threatening. Otherwise, I will be seeing him next appointment.

I gave the surgeon my records because he told me he would do the surgery—first by through the stomach and then if that looked to be too life-threatening, he would shift over and go through the ribs. I'm just wondering if he shouldn't just go through the ribs in the first place. But, I'd rather he go through the stomach so if that works out, then the gamble would have been all right. He said he'd seen one or two of my tests. I gave him a lot of records. He needs to look at all the recent tests. All my records were very educational and were loaded with information from a different hospital than he was working in so they had to have been very helpful to him on several fronts. He said "come back in four weeks". He'll have plenty of time, then, to go through all my tests and records, figure out his schedule, and figure out what he wants to do. I'll write down questions to ask him so I don't forget to ask them. This particular surgeon likes to be in command of the conversation (he probably has to be because of his work) so I hope I can squeeze in my questions. He will probably be my surgeon, or so it seems right now. It's scary to think about all the things that he'll have to do. He's an older man, and he seems like an all-right physician to me.

My main symptom right now is inability to eat normal-sized meals. I can only eat a certain amount of food at a time, and it is about one or two full, pressed down cups of most anything, if most of the previous food has already been digested. If I wait a couple of hours, then I can eat a fair amount. I end out being a grazer of sorts. I periodically snack throughout the day because that is all I can do. I don't know how good that is for my overall digestive system. I've been able to only eat smaller amounts for some time; I'd not given the matter any thought, though, which now seems strange to me so I've probably had this condition (that recurred) longer than I realize. Why hadn't I realized this sooner? I should have realized <u>much</u> sooner that the first surgery had ruptured or torn and that I had the same problem, once again.

I didn't want to have my second surgery right away. I had an approach-avoidance conflict. Plus, my symptoms weren't at all debilitating. At first they bothered me, but that was because I'd eat too much and food was then above where the stomach bended. The pressure from that was painful. Once I got used to eating only so much at every sitting, I could live with that symptom. If I lifted heavy items too often or walked too much, I'd get a pain in the upper stomach area so I stopped lifting heavy items and walking too much (for me). I could walk short distances, then rest, then walk again. For this reason I could shop and go to the grocery store because I'd 'start and stop' when I was walking. Strenuous walking was out of the question. Mainly, though, I had to stop lifting whatever was somewhat heavy, or even bulky. Walking within normal limits (for me) wasn't the problem. Lifting heavier items was. In that I had so many items in boxes—items for a book store, a museum, and for a second place (where the museum was to be)—I was up the creek without a paddle. As noted earlier, I also had problems with breathing from time to time. I believe a lung was being pressed.

I wanted to wait for as long as possible to have the operation. All along, I didn't want my gallbladder removed and the doctors at the hospital had wanted to do that. It was <u>my</u> body part. If I ever did have it out, I wanted to delay its removal for as long as possible. I wasn't even sure it was all that bad and so why remove it? Quite frankly, tests could not reveal how many gallstones were in my gallbladder or how large any of them were. Possibly no test can, at this point in time. For all I know, there were few, there, and they were small. For all I knew, I could go until death from old age without really needing my gallbladder out. Just because I passed one stone, that caused me to have pancreatitis (both the stone and the pancreatitis passed), to me, is not indicative of my having lots of stones, some of which could be on the large side. If I did, yes, go ahead and remove my precious body part (the gallbladder), but the doctors didn't even know the amount or sizes of gallstones setting in my gallbladder, and, that is key.

Several of the doctors wanted my gallbladder out. When I was hospitalized, had I not wanted to get home to take care of my indoor cats and the stray cats,

227

outside, they would have pressed me even more to have it removed, right there and then. Yes, it's a gamble on my part to hold off but they don't know, nor do I, if it is genuinely needed. Now, if it had been my second and third bout with a stuck gallstone, it would seem a little more likely that I had more than a few gallstones, but one gallstone, no, absolutely not. I won't have my gallbladder out for just that. Also, because so much is re-arranged inside of me because of the hernia, it is possible that the gallbladder is more vulnerable to pushing out gallstones, so, any that are pushed out may not, necessarily, be indicative of the number of stones that are in there. I do not lie down or sleep on my stomach anymore, just to be safe, as that is what I'd been doing right before, and then had the gallstone flare-up. Sleeping on my stomach may have had nothing to do with the gallstone incident, but in the event that it did, I will just sleep on my back or side. Besides, sleeping on my back helps my back to straighten. It's better for my back. It's curved too much as it is. I prefer sleeping on my back, and sleeping on my side just gives me an occasional break from sleeping on my back, which I do, now, most of the time.

I think it's possible to have a gallstone get stuck and press on the pancreas (and have pancreatitis) and then have the same gallstone reverse itself and temporarily rest somewhere else and then go back over to the pancreas area and rest on the area and cause a pancreatitis flare-up, again. So, it's possible you could have two pancreatitis episodes in close sequence because of only one gallstone. The second episode would happen within several days of the first one. I believe that is what happened to me, and so, I've technically only passed one gallstone. The first incident only lasted a couple of hours, then it went away. I thought it had related to digestion problems, so the incident did not plague my thoughts. Well, it did, and it was quite disturbing, but it stopped and didn't return so I forgot about it. In any event, the same thing happened a little later but that time, the pain stayed around. I truly think it was the same exact gallstone. I assume it passed through and ended out in the toilet and didn't somehow go back into my gallbladder. When I got to the hospital, the stone had passed but by then I was in a bad way. That was in early October of 2014 and since that time, I haven't passed a gallstone that I know of because it's possible to pass gallstones unknowingly. Several years have, now, gone by. Gallstones go through the bile and are dislodged by way of fecal matter so how can anyone know. Also, they aren't all that large, even the larger ones, so you can't readily see them in the bile.

The surgeon I currently have told me recently that I couldn't have my gallbladder out on its own without having the hernia surgery done. Everything is so pressed in, I assume that's why he said that. But the gallbladder isn't diseased, I don't think, and nobody knows how many gallstones there are or how many there are. How can I consent to having my gallbladder out, until I've had at least two or three definitive episodes of pancreatitis? Then I'll really know there's a problem. But, the surgeon I now have wants to remove my gallbladder at the same time that he does the somewhat complicated hiatal hernia surgery. So, I want to procrastinate on that surgery, too, i.e. wait it out and let the days roll by. I just don't want to let my gallbladder get cut out—not just yet. I know the doctors are trying to do their best for me. They live within their world. I live within mine. They usually know best, but not every single time. There's some fallibility there.

I know that some people live with gallstones for a long time. I'm not sure living long with gallstones should be recommended, necessarily—i.e. if you keep having them get stuck. I hope, one day, they'll be able to find a way to remove gallstones from the gallbladder so gallbladders don't have to be removed. If the gallbladder is removed, the liver takes over and essentially does what the gallbladder does but if there is malfunction of the liver, therein is the problem. Some people have a fatty liver that is enlarged but if they stop drinking alcohol and eating certain foods, especially sugary foods, their liver will go back to being more of a normal size. Heart problems will be less apt to occur. The gallbladder will not be so overworked. People have lived into old age with their gallbladders out, so I really do see the larger picture. I'm just not sure that my gallbladder needs to be removed just yet. I think it is better to hold on to it for as long as I can. Again, if I have another episode with a gallstone, then I'll think about it more seriously. Even just one more episode would help me along in deciding, but I've only had one episode, in so far as I know and realize. True, I ended out in the hospital, and might again, but if I possibly can, I'd like to save my gallbladder, since I don't really know its true condition nor do the doctors. So, I'll live with the gallbladder, and the hiatal hernia, for a little longer and maybe until I die.

The gallbladder is an important organ. It is right next to the liver, which is on the right side of the upper abdominal area. The gallbladder is useful because it functions as a detergent would, when breaking up fats and the like during the digestion process. The liver can become fatty and therefore enlarged by the eating of too much fructose, for one thing. Drinking alcohol will enlarge a liver, too. If you stop drinking, the liver will become reduced and will no longer be fatty. Eating sweets should be reduced, a lot. Fruits actually have to be eaten in moderation (because of fructose). Foods good to eat are broccoli, first, then cauliflower, cabbage, garlic, onions, and a few other natural foods. An apple or some applesauce a day is good, and you need a banana two or three times a week for the Potassium. Fruit is OK, but in moderation, as exists in a balanced died. <u>It is always better to take care of yourself in best ways so you can avoid surgeries</u>. Avoiding surgeries can be done and is key.

If your liver is compromised, and fatty, your gallbladder can also be because they work in tandem. One book, *Dr. Bob's Guide to Prevent Surgery*, is a must-read. Some of the foregoing information is in that book . . . and much else is. If you take good care of your body, you can, more often than not, sidestep having surgery. Being in an accident would, of course, be an exception.

I had yet another gallstone attack about six years after my first attack. This gallstone took less time to pass than the first one had but it brought with it great pain, and rendered me near-immobile. The pain, as with before, went all around my torso—back to front—and it was one of those high-up-there pains. At the time when it was happening, I would have said "10" to the pain, but I know other pains likely surpass gallstone-passing on the pain scale. The severe pain went away after about five hours.

I ended out lying on my back because doing that made me feel better. By that time, it was about four in the morning. I slept for at least six hours and when I woke up I had a high temperature and felt weak and achy. I ambled about, slowly, for a short while, trying to tidy up my home and got so tired I had to go back to bed and I ended out sleeping on and off for a couple of days until my temperature broke. It took two days for my temperature to break.

When I was in the hospital for the first gallstone incident, they put me on antibiotics to fight whatever was needed to be fought because of the gallstone disruption and possible internal damage. This time, my body had to fight what it needed to fight, on its own. I had no antibiotics. Hence, there was the raised temperature for those two days. I was tired and drained.

A friend of mine's husband also gets gallstone attacks (i.e. a stone drops out of his gallbladder and makes its way out of his body from time to time. He drops gallstones more than I do. She told me that he just 'rides them out'. (I don't think he has health insurance but I can't be sure.) He just suffers and expects they'll pass and when they do, he goes through recuperation time, at home. I guess he's had several of these attacks, and yes, they do seem like they are actual attacks. They come on suddenly, in a full throttle of pain, and there is no warning.

There are three phases to this horrid ordeal. First there is the onset of the dropped gallstone and its going through passages in the body and then, its elimination. This is the real painful part and it is traumatic. Because it is quite traumatic, it, literally, leaves you in shock mode, for a time. Both your body and your mind have to rest, for a time, after the stone has passed. The shock you feel, because of the sudden pain (and continued pain) is similar to shock felt when you get hit hard by a car. I am very aware of this kind of shock, since I had been the victim of a pick-up truck that was exceeding the speed limit and hit my car. Who knows when another gallstone attack will hit? I may never have another one, before I die. Two has been enough.

I don't know exactly how long I've had the hiatal hernia, this second time around. The last time, it was five years between when the accident that caused the hernia happened and when I had the surgery. It may have taken a while for my stomach to make its way up into my chest and go above the diaphragm. I'm sure the surgery my surgeon at the VA did held for at least ten years; then somewhere in-between that time and when I had all the tests done during my hospitalization for the pancreatitis, the diaphragm had re-torn (or even stretched) and the stomach went up above the diaphragm where it remained and caused eating and breathing problems. I could conceivably live with the hernia for some time and even indefinitely, and the same with the gallstones (however many there may be). If I live with both, I don't think my life will be shortened or that I will get cancer. I don't think I will get an ulcer, either. So far, I don't have significant throat problems—just an occasional dry cough, that could be from allergies in the air or cat dander. I also have sniffles sometimes so that would be allergies. Even though my heart and left lung are very possibly being pressed by my stomach, neither situation is going to harm me in so far as I know. I get a little short of breath, but that has not been a problem. I just go about doing things more slowly. Bending too much is a big problem, though. I can only bend a little and not over and over, like you do when you vacuum.

The diaphragm tear is around 8 cms., I believe. The diaphragm has been even more ripped since I was told it was about 8 cms., likely, and the hiatus has certainly been more stretched out. The surgery might take longer for that reason, too, in other words. That's also something that sticks in the back of my mind. I read on the Internet that some doctors don't even recommend the surgery (so you just keep on living with it), but likely that would be on a case-by-case basis. Since the hiatus is now even more stretched, it is more possible for the stomach to go back up in the chest, after any second surgery was done. Again, the surgeon I currently have on hand (who may eventually do the surgeries) does not think that anything will twist, and, that it would have twisted by now, but of course there are no guarantees about that, he added. The likelihood is not too great, though. If I end out in emergency again for a gallstone, will I even need to have the hiatal hernia surgery, then? After all, I didn't have it at the hospital the first time. The doctors would want to do surgery, but would I really need it? If anything twists, yes, for sure I'll need fast surgery. If I have another bout of pancreatitis, I really might not need surgery even then and could keep on living as I am, assuming the gallstone were to pass through like it did the last time. If they have to actually go in to remove a gallstone because it wasn't passing, that would be a different situation. Something could be different relative to the whole scenario so my resolve could change. Strangely, I have no significant heartburn yet—no significant GERD. Since I'd had that right before my first operation, which was one reason why I had the first operation.

When I do have the surgery, it may go slower than the first one did. After the last one, right afterwards, I had to sleep on my right side for a long time, so anything that had been put back in 3its normal position, shifted over a little to the right and grew there, causing me some internal asymmetry. Plus, the diaphragm and hiatus is likely more damaged now so during operating, that could also slow things down, some. Some things in the stomach and thoracic area will have to be detached by cutting (to separate everything), because they have grown or adhered together. Then they will have to be put in place, as is normal and in line with correct internal placements and positions. I hope everything will be put back into position with no complications but who is to know if it all will?

Again, the surgeon won't know until they actually get into the area and see everything, how everything might go. Sometimes surgeons have to wing some things once they cut someone open and they get inside. They study and plan out their surgeries, but there can be some unknowns and surprises they encounter. There will be a main surgeon and an assisting surgeon, assumedly, so that is comforting. Since there has been some scarring from previous cuttings and related separatings from the previous surgery, any scarring can be quite problematic when it comes to cutting and separating, a second time. Cutting through scarring can be done and is done, however. Could there end out being perforation, in other words? Yes, there could. Can a surgeon sew through scarred areas all that well? I don't know how much scarring there is inside my body, nor do any of the doctors I've seen know, but they are all very aware of whatever the dangers are, relative to cutting through scarring. At least, I assume they are.

One doctor informed me that scarring tends to be easily seen so that's encouraging. I hope it all can and will be, if I have a second surgery. I know for sure that there is scarring on the lung but scarring is at a number of other places, too. I could guess at the spots but I could be wrong. My first surgeon might know, but maybe not. It's been so many years, for one thing. And for another thing, he's no longer living here. He's long gone . . . to another state. I know there are several small scars here and there, and I assume none are very large but that is an assumption. I assume any larger scars can be seen but what about the smaller scars?

From what I understand, men's hernias are essentially the same as women's hernias. The anatomy is just different relative to the surgery (but not as much as you'd think). Muscle tone and even thickness is different, and muscle must be cut through. Also, there are different kinds of hernias and some are more severe than others. Some hernias cause more symptoms; some hernias can have more acute symptoms. So far, I have several symptoms but none are acute, except for the eating-amount one, and that one is not problematic unless my stomach gets filled past a certain point, which I don't let happen.

If the surgeon were to cut through my scar on the side (the scar that's there now from my earlier surgery), there is scar tissue there, so I have to assume he will have to do a new cut to the side of it. I surely don't want any such scar—a double scar—but I may end out with one. Perhaps he will cut right through it? The very thought makes be shudder.

Right now, my desire to not have the surgery well exceeds my desire to have it. Furthermore, as far as I know, there is no significant danger if I wait for a time. That is as concerns the hernia repair. (As for my gallbladder, it is presently a gamble.) That is where I am. It is frightening to think that I could be cut into, in front, and then during the same operation, turned over and cut into on the side and have my ribs split open. And, are my rib bones more vulnerable now so that a rib would break? For one thing, the cutting would be into several muscles, and lots of tissue. Could I physically withstand both incisions and the related surgery? Subsequently, the healing would be so difficult. I also know that doctors sometimes cut into a person more conservatively, with a smaller cut, only to ascertain that they must make the cut larger, and so they do. How large is that front cut going to be, I wonder, and will it have to be angled or increased in size? It will be dangerous even making the main incision because everything inside is presently placed in such a helter-skelter manner. Assumedly, the surgeon has to know where everything has shifted to before he does any cutting. He can't be cutting through anything that's vital.

I learned, at some point in time, that surgeons feel around and look carefully before they do any cutting. They don't always assume it's free and clear to cut somewhere. I assume surgeons realize there could be placement anomalies of anything in a body. I assume they <u>all</u> feel around before cutting anything and do so all of the time. Anything could be in an odd or unusual place or off-kilter, somewhat. In my case, several internal parts are not where they are supposed to be.

I'm no longer a 'Spring chicken' age-wise, so how I'm going to be able to withstand the surgery, I cannot say. It will be more difficult compared with the first one—this I do know and it's what the surgeon said, as well. When I had the first surgery, I was not a senior citizen. Now, I am. I assume I can live through a surgery, were there to be two long cuttings (one in back and one to the side), and also rib splitting. This is where one must really trust the surgeon and surgical team in the operating theater. Again, another surgeon will assist the primary surgeon. At this point, I have no idea who that secondary surgeon will be. So far, I've been able to avoid the endoscope, which very much scares me, especially after the death of the comedian, Joan Rivers. The endoscope went down her throat and the movement of it somehow bumped an area and caused inflammation which blocked her breathing ability; so, she stopped breathing. They didn't have emergency equipment there, either. In a nutshell, that is how she died. So, now, many people don't trust endoscopy for any purpose, and it's not just me. It has more positives about it than negatives, though, and allows some visibility of certain areas that cannot otherwise be seen or seen well.

Apparently, if a gallstone stays stuck on the pancreas (or elsewhere) and you end out in emergency, they may well use a scope to somehow, subsequently, go in to find the stone. Possibly endoscopy can aid in getting rid of the stone. You may not have much choice. I'm not yet sure exactly how this all works but if they cut into the duct, that sounds a little too chancy for me and is, really, going to end out being precision surgery. A scope merely views the area. So, how exactly is the stone removed? During the throat endoscopic process, the patient has had their throat area sprayed and has been sedated because of the endoscope, which goes in the mouth, through the stomach, and into where it needs to go. With a gallstone, the dye would go in (via the same tube) and fill several areas of the bile duct, whereupon X-rays or filming is going on to ascertain what is going on inside (relative to the discovery of the location of any gallstone found somewhere in the bile duct). Any X-rays or filming is seen on a nearby screen that shows what the endoscope is picturing as it moves along. Any actual surgery to remove a stuck gallstone is what I'd like to avoid. Perhaps this is why surgeons want to remove the whole gallbladder. They don't want to have to go in later to remove a gallstone that is stuck somewhere. If that's the case, why didn't anyone explain all that to me? They have to remove a gallstone by surgery. A kidney stone is something different. There are ways to remove a kidney stone without having surgery.

Some stones, however, actually dissolve before or even while they are lodged somewhere and have caused blockage. Or at least, they dissolve enough. Many of them just go ahead and pass on through, which can take a very short time. Usually, they are menacing and painful for a certain period of time, when they get stuck. You need to get to the emergency room right away and will need medical-removal intervention. In my case, when I went to the hospital, I was still in pain even though the gallstone had passed, and so I thought the problem (whatever it was) was still going on. The emergency-room physician at the second hospital told me what the problem was and that it had passed through. I don't recall how they realized it had passed, before the Ultrasound, but the emergency room physician seemed to know. If it had passed, why did I even need an Ultrasound, I now wonder? I had an MRI and CT scan because of my hiatal hernia (which I'd mentioned to them to look for), but the MRI also picked up on my gallbladder issue. I guess they needed to see the condition of my gallbladder and also any ducting where a stone could have lodged, if they were able to see it. They likely wanted to see that everything seemed intact and that nothing had not been damaged. I continued to be in pain after the stone had dislodged because my gallbladder and pancreas had been so compromised. There was inflammation, and probably some infection. My temperature was up. The CT scan was done so the anatomy of all my internal organs could be looked at. I had all these tests but recently learned that from a third to a half of the people who have a gallstone episode never have another one so I wonder, am I going to be one of those lucky people? I sure hope so. This is something that should be confirmed by a doctor, though, because gallstone episodes are dangerous. Tests are needed, in all cases.

Gallstones are formed by bile crystals that form in the gallbladder. The gallbladder can become diseased—cholelithiasis. Any gallstone blockage causes irritation and pain, inflammation, and probably infection. That is especially why hospitalization and medical treatment is needed. The stone travels down the cystic duct to the bile duct, where it can get stuck. When stones move around a lot, in the gallbladder, that can scar the gallbladder. After all, they are hardened stones. Bile backs up into both the liver and the gallbladder. This is why infection can develop but it can also happen when stones move back and forth because stones are harsh on the inner lining of the gallbladder and on any duct area, if they are scraping any inner lining whatsoever. No one stone is alike, though; they're kind of like snowflakes in their individuality.

Dietary fats and cholesterol relate to stone formation, which is why everyone should eat well early on, even when a child. Veggies surely help. More females get gallstones than males do—two times as many do. Women who tend to have some extra weight on them and who are middle-age or older are the most stricken. Eating more vegetables lowers one's chances of getting gallstones but you have to start doing that when you're younger. Being overweight ties in with added cholesterol. Certain kinds of fat have to be avoided. The more formed, and the longer a gallstone has been being formed, then the less apt the gallstone is to dissolve. It is really an increase in triglycerides that is the culprit, relative to the increasing number of gallstones.

Removing the whole gallbladder with the gallstones is sometimes the solution. A laparoscope goes into the belly area after a small incision is made. You'd think by now they could go in and somehow remove the gallstones without removing the gallbladder. So often, the gallbladder is still in generally good shape. With gallbladder surgery, the gallbladder is cut, removed (pulled out), and the connection, there, is clamped. What is going on is seen on a nearby screen or monitor. Not everyone should have a laparoscopic cholecystectomy, however, because complications could result. The doctor assesses the overall situation and internal placement of everything and decides what to do. Some are not so 'conservative' about removing gallbladders, though. The laparoscope has a type of video camera attached to it. During this procedure, the doctor has to pay particular attention to all internal organs, including the liver. The gallbladder is actually dissected from the liver. The cystic artery has to be divided. No damage, at all, can come to the liver because the liver will do what the removed gallbladder was doing so without the gallbladder, if the liver is damaged, there would be a big problem. Anyone who has their gallbladder removed should not be drinking much alcohol, because excessive alcohol can play havoc on a liver.

If there are large stones and a gallbladder is diseased, a general surgical procedure (an open cholecystectomy) needs to be done and the incision will be about six inches long. If a stone is still in the bile ducts, additional surgery will need to be done to remove it. This can end out being a problematic surgery, at the time and after close-up. Right after a bile-duct stone-removal surgery, a drain has to be inserted so bile can drain until all is safe in the system. A liquid substance can be injected through the drain, too, so X-ray results will show up during and after the surgery. Please do not hold me to all this medical knowledge, though, because it was second-hand learned and I am not a doctor (though I believe, now, that I could have been some kind of a doctor, in that there are many kinds of specialist). You have to be a very serious person to be a doctor. I think of the doctor with autism and savant syndrome, Dr. Shawn Murphy, in the TV series, *The Good Doctor*, and he is about as serious as they come (except for when he goes off in a flashy car on a road trip with his female neighbor). Over the course of years, there have been many medical TV series, and doctors on those shows are the more serious individuals, relative to TV series in general. Some of the detectives on TV series have been pretty serious, too, but the doctors on medical TV series have the responsibility of keeping people alive, for as long they can.

In *The Good Doctor*, the doctors live and breathe whatever is medical. You see where they all constantly pool ideas and diagnoses. It's been said that the medical and hospital goings-on seen on TV is not at all like real life and what really goes on in the medical world and in hospitals but I have to note that the medical knowledge and expertise seen and discussed on that TV series surely does seem right on and more than interesting. The somewhat long British TV series,

Doc Martin, with Martin Clunes also has some excellent and accurate medical knowledge on it. They consult with medical people. Some of the surgeries they end out doing in *The Good Doctor* (an American TV series) seem somewhat unusual, at times, and the surgeries are varied because the conditions and diagnoses are varied. Such shows aren't always realistic. Surgeons surely must upshift and downshift all the time. These kinds of TV series give people a glimpse of what the medical world is like and what doctors have to go through. Each TV series is a little different than the other ones are. These medical TV series have been going on since the 1970s especially. They somewhat replaced Westerns.

A process known as ERCP, or endoscopic retrograde cholangiopancreatoscopy, is what is done to remove a stone without surgery. An endoscope goes into the mouth and is run all the way through to the biliary system, including through the duodenum.

Gallstones can only be removed by surgery, shock-wave fragmenting, and chemical and dissolution bombardment. There is an oral bile acid litholysis—a medication that can help dissolve small stones having a predominant cholesterol make-up. Around 75% of the time, with people who receive this treatment, there's success. There is also shock-wave lithotripsy—waves go through and break up a stone. Such treatments have to be repeated before the stones are fragmented and cleared. Only if there aren't many stones should this be done. Effects can cause pancreatitis and cholecystitis, though, that has to be medically treated. The method is known as extracorporeal shock-wave lithotripsy and there are several types of lithotripters. There can be some damage done with this method so options and possible after-problems have to be learned and discussed with a doctor. But, you will be in pain at the time and in need of urgent care.

MTBE, or methyl tertiary-butyl ether can be used to dissolve and disrupt a gallstone. It is a chemical solvent. Direct chemical infusions have an almost 100% success rate and the infusions can go on for around five to ten hours. Even if a stone or stones are removed, there can be residual stones in the system, and, there may have been bile duct damage due to stone abrasiveness. Regarding gallbladder removal, with laparoscopic cholecystectomy, there is less apt to be residual healing problems, compared with the open cholecystectomy surgery.

With the former, the patient can go right home afterwards, but with the latter, there will be about a five-day stay at the hospital.

With me, assuming the hiatal hernia surgery and the open cholecystectomy surgery are done at the same time, the hospital stay would be almost a week, probably; it could just be five days, though. Tests are always done before a patient is released and the release is predicated on the test results. Most gallbladders (90% of them) are removed by the laparoscopy method, but mine will likely be done at the same time I'm opened up for the hiatal hernia surgery, if I end out having that surgery.

As I think about pancreatitis occurring because a gallstone gets stuck in a very tight spot inside of the bile duct, what stands out most is the overall pain it generates. The pain is not in one spot, it's all over, like labor pains are (except that this pain stays, whereas labor comes in and out—but will escalate). After-surgery pain stays, too. It is chronic, in other words, until it subsides enough to not be all that painful. It becomes a discomfort, for a time, and then it generally, but slowly, fades out. I wrote a poem earlier in the book that was about pain, and I have this other one, now, to insert. It is a personalized poem (which I rarely write), but it is for any and all people, really. This one is blank verse or non-rhyming. The poem relates to any and all pain that anyone can be experiencing.

Feeling Real Pain

The pain is back–how it comes and goes.
I never know when it will visit.
I climb up the wall, and have to stop,
And can go nowhere when pain's on me.
I cannot think well when the pain hits;
All I can do is feel intense pain.
I want, so much, for it to go away,
But it grips me and makes me its slave.
Some invisible stairs, I must climb
To escape the pain when it's present.
The pain may not leave, or may not end;

Pain will stay just as long as it wants.

I can't kick it out and say "be gone".

Right now I hurt and need some relief.

I'm flushed and weak and I cannot move.

I wish I could take a painkiller.

If I could go to a warm climate,

The sun's rays would feel good on my skin.

Oh I did not want this pain again.

Is my body now hurt from these bouts?

All I can do is wait this one out.

I can't sleep 'til the pain goes away.

Would it help to hear nice music?

Would it help if I watched a good film?

Bad pain can affect the whole body;

It's mental stress and also anguish.

It's something you must try to get through.

You want pain to cease and to be gone.

It will help to find some distraction

When the pain starts to be excessive,

But I still feel pain when it is there;

The pain has too strong a hold on me.

If I sit up, walk, or I lay down,

It's the same–I shake and I feel hot.

God please come and take this pain away

So it becomes something that is past.

When the pain leaves, you are so relieved,

And you then hope to keep it at bay.

You don't ever want it to return.

The ordeal has left you so crumpled.

You may have to give up hopes and dreams

If pain stays around all of the time.

Even though you have set certain goals

You might have to change some of your plans.
If you tell people about your pain,
Most of them cannot relate to it.
They cannot completely understand.
You have to weather the storm alone.
This visiting pain just now got bad,
But I took some pain medication,
So I do not now feel too much pain–
When I move about, I can be free.
Light is glistening on a large lake.
It's nice and warm, and bright and sunny.
For now pain's gone and I am relieved.
How much longer am I going to live?
I could live longer than I expect.
I am thankful for every day.
My senses are tuned into my world.
I want to live as long as I can.

One thing that is a bit psychologically distressing about the stomach being so high up is that part of my bowel is now up somewhat high and not where it should be (which is one of a number of reasons why a surgeon will have to very carefully look and feel around before cutting into my body. Fortunately, my regulation is good, though, and so far I have no problem with urinating or defecating. I can eat anything, too, and again, stomach acid amount seems to be in check. If and when the stomach acid gets up high and causes day-to-day problems that cause heartburn or GERD, that is when I'll have to have the surgery. I suspect that that day could come.

A lot of people get ordinary heartburn from time to time because of foods they eat. Heartburn is easily treatable with certain over-the-counter medicines and with the choosing of certain foods to eat, and to not eat. Having GERD or Gastro Esophageal Reflux Disease is more severe. Acid-reflux happens more frequently and more on a regular basis. It can be continual and will require medical attention.

GERD can interfere with a person's day-to-day activities. There can be a number of reasons why a person has GERD; it can have different causes and become quite distressing and affect eating habits. Food can go up too high in the esophagus and there can be a burning feeling. Having milk or milky drinks helps coat the lining and relieve the burning or irritation. Milk of Magnesia® helps. People who have GERD may need surgery, of some type. Obviously, people with hiatal hernias are prone to getting heartburn and even GERD because the stomach is pressed up higher and closer up to the throat, but it depends on how the esophagus lays and lines up as to whether or not acid goes upward and doesn't stay in the stomach because the food content and hydrochloric acid gets pressed upward. Sometimes pregnant women get Acid Reflux because of the squeezing upward of the stomach, esophagus, and stomach contents. Also, hormones at the time can cause digestion slowdown.

With people who have GERD, stomach and esophageal contents are usually up higher, compared with people who simply get occasional heartburn because of acidic foods. There is a sphincter a little lower in the esophagus that may be affected, too, and it may not open enough or at all. The sphincter valve may not open well or at all and if certain foods have been eaten, there can be acid accumulation. Any kind of chocolate is but one of the foods that should be avoided. Sometimes a person has a problem with digestion and food stays in the stomach too long. This can be GERD, too. Sometimes food gets pushed back up the esophagus, causing irritation and this can be GERD. Irritation can be periodic, or chronic. If it is chronic, see a physician, for sure. If it is periodic and you change to milder foods and it continues, see a physician, but it would be more advisable to go see a physician in the first place. There can be more than one reason why GERD is occurring.

With GERD, you have to avoid anything vinegary because it is so acidy. You have to read what the ingredients are before you even buy a food product. With some food products, you really cannot taste the vinegar. Where vinegar is listed in with the group of ingredients, is important; if it is early in the listing, this obviously means there is quite a lot of vinegar in the food. Absolutely, mustard should be avoided, even the Dijon type. It is loaded with vinegar. Pickles and pickle relish are stay-away-froms, too, as is horseradish and certain salad dressings, sauces (including ketchup), and even marinades. Pizza sauce can be a problem for most who tend to get heartburn. Vinegar acts as a preservative as well as creating a certain taste (mainly when it is mixed in with other ingredients, including spices). Vinegar is an acid-acetic acid. There are different kinds of vinegar—twenty or so—around the world.

My surgeon mentioned possibly doing a Wrap over my stomach during my surgery (if I were to ever have it). They have done these wraps for some time. They were not done when I had the first surgery but my surgeon never mentioned them to me, nor was one done, even though I'd had 'some' acid indigestion but perhaps not actual GERD. After my first surgery, I did not have heartburn or acid indigestion, at all, and certainly not GERD. The Wrap (that sometimes gets done) goes around the esophagus so GERD will be less apt to happen. The wrapping together (and sewing) is supposed to strengthen the valve (between the stomach and esophagus). One has to wonder what the valve looks like, and how it could possibly be strengthened. I would have to totally understand and be able to visualize the Esophagus Wrap before I consented to one being done, and even then, I'd probably think twice about it, because there is sewing involved and also, they may not last. The procedure is done so there would be little to no acid reflux after the surgery, but, I don't have that now, and I didn't have it after my previous hiatal hernia surgery. So, why would I want or need a Wrap—or fundoplication surgery is what it is more formally called. I think the surgeon is going to have plenty to do with just the hiatal hernia surgery. I want 'that' to be a wrap. I don't think I want this other Wrap.

Again, I don't now have GERD, and, there could be too many risks tied in with this Wrap—some pretty big risks, even. Who knows how long it will last, too. Like hiatal-hernia surgeries, the wraps can 'give way'. GERD is a nuisance but it isn't usually dangerous to have it as long as it is well managed. Certain problems can come about after having the fundoplication and if it fails the first time, the second fundoplication is harder to do, more risky, and may also come apart. Because sewing is involved, it can rip out and everything can come apart. Who wants that? Of course, it could last a long time, too. The particular problems that can result if there are problems with the fundoplication can be quite severe. Still, certain doctors do these wraps periodically and swear by them, and really, there have to be plusses and positives to having this done. They've probably improved on these wraps, over the years.

The surgeon here has determined that my symptoms, so far, are not that bad and he has not pressed for the hiatal-hernia and gallbladder surgery but he would were symptoms, pain, and inconvenience to reach a certain point. I'm fortunate to not have the heartburn or GERD yet, like I'd had right before the first surgery. I'm not sure why I have no heartburn or GERD, quite frankly. If I did have heartburn or GERD, I'd be taking Nexium®, Prevacid®, Aciphex®, Pepcid®, GasX®, or Rolaids® and I would eat nothing tomatoey or greasy or drink anything with caffeine. I'd avoid certain spices. I should have heartburn or GERD, but I don't. My stomach is above my diaphragm so I should very definitely have heartburn or GERD. I don't know why I don't. Is the esophageal sphincter that holds down the acid being damaged, I wonder, because of my condition? I sure hope not. Why did I have acid reflux the first time and do not have it this time (so far)? Knock on wood. It could be the way everything is set and also because I only eat partial meals.

I used to think that surgery via the stomach was easier than surgery through the ribs but it may not be; it all depends and would be case by case in all probability. I read somewhere that a Chiropractor can push stomachs back down into place if there are hiatal hernias; if the stomach goes back up (and it may happen again, after a time), the Chiropractor simply pushes it back down. I imagine this remedy could be applicable to only certain cases. I doubt it would apply to my case, and wouldn't you need an anesthetic? I suspect that doctors would most likely disapprove of this, especially surgeons. I don't imagine everything would slide down and move easily, in every case. If the hiatal hernia has been there for a while, would everything detach? It probably wouldn't, not is there had been bonding and adherence. Chiropractic care is generally not compatible with Medicare and so many older people rule it out as a remedy path because of 'no coverage'.

With hernias, everything internal is still there, and everything is still functioning; everything is just in different places and positions. Supposedly, there are even some massage therapists who can push a stomach back down below the diaphragm. They somehow bring the stomach down by hand. I do not wish to try either a Chiropractor or a massage therapist because my case is too complicated. I wish I could go that route, but wisdom tells me I can't, and shouldn't. The diaphragm tear will always be there and therein is the problem. It has to be repaired. Any surgical repair will hopefully last at least ten years and maybe longer, if I am very careful, and if I have the surgery.

Someone said just drink a really large glass of water and the stomach might go back down, which seems absurd. If I did that, I would be in such pain, and I doubt the stomach would move just because it was so filled up. It would be more apt to move with manual manipulation, than with an over-fill of water. There are even exercises for people who have hiatal hernias. I don't yet know if any of them work, nor why anyone would even do them. One of them is that you first lay down on your back with knees bent and feet flat on the floor, as with your shoulders. You lift your back and buttocks off the floor and gently lower yourself back down and do this around ten times each time, from time to time. I suppose some of the stomach could be moved, somewhat, but it's doubtful that anything would be major or permanent. I'm not sure you could get much relief from this exercise. Because of my gallbladder issue, I don't wish to do any exercise other than walking. I wouldn't want to push out any stones. Again, I won't even sleep on my stomach, since that is what I'd been doing right before I had my major bout with a gallstone that went wayward—a rogue gallstone. Sadly, I know that once the gallbladder gets filled up with enough of them, they're going to start coming out. It can be a waiting game. Then again, I may never have another bout with a gallstone and pancreatitis.

Hiatal hernias are deceptive when it comes to diagnosing. They imitate other disorders such as heart attacks, ulcers, asthma, and acidy stomachs. Frankly, it can be years before a hiatal hernia is even diagnosed. This delay is quite typical and common. Symptoms of hiatal hernias can be hoarseness and coughing (it's a dry cough), acid indigestion, breathing problems, and pressure below the ribs. (There are others because there are different kinds of hernia.) Such symptoms can point to many disorders or problems and doctors have often diagnosed incorrectly and that is a fact. I ran into this myself, more than once—until the chest X-ray was done. A chest X-ray must be done, always.

Another symptom of hiatal hernias is that one arm and shoulder can tingle or feel like it's somewhat burning. Quite a few people end out with this symptom, actually. I never did the first time; I did the second time but only because I'd allowed one of my cats to rest on top of my left arm while I was writing with my right hand. My desk area is large enough for one, even two cats, to rest next to me. This kitty laid down on my lower arm and pulled hard on my upper arm without me realizing it and the next thing I knew I had tingling arm and shoulder syndrome because of nerve pulling and possible damage (but it got better). It is the left arm that tingles or burns when you have a hernia (but not with all people). It took a long time for the tingling to cease, months in fact, but right after it started up, I assumed it was due to the hiatal hernia (because I'd seen that symptom noted on the Internet). The symptom so distressed me that I made an appointment with the doctor and was near-ready to have the surgery. When it gradually dawned on me that the tingling was in process of ceasing, I connected the dots and realized that one of my cats had caused the nerve damage. He was a somewhat heavy cat, and he rested and slept on my arm for a long time, and more than once (which, he doesn't any more). I like to be close to my cats so I didn't mind or really think much about it, since I was concentrating on my writing and I write with my right hand. I'd had no idea he was pressing or pulling on and messing up a nerve. (Something had been crimped or pulled because of his weight, I believe.) So, I cancelled that appointment and made one for later on. In retrospect, it's quite funny. I was truly panicked and upset at the time, though.

Arm and shoulder tingling is a symptom of a heart attack, so I was quite upset when this occurred because I thought, at first, that I was about to have a heart attack. Then I read that it could be a symptom of a hiatal hernia. Just why it crops up in relation to a hiatal hernia would best be explained by a physician because it's beyond common-sense assuming. Could it have something to do with the stomach pressing up against the heart? I just don't know that answer.

Needless to note, now none of my kitties are allowed to rest on my left arm while I am writing at my desk. They get whisked away if they try. Two of my kitties are on my desk right now and so writing space is a little meager. My cats will be with me at home after I have this next surgery (if I have it and I likely won't unless it all turns into an emergency), but they won't be in my bedroom, not for the first several weeks while I am healing. Having the second surgery could be inevitable. I suspect that something could worsen or even suddenly happen, to put me in the hospital. I'm going to hold off for as long as I can, possibly for all time if I have my way. Absolutely, I don't want them to take my gallbladder unless I'm shown why on a screen and everything I see on the screen appears valid and makes sense. The doctors at the hospital I was at failed to prove to me that having my gallbladder removed was at all, or even a little necessary. It may well be the case, but they did not show me anything clear and evident to go by. I surely never saw that on any screen. The screen was so unclear. You couldn't even tell what anything was. I saw nothing that was convincing and obvious. I got no adequate educational analysis.

In any event, I can't help but wonder if living with my hernia and gallbladder situations are going to shorten my life? My biggest concern is that the surgeon who I'm now working with will be gone when I really need to come in for surgery. He retires in five years. He knows my case, inside and out. I trust his expertise, but he may not want to do it, as previously noted. If I end out in emergency, he will answer the call and come and do the surgery, or, I can elect to set it up for him to do the surgery at any time prior to an emergency, but he will be wanting to remove my gallbladder, too, and he could possibly end out doing two large entrance incisions, and not just one. Can I find a surgeon who will just go through the ribs (I'll have that double scar), and do I even want to do that? Such a surgeon may not be around, truly. Rarely do they go through the ribs at civilian hospitals, at least initially. I'm sure all hospitals have rib-splitter apparatus, however. You find rib-entrance surgeries more at Military hospitals because so many Military men get hiatal hernias from blasts, explosions, collisions, and accidents.

I am now under Medicare, so a Military hospital is out. (You cannot have it both ways.) Most civilian doctors go through the stomach when it comes to hiatal hernia surgeries. And again, I worry about such things as rib breakage (should they end out having to, also, go through the ribs), my Serratus anterior muscle being messed up again and messed up perhaps even worse than the last time, and that there will have to be a second scar right next to where that first scar is. Again, there can be problems if they try to do stitches over already scarred spots. I also worry about the cost to the government, relative to Medicare, and regardless of how I proceed. I don't like to be a burden to the government. The surgery will be quite expensive. My hospital stay alone, when I went in for emergency care because of pancreatitis and all the diagnosing, cost around what my first surgery cost, all total, and there was no surgery during that hospital stay at the time—just tests and nurses' help and doctor visits...and all the tubes and the room, etc.

I've not really been fighting having surgery, per se. I've been looking into it, over time, and looking into it very seriously. It has taken time—by having some doctors' appointments, and by checking things on the Internet. When I saw my doctor recently (my prospective surgeon), he seemed to be 'so' in a hurry and even impatient. He's got so much on his plate and he must have waves of stress always hitting him. He didn't answer many questions and he gave me but ten minutes, maybe fifteen, and during that time he left to make a phone call and to do something else; then he returned. I believe he was pre-occupied with something else—perhaps an emergency, since he gets called in to do emergency surgeries all the time. He probably does more surgeries than others do because he is older and has an established reputation and has more patients than other surgeons have. I could be wrong, but he has been a surgeon for a good many years. There has to be more than meets the eye in the world of surgeons.

An appointment with a surgeon costs around $200, even if it's just a quarter of an hour. The life of any surgeon must be busy, tense, pressurizing, and sad, actually, because some people he meets have terrible medical problems. Many die. They must also be and stay on top of everything and this can be very taxing. Also, many employed people are dependent on him—office staff, nurses, medical suppliers, et al.

Since the heart is in the thoracic or chest area, my surgeon is a specialist about heart matters. I know he has to be because he does heart surgeries. He also comes across cancer a great deal, and may or may not refer cancer patients to other professionals. Oncology is a separate field. My other surgeon (who did the first surgery), was in the Air Force, and he did the same work. I just hadn't realized how extensive his work was, at the time. He was a nice Mormon man—a very kind professional—but he's now in Caldwell, Idaho (in a Mormon community). He worked with me very well, as his patient. I believe he did the best he could for me, relative to the operation. It's possible I could arrange for him to do the second surgery. I'd have to fly in, and then fly back after having the surgery. Pretty soon, though, these doctors are going to retire.

The Air Force surgeon chose to go through my ribs in the first place so he would be able to work higher up, better. He knew he could go through the stomach but chose not to (even though I'd implored him to because it would have been easier on me). He very possibly made that decision because there'd been adherence of my internal tubes and organs in places where they shouldn't be (in other words, up higher). If by going through the stomach area the stomach itself could not be pulled down from the heart and lung area because of adherence, then he would have also had to have gone through the ribs, immediately afterwards, and what a mess that would have been, I can well imagine. I would have been cut open in two places. Ouch.

I'm not so sure that going through the stomach will enable the current surgeon to work higher up, should he need to. A surgeon at the hospital was the one who told me that, from a stomach-area incision, the stomach (et. al.) might not come down when being pulled down. It may be stuck up there and that is why rib entry might be best in the first place. I'd somewhat already known that, but he brought it all home to me, as being a reality. The surgeon may not be able to see where to cut to separate anything up higher by going through the stomach area. But, if the stomach were able to be pulled down, the gamble of stomach entry would pay off and be so much better.

Something else that added fuel to the fire of my not wanting to have surgery right away is that I fell flat and really hard again, on my previous surgery site, so that, even though it had been over ten years since the first fall, the area was still very tender and vulnerable to being damaged—more damaged than had I fallen on the ribs on the other side, in other words. The fall left me very sore in a few places—where the cartilage held the Serritas anterior muscle, along the side (probably the area where the ribs had been split but had come together and also where the scar was), and a sole spot on the side, which may relate to damaged cartilage.

The acute-pain areas were that one side spot and the spot in front, where cartilage held that front muscle. There was general pain all over and along where the scar was, but there were the two main points of acute pain. It took some time for the pain and discomfort to go away.

When I tried to lie down to rest or sleep, those areas were so painful I could only move slower than a turtle to position myself. I could just barely lie on my back, but for sure not on my left side—no way. I could easily be on my right side but even then, any movement at all was with some pain. The first night after my fall, I could not sleep. The whole side area was considerably painful and very swollen. I was stressed, psychologically, and my temperature was up.

The accident happened on a Sunday—Mother's Day—on a restaurant walkway having concrete sections. I tripped where there was a crack, but the crack was not very raised up. I must have caught it just right. I'd been walking in full gait when down I went. As I'd turned to the side somewhat, to speak with my son, it was down on that side that I went. I was extremely dazed when it happened. You somewhat have brain blank when you fall and hurt yourself like that, or are in an accident. You're in some degree of shock. If I had just fallen straight on, it would have been one thing, but I fell full force on my previous surgery site and that was extremely distressing. My son and a man walking by helped me up.

I went in and had a meal with my son but only felt some pain, since I was sitting and hardly mobile and since it had just happened. Also, I had wine with my meal. I felt it more when we were walking out of the restaurant to the car and getting into the car, and I felt it that night. The whole area was swelling up and sore areas were revealing themselves. What was worse was that it was near impossible to lie down because of the pain. It was even hard laying down on my right side; that was about all I could do. I could tell that the particular pain I was having was not going to heal up very fast. It resembled the pain I was having after my previous surgery, which I thought was strange but perhaps not that strange (i.e. that the pain was as much as it was).

The next morning—a Monday—I called to make a doctor's appointment because I was concerned I'd broken one or more ribs. Also, I wanted a prescription for painkillers, but I did not want strong ones, just pain reducers, really. Stronger drugs tend to scare me. I had some right after my surgery (and during it), but I coped afterwards with very few painkillers for a short amount of time. I believe in antibiotics more than I believe in painkillers. Rather, there are times you absolutely have to have antibiotics. There are times when you should have painkillers, too, but many times you can opt out and take few to none or take something less strong to get through any pain and go through a time of healing.

Too many painkillers are being prescribed these days, and doctors are slowing down on prescribing painkillers. Celebrities have died from prescription medicine and so have many others. The opioid crisis has hit and doctors are having to deal with that. As long as they don't start under-prescribing pain medication, everyone will be fine. Surgery patients will always need pain medication for a while after they've had surgery. I only needed pain medication for a short time. Something strong is needed when you first get home. You never need to take more than the doctor prescribes but some people think they need to take more than they should, and take the prescribed med more frequently than they're supposed to. This is how some people get addicted.

Surgery patients are going to have to cope with some pain but if they move around slowly, do not stretch or twist, and are careful about all their movements and about where they are walking, they'll be fine. Some people talk themselves into needing more pain medication than they really need. You only need just enough and no more than that. Pain will pass. It gradually subsides. Slow down on any and all pain medications, as it does. Keep yourself from becoming drug dependent. When you sleep and lay down, you might need a painkiller. You move around when you sleep. After a time, after a surgery, some people will take only a half a pill or half the dosage. I wouldn't let myself stay on painkillers too very long. You can say no to yourself. Use painkillers very sparingly and only as needed.

I got my prescription filled and only took a half a one a couple of times. Then, I checked the Internet and found out that the Tylenol 3 with codeine had caffeine in it, so I didn't take any more. I was still in pain, though, especially when I'd go to lie down, actually lay down, and then go to get up. Ouch. Ouch. Ouch. That whole area would be strained and again, I could only move very slowly. Once in position for sleeping, I did not get up unless I absolutely had to.

It hurt greatly if I coughed or sneezed; it hurt a little less when I'd take a deep breath but it would still hurt. I had to wear a looser bra than usual and had to push the band on the left side way up. Nothing could touch that very sore site. I was surprised it hurt as much as it did, when muscles got strained and especially when I would lie down. For many nights, I had interrupted sleep, which meant that I was somewhat tired during the day.

Also, I noticed my temperature would rise a little when I exerted myself and felt a little pain. It would stay high for a while, and go down after a time; then, when I'd move around and exert myself, it would go back up. It would only go up a little and I found this trend and phenomenon strange, never having had experienced it before. I'd never heard of this phenomenon or heard anyone ever talk about it happening to them.

From this experience, I have to conclude that an increase in actual temperature can relate to physical stress and exertion and to pain, itself. When pain begins, your temperature goes up. The temperature doesn't relate to a virus or bacterial illness, it relates to stress that comes on from feeling pain. The temperature increase tends to be slight but if you are focused in on it happening, you will notice it, as a cause-and-effect pattern. I really don't know why I haven't heard of this pain/temperature increase syndrome nor do I know why, specifically, it happens, but I know it's real. My own temperature would go up, slightly, and be noticeable but not significantly noticeable whenever I would move around or lie down and any pain would be generated. Someone in the medical field should do some research on this. The rise in temperature didn't make me feel too badly. It triggered the thought that I should slow down and be more restful, even if just sitting somewhat still and working at my desk. This, I'd planned to do anyway, all summer long, since I needed to read through some of my writings needing final editing.

I know the pain will gradually subside and then go away. I'm just not sure at what rate or when. My pain is nothing compared to the pain of many people, like quite a few disabled veterans have had to experience, for example. Some vets healing from some severe damage don't like taking painkillers, either, unless they are absolutely needed and unless the dose is as low as possible. In truth, though, some veterans really need to have painkillers. They're in so much pain. I don't really like writing about my pain but I have to, to move this surgery book along. What I learned from the fall and its related pain is that I now know I do not wish to ever be opened up through the ribs again because that area has never really completely healed (because it had been so damaged from the cutting, rib splitting, and the pulling and stretching of cartilage). My prospective surgeon now knows that I may not consent to a through-the-ribs surgery, which wasn't the way he wanted to do it anyway. He'd wanted to go through the stomach area, do what could be done, and then, if necessary, also go through the ribs. But now, I may only consent to part one, not part two—no matter what. If I were to suddenly need to have the surgery, my whole left-side area is too compromised right now, anyway. Even when it generally heals (and I'm guessing it will take two or three months), I still do not want it to ever be cut through there again. The surgery is on the back burner for now. Just how long it will be, I cannot know and I'd like to avoid having it indefinitely.

My first surgeon affirmed so strongly that the stitches would hold and he made me feel invincible. Based on that affirmation, I still may have lifted too many heavy items, including boxes. I may have bent, twisted, and turned too much. I may have done more than I should have. Someone said—much later—that diaphragm/hernia operations don't always hold. By the time I heard that, I'd perhaps lived too 'normally' and had over-exerted myself too often. I'd obviously thought I was invincible.

When I had my first surgery, I had no concerns about 'medical mistakes'. There have been whole television documentaries about these, and they are scary. Infection problems were on the list, some of which were caused by instruments not being sterilized enough, but infection can come about many ways. You can also get staph infection in hospitals. On rare occasion, something can be left in a body after a surgical procedure. A surgical sponge, a clamp or retractor, for example, have actually been left in the body, after the surgery close-up. When there is a surgery, someone is supposed to keep count of everything that goes in and comes out. But, doctors are supposed to pay attention to these things, too.

Excessive radiation has sometimes accidentally occurred—sometimes because of arithmetic errors and sometimes because of not running a machine properly. Patients can go from being bald to getting cancer, when there's excessive radiation. Sometimes there's been patient mix-up because a name is similar. Something gets done on a patient that shouldn't have been done. A wrong body part has even been removed. The wrong patient has been treated, on occasion. Sometimes the wrong band gets put on a patient and a wrong name or barcode gets read. We have all heard about baby mix-ups and switches (not to forget to note the occasional baby snatching that happens at hospitals). Typists and nurses cannot be too careful. Transfusion mix-ups or errors have also occurred and diseased blood or the wrong kind of blood has been put into a body. Sometimes, body parts transplants have been problematic to begin with. They've been mixed up with other ones that had some kind of problem. You wonder, sometimes, if there is enough double-checking going on in medical fields. There can be many kinds of mix-ups. It can even happen in a pharmacy, and has, many times. Medication has also been confused and given to the wrong person . . . and much worse has even happened, because of patient mix-up. There have also been dosage-amount mix-ups and the dosage was misread or mistyped. Death can so easily result from these mishaps. Surgery on the wrong body part has even been done. For example, one doctor operated on the wrong eye, another doctor removed a lung that had been fine, and so it has gone. Diagnoses have often been wrong or wrongly interpreted because of poor note-taking, patient mix-up, or poor recordkeeping. Misdiagnosis is more common than we like to think it is. Doctors don't always 'get it right' but misdiagnosis can happen when there are typing or encoding problems, or the switching of information occurs. Biopsy mistakes have also given doctors problems.

There have been IV mix-ups and wrong substances put into bodies. (Tubes can sometimes look alike and get muxed-ip. Awful damage can be caused when tubes or lines are wrongly used.) People have ended out getting internally burned because of wrong hook-ups or excess use—badly burned, too. It can happen in a throat, a heart, or anywhere, really. Much around clinics and hospitals is electric and can overheat. All that hook-up apparatus is electrical. Also, air bubbles have somehow made their way into blood, and air bubbles cut off the blood supply and so people die because of them (and sometimes die quickly). Lasers, and sometimes cables have burned patients—both inside and out. Techs and nurses, as well as all doctors, have to always be focused, and concentrate. They can't let themselves get distracted. Such oversights or undersights ended out bringing about unbearable pain for a number of patients, and even some deaths.

There can also be problems that relate to anesthesia. Something about the anesthesia that gets administered may not be right, while the surgery is taking place. Not enough anesthesia may be being fed in, through the lines. This can be unbearably painful. When this happens, patients can feel all the pain and the moving around, pressing, snipping, and clamping, but they cannot move or talk. The operation will keep going on while they are screaming in their minds. This kind of thing happens more than the average person realizes, and how not getting enough of the anesthesia even happens can be hard to determine but it's usually the fault of the Anesthesiologist and sometimes a machine. The machine may not work right or read right. Something may not have been monitored well enough, too, so the fault can even be on the surgeon. Surgeons are supposed to check everything. Quite a few catastrophes can happen because of anesthesia. It has to be administered at right times, in right amounts and right proportions. Everything has to be ready to go. Everything has to be well prepared. Poor preparation and snags can mean delays during surgery, the worst case scenario being that they get part-way through a surgery and then have to close back up without completing the surgery because of some delay due to poor preparation.

Something else that has happened at times is that certain items or objects were not detected and were overlooked when the MRI was in use and the MRI, being highly magnetic, lifted up or drew in those magnetized items. Harm can be done, in other words, when the MRI is in use and someone is inside the machine. Objects fly and they fly hard if they're loose. You don't want someone coming in with a metal water pitcher, in other words, when the machine is on. All jewelry has to be removed…and does the patient have a metal pin or some shrapnel in their body? Nothing can be overlooked, but on occasion, some things have been.

There are even more types of these mix-ups and accidents but I think I've done all-right in including the ones I did. There have also been problems relative to ambulances, waiting rooms, and releasing patients. There have even been some fake and unlicensed doctors, here and there and on occasion. There have also been rogue doctors, nurses, and general hospital workers that tend to be secret misanthropes. Some have done some awful things but these workers are few and far between. The trouble is, they sometimes don't get caught or apprehended fast enough. The computer helps, but a rare fraudster slips in and can end out killing people. Unfortunately, credentials can be falsely fabricated or stolen or fraudulently obtained. Even when a credential is authentic, some doctors can go rogue, and do damage. It's not common, though.

It is not good to completely close up about medical and hospital care, though. Way more patients have satisfactory experiences at hospitals than don't. The point is, though, that patients not only have to be wise and aware, but they also have to be alert, cautious, and wary at every bend and turn, when they end out at a hospital and sometimes even at a clinic or doctor's office. Patients have to check things out or have them checked out, all along the way. Patients should ask about how things are reading, and how things are being interpreted. In general, they need to question things along the way. If something is about to happen, a patient should ask many questions and even pin down some medical professionals people so the patient can get their answers.

In conclusion, I'm not so willing to have surgery unless it is absolutely clear that I must. When symptoms worsen to the point where surgery becomes a must, then okay, count me in. So far, any symptoms haven't worsened, and everything is manageable. It doesn't seem like any damage is being caused.

In any event, am I lollygagging? Am I overly cautious? Am I being foolish? I'm trying not to be. I'm very much trying not to be. My body is at stake. My life is even at stake. I could die on the operating table, especially since I am older now. Also, I well remember coming out of the hiatal hernia surgery the last time as a tube woman, having chest tubes, an epidural, IVs, and a catheter, and that was unpleasant and radically distressful. I got through it all, but it was no picnic in the park. I well remember that experience, and I also know I can get through it again, even if the waters were to end out being rougher. There's little I could have done about the whole scenario. It was all so very real. It came upon me, overwhelmed me, and I had to deal with it.

Presently, God is steering the boat; He's the Captain—Captain God. As long as my symptoms remain generally minor, my present decision is to coax along. Again, I do not have heartburn or indigestion. I sometimes have problems breathing but that can sometimes relate to allergies, too, and not just be happening because my stomach is pressing against a lung and esophagus. Eventually, I may have to have all this double-checked. However, the longer a period that goes by and I'm able to still live generally satisfactorily, and, the older I get, the less likely it will be that I will have to have this second and repeated surgery.

If my symptoms stay minimal and are able to be easily managed, I will continue to limp along, but could possibly have to have this surgery done again should any symptoms flare up. There are bothersome symptoms. Those you can sometimes live with, as long as they aren't too distracting. But, then there are the irritating or painful symptoms that are distracting—sometimes considerably so. What I have now are bothersome and I can work around them and I don't believe they are reducing my longevity. That could be happening, though, with the breathing problems, that are especially problematic when I bend, but I stand, sit, and walk just fine. It's bending that causes me problems, especially with breathing. I do better when the air is humid, but that could relate to asthma. In any event, is it best to, therefore, have the surgery? I'd rather not, and to live as I am, but I know that the older I get, the harder any kind of surgery will be on me. I have to watch my bending, and my eating. (I have less stomach capacity, because of the way the stomach is now situated. My exercising is confined to non-vigorous walking and to normal household chores. Lifting and bending both have to be less than minimal.

If I do have the surgery done again, it will be a 'second verse same as the first' situation so I won't have to write another book like this one. There'd just be too much repetition. Not much new would come about, but it is apt to be a more difficult and dangerous surgery. I would hope that there wouldn't be too much that could happen that would be different, along the way, and so, I think, that this book has well been enough. I will likely die, never having had a second surgery.

I've tried to relay authentic experiences that I've had during my medical-related journey, and sometimes I've relayed impressions I gathered after having had the surgery experience. I'm not being disparaging of any one professional I may have noted in the book and besides, there is no one I can find fault with—not really—and there were times when I purposely did not note a name because the name was not important. The content was. Any doctors went out of their way to help me and I have no negative thoughts relative to their expertise. At any time while reading this book, if the shoes have fit, then it's probably good to wear the shoes. If they seem to fit later on, it's probably good to wear them, too. If the shoes don't fit, don't bother to even put them on. Perhaps they'll fit somebody else. You cannot wear shoes that don't fit you. I'm just thankful I got around twelve years usage out of that difficult surgery before my stomach went back up in my chest.

That's all I wish to report for the time being since everything 'seems' to be finished. I am definitely deferring surgery, hoping that nothing worsens. Of course, I still have to be careful about everything I do, but I'm used to that by now. There is still one last chapter, though, and it follows and is not too long.

CHAPTER 12
Twenty years after the surgery

It's a risk, the older you are, to have surgery. It's a risk at any age, really. I have been living, year after year, without having had the second surgery. So far my symptoms are not intolerable. My scar area is still vulnerable and were I to bump the area, it would hurt quite a lot but it doesn't bother me now. My arm somewhat protects that area, since I had been opened up on that side area, and to the back, some. I don't feel anything there so all's well. My breathing is, at times, difficult. Bending downward is a big problem and it causes me immediate breathing problems when I do. If I bend at the waist (like you do when you pick things up), my breathing will suffer, thereafter, for a time. I cannot exert myself too much, either. My breathing becomes more labored than it should, but I do not faint. I cannot lift heavy things. If I do, I have breathing problems. If I breathe normally, I'm OK but if I exert myself, I breathe more heavily than other people would. I try to not bend but there are times when I have to. Really, it's one or two quick bends that is the problem. I can bend on occasion, but only once or twice at a time and then I have to stop because any more bending, and I will have noticeable breathing difficulties. One of my lungs is being pressed against (because my stomach is pressing it, since it is back up in my chest) and the one lung, and perhaps both lungs, are being constricted so my breathing can get to be difficult, at times. I get less oxygen and this tires me out, some. I breathe less well but that has not been debilitating, as yet, as long as I go about everything steadily, and I'm cautious. I can't exert myself too much. I can eat, but only about half of what others my size can eat when having a meal. If I eat past a certain point at one sitting, I am in considerable pain (it is pretty bad) but I know not to eat past that point so I don't but I have accidentally done this a few times and when this happens I must lay down and let my food digest past a certain point before I can get up and start moving around. If I eat past that point (and I generally don't, anymore), pain will subside as food digests. I absolutely have to lie down, though. When all is well, I am able to walk all around a grocery store, or any large area, but I can't run. I can never run, but I don't need to run. I am living with my condition, which is actually a boni fide handicap. Not being able to breathe well or all the time can be a handicap. I don't quite get enough oxygen so I tire more easily. I breathe differently than others breathe—I have to breathe out more slowly so air leaves my lungs more slowly. If air leaves fast, I gasp for breathe. Breathing out more slowly is not hard to do.

I have no small pains anymore from the actual surgery, like I did for a long time after the surgery that I had close to twenty years ago. For years I had those pains, although they became more aggravations than pains and they kept reducing in magnitude as the years went by. Now, they are gone—except that front muscle over my left rib sometimes gets dislocated if I twist a certain way and so I have to turn a certain way really fast to get it back into place because this causes a sharp pain. Sometimes I have to lift my arms up and stretch the muscle back into place. The area hurts, until I got the muscle back into place. This doesn't happen too very often, and the condition has been manageable.

I'm quite sure that the main reason I've avoided the second surgery is because I don't get G.E.R.D., or the acid indigestion, like I did before I had the first surgery. Some foods give me acid indigestion but that isn't exactly chronic G,E,R,D. because it isn't chronic My stomach is now set in a certain way, up in my chest area (and not below the diaphragm where it is supposed to be), but it does not seem to cause my esophagus to be affected by its particular placement like it had before the earlier surgery so I got that stomach contents backflow and the accompanying acid indigestion. If I did get that, I'd be on the surgeon's table, forthwith. That is what happened the first time and so I had no choice in the matter and had to give that surgery a chance. Now, even with the inconveniences, and even disability, a second and repeat surgery is optional. I do not need to have it. I can wait it out and hope nothing worsens. So far, there's been no acid indigestion.

I had yet another gallstone attack about six years after my first attack. This gallstone took less time to pass than the first one had but it brought with it great pain, and rendered me near-immobile. The pain, as with before, went all around by torso—back to front and it was one of these high-up-there pains. At the time when it was happening, I would have said, "10" but I know other pains likely surpass gallstone-passing on the pain scale. The severe pain went away after about five hours.

I ended out laying on my back because doing that made me feel better. By that time, it was about four in the morning. I fell asleep. I slept for at least six hours and when I woke up I had a high temperature and felt weak, and achy. I ambled about, slowly, for a short while, trying to tidy up my home and got so tired I had to go back to bed and I ended out sleeping on and off for a couple of days until my temperature broke. It took two days before my temperature broke. I knew I'd passed the gallstone so I did not go to the hospital that time.

When I was in the hospital for the first gallstone incident, they put me on antibiotics to fight whatever was needed to be fought because of the gallstone disruption and possible internal damage. This time, my body had to fight what it needed to fight, on its own. I had no antibiotics. Hence, there was the raised temperature for those two days. I was tired and drained.

A friend of mine's husband also gets gallstone attacks (i.e. a stone drops out of his gallbladder and makes its way out of his body from time to time. He drops gallstones more than I do. She told me that he just 'rides them out'. (I don't think he has health insurance but I can't be sure.) He just suffers and expects they'll pass and when they do, he goes through a recuperation time, at home. I guess he's had several of these attacks, and yes, they do seem like they are actual attacks. They come on suddenly, in a full throttle of pain, and there is no warning, but no one ever knows how many stuck and slow-moving gallstones they will get during their life. It could only be one . . . or it could be many more than one. It could only be two or three.

There are a couple of parts to this horrid ordeal. First, there is the onset of the dropped gallstone and it's going through passages in the body and then, there is its elimination. If it gets stuck anywhere during its passage, this is the real painful part, and it is traumatic. Because it is quite traumatic, it, literally, leaves you in shock mode, for a time. Both your body and your mind have to rest, for a time, after the stone has passed. The shock you feel, because of the sudden pain (and continued pain) is similar to shock felt when you get hit hard by a car. I am very aware of this shock, since I had been the victim of a pick-up truck that was exceeding the speed limit and hit my car (and, the driver had no driver's license).

How long I can live with my stomach being in my chest, I do not know. I generally function OK and can do everything I need to do. I am coping with the intermittent breathing problems. When I exert myself too much or bend too much, I have shallow breathing and struggle to breathe in varying degrees, depending on how much I did either, all in a row. This can get a little scary sometimes. It is inconvenient, as I must stop everything I am doing and rest. Even with just normal breathing, I labor to breathe more than other people do and so I get less oxygen and consequently get a little more tired, compared with other people. If I don't exert myself too much, I'm okay. On top of my breathing problems, because one or both lungs are being pressed in by my stomach, I also have asthma, but I always have a nebulizer around for that. I've been hit with both problems at the same time. When that happens, I have to sit and rest for a while, after using my inhaler, which is Symbicort®. I sometimes get allergies, too, especially in the spring. It's all good though. I've learned to live with both situations. Time has been what I needed. Time is always what is needed. You learn so much along the way.

I am ever concerned about having surgery again, period, but I also don't want to have it again because of complications that can show up after a surgery and as a result of a surgery. You can be alive when you wake up from a surgery, so you got through the surgery, but you could die because of surgical complications (whatever that or those could be). They can enter the picture after a surgery. Infection is one well-known complication. It can take over a body really fast, whether you're in the hospital or at home. Before leaving a hospital, there is the vitals check for any trace of infection. Internal bleeding is another possible problem. It can also happen after a patient leaves the hospital. Blood-flow blockage is another. For example, a blood clot, or embolism, can form. There can be other kinds of blockages, too. Some complications come about because of medical error, but certainly not always. Most of the time there are no complications whatsoever. There is medical competence out there—big time—but we all know weak links can be anywhere. They are few-and-far between but they're out there.

I am also ever-concerned about having surgery again (and want to avoid it) because I have so much I still want to do with my life. I want to keep going at a good pace and a major surgery, right now, would slow me down and could even cause me harm…because of my age. Every day is important as I continue with my writing and plans to go full-scale ahead with establishing a museum for families and children. I have to finish all my writing. I'm on a work treadmill. My age is against me, too, when it comes to having surgery. Twenty years ago I was in better shape and more resilient. I didn't know, then, what I know now. If anything were to become too problematic and difficult, I would have the surgery, but so far, so good, and I can cope with the problems, though life can be rather difficult for me at times. I could have the surgery. I have the insurance. I don't like costing the government money unless I absolutely have to, though, and this is also something that I factor in. I'm a minimalist, there, and that is another reason why I am holding back. Time will tell what the future holds, though. Again, if my condition were to suddenly worsen, in any way, I would have to have the second surgery, and go into it, in faith. I give everything over to time. What is to happen, will be revealed. <u>Sometimes all we can do is wait—wait and see if something changes</u>—but again, so far so good and, to date, it does not seem like anything is going to worsen to the point of catastrophe (and a second surgery).

I guess this is a good time to end the book because at my age, the odds are that I won't have the surgery again. I worry about any surgeon's cuttings, too, because nothing in my body is exactly where it should be, not anymore. Everything's been shifted. Some of my organs are pressed in together. Plus, some areas may now have thinner walls because of previous cuttings and separations (done during the first surgery) so any new cuttings in those areas would be more dangerous to do. If something were to internally change and then become problematic, will I have to have a second surgery? Yes, I would, which is why I am now more cautious about my movements.

To emphasize and in conclusion, I still have breathing problems and cannot exert myself. I can't bend, pick up anything real heavy, or walk too fast. I cannot run. If I pick up something that is heavy, I absolutely cannot carry it very far. Big bags of cat food and of cat litter, I can lift them up to the top of the cart and push them over, but it is a strain and causes a short-term breathing bout. Sometimes I get help putting the bags in my car. Because I feed so many strays, I buy the thirty-five pound bags of dry cat food. Some things, I just can't stop doing.

I have noticed a worsening of my breathing, but it only occurs twice a year—pre-summer and post-summer—which means that it occurs in the spring and the fall. I'll have to explain this as best I can. It relates to particles floating around in the air. At first, I thought it was because of my stomach-placement problem since that has caused me some breathing problems, but then, I figured out what was adding to and intensifying my breathing problems and it related to asthma.

I could not make it through April to October without my evaporative cooler. It gets hooked up mid-spring, really, and once it is in operation, it acts as a humidifier because the air moisture weighs down the dust and allergen particles and this allows me to breathe really well. Just before it gets warm enough to start using the evaporative cooler is when I have added trouble breathing—sometimes for a whole month. Coolers are disconnected every fall—the pan is drained and cleaned and sometimes tarred and the cooler is shut off from water usage. In the winter, it gets re-connected. The pan gets filled, the float is adjusted, and the water handle for it gets turned back on. At the end of the season, when the evaporative cooler gets disconnected, I have added trouble breathing for a short time, since dust and allergen particles aren't being weighed down by the cooler moisture anymore and because it is still warm outside (and inside) and irritating particles are floating around more, in the air. As soon as it gets cold enough, though, the particles get weighed down and I can start breathing better again. Consequently, through the winter and the colder months, I'm OK with my breathing. My asthma is under control But then, it starts to warm up in the spring and the dust and allergen particles start to swirl around again because of drier air, I end out suffering for a month or so again, until the evaporative cooler gets hooked up. So, there are the two interim periods, and I have more problems breathing during those times. I use my nebulizer much more, during those times.

Whatever is in the air is what agitates my breathing. It is down to general particle irritants—a mix of whatever happens to be in the air—and not down to anything in particular, like Ragweed, for example. Many particles get in my home from the outside but many originate from inside, too. They all add up. Again, I definitely have partial lung use, too, which does not help when I have allergy problems, too boot. Both situations can be debilitating and so I sometimes wonder—should I have this second surgery or shouldn't I? But, in the main, I have decided to not have it, and to keep on living as I have. I'm not horribly debilitated and non-functional so why not keep on living with it? It is hard on me, sometimes, and I can't bend over very much—that really gets me—but I can live with it and work around it. I cannot exert myself but because I write so much, I am sedentary, anyway. I do not expect anything to worsen, but I suppose it could, but, it hasn't yet so the odds are (I assume) that nothing will worsen. Fingers crossed. Knock on wood.

Thanks for bearing with me, while reading the book. Please forgive any repetition. This book has absolutely not been an example of my best writing, and I jump around because I wrote it at different times. I know I've gone round and round about having this second surgery, too, but that is because that is what a person does, whenever surgery is optional. This one has been optional for some time and there has always been more than one place where I can go to have it. In a few places when I wrote the book I was in pain and was possibly on painkillers, but even with the problems with writing the book, the book is a one of a kind, I think, and I hope it gets out to people who are in need of such a book and who will be happy to acquire its contents. You cannot say it is not informative. Not many people I know of have written about a particular surgery experience that they've had.

Again, I also wrote a book about my experience with Shingles—start to finish. had. There is also one out about cataract surgery that I completed. People have surgery. People get Shingles (and they have cataract surgery). My writings are from experience and I wrote the surgery and the Shingles books as I was going through the medical ordeals. Outside people have a right to know what goes on, what happens, and what can happen. Different people, put through the same ordeals, might have different experiences, though, so always realize that, and also realize that it is important to be under a physician's care when it concerns anything medical. They are specially taught and trained. Check out different doctors, if you believe you must have any kind of surgery. Any surgeon should be available to address any of your concerns.

I had to be especially careful about COVID-19 and its variants after it entered around January of 2020. It spread like wildfire and killed many people of all ages but more particularly, it killed the elderly. (I am now elderly.) I believe I got it quite early on but fought it off but could never be sure that it had been COVID. Because I had less lung capacity than was usual and had breathing problems to begin with, I had to be more isolated than others were. Luckily, I needed to keep writing and so I stayed indoors. Others people were not so fortunate and ended out dying, which includes many brave COVID-related workers. COVID stayed around for a long time, even with the immunizations and boosters.

Victims of COVID are missed. COVID brought about some medical advancements, so that part has been good. Are all the labs that work on these viruses really safe, though? Are all of them supervised and regulated well enough? Stay tuned.

Hospitals were so full during COVID that even if someone wanted to have surgery, they would defer it until later if they could. I'll probably keep deferring this second surgery up until I die, but my breathing problems are aggravating because my stomach presses my lungs in. my life has been modified because of limitations. I do not know why the first surgery did not hold. Some surgeries hold and others don't. Probably, most hold, but in my case, my stomach even back up into my chest so I'm now stuck with that. It didn't slow down my writing and it caused me to keep writing so I'm content, though life has its difficulties.

INDEX

278

M

machines 53, 69, 201, 203, 216, 217, 218

Magnetic Resonance Imaging 201

Maine 9

maintenance 6, 188

major surgery 60, 87, 142, 265

Malpighi 65

Malpighi, Marcello 65

manageable 107, 154, 186, 257, 262

management 52, 82, 87, 165

managers 110

Marcello Malpigni 65

marijuana 87

Martin Clunes 239

M*A*S*H 137

masks 48, 57, 75, 140

Massachusetts 65

massage therapist 246

material xi

material items 173

materials 149

mathematics 65, 79

maximum healing 145, 156, 158

McDowell 65

McDowell, Ephraim 65

MD 88, 109

meal 24, 25, 34, 68, 102, 113, 114, 188, 251, 261

meals 24, 32, 38, 102, 113, 114, 118, 157, 158, 182, 185, 192, 214, 226, 245

measurements 9

medical advancements 167

medical background xiii

medical facilities 87, 109, 138, 139, 167

medical facility 23, 24, 110

medical insurance 59

medical marijuana 87

medical museum 70

medical plans 167

medical profession xiii, xv, 72, 75, 86, 110, 166, 188, 203, 257

medical professionals xv, 72, 75, 86, 188, 203, 257

medical records 24, 25, 111

medical research 66, 67

medical school 49, 111

medical tests 43, 71, 202

medical TV series 238, 239

Medicare 207, 219, 245, 248

medication 74, 85, 91, 93, 100, 101, 102, 103, 117, 131, 132, 133, 135, 142, 195, 239, 242, 252

medications 223, 252

medicine 61, 64, 66, 68, 70, 101, 109, 133, 134, 160, 167, 168, 252

Medicine 37, 49, 62, 63, 66, 68, 69, 70, 110, 111, 206

Medi-Vac 137

melting point 211

memory 49, 58, 73, 188

Mental Assessment ii

mental dependency 168

Mental health 137, 176

mercy 44, 198

mesh 41, 78, 81

metabolize 204

metal 93, 95, 201, 204, 216, 257

methods 64

Mexico 138, 139, 167, 176

Microbiology 49, 66

microorganisms 66, 67, 68

microscope 49, 50, 65, 67, 68

military 64, 138, 207, 223, 248

Military 207, 248

military hospitals 223, 248

military surgeon 64

Milk of Magnesia® 243

minimal 74, 122, 128, 174, 208, 258

minor surgeries 53

misalignment 178

misanthropes 257

Mississippi 138

mix-ups 255, 257

mobile 71, 86, 95, 114, 118, 121, 157, 177, 181, 197, 251

Mobile Army Surgical Hospital 137

mobile meals program 114

molecular biology 211

Monounsaturated Fat 210

286

X

x-ray 26, 27, 29, 31, 32, 35, 71, 160, 168
X-ray 26, 27, 29, 31, 32, 35, 71, 83, 160, 168, 201,
      202, 203, 216, 236, 238, 247
x-rays 29, 35
X-rays 29, 35, 203, 236

Y

yard 20, 162, 163, 175, 191

yards 10
yard work 20, 191
yellow 1, 3
Y-shaped 7

Z

Zimbabwe 167

Printed in the United States
by Baker & Taylor Publisher Services